CHURCH

the

REASON

for

ALL

T0367340

by Clement B. Talipan

AuthorHouse™ UK Ltd.
500 Avebury Boulevard
Central Milton Keynes, MK9 2BE
www.authorhouse.co.uk
Phone: 08001974150

First published by AuthorHouse 12/24/2010

ISBN: 978-1-4567-7223-9

CHURCH

the

REASON

for

ALL

by Clement B. Talipan

CONTENTS

Contents

Contents

DEDICATION

It is my pleasure and honour to dedicate this book to my dear wife Florina Talipan (Mrs), and my dear sons Joshua D.Talipan, Victor E. Talipan, IsPeniel T. Talipan and daughters DeHaine D. Talipan and JoyHert B. Talipan. Though it has been a very noisy and not welcoming environment with all the kids playing almost every hour as I wrote this book, I have accepted the fact that the children have come to be part of me forever. I am more than happy to dedicate this book to my wife and my children; for they are the only precious people on earth God has given me that I be their father and they be my household.

Visitors come and go and other friends are friends only when you need them. Even our extended family members fall under this category. The only closest people one could ever have are the members of his or her own nuclear family. I would therefore, rather dedicate my first book to my wife and my children than to any of my best friends. To God be the glory forever and ever; Amen!

ACKNOWLEDGEMENT

I have realized and experienced that writing a book is not an easy task as one may think it is. For my book, it involved so many bits and pieces that without them; this book wouldn't have come out as it is. I would therefore, like to acknowledge not every body but few who have contributed some kind of support in its initial part of drafting and publishing. I also pray that the following be blessed in whatever they do that they may continue in their support ministries, to extend the Kingdom of God.

I acknowledge Messrs Max Yallon, Danny E. Korakali, Gideon Korakali, Freddie Korakali, Kenneth Korakali, Raphael Poko, Jonathan Walen, Daniel Bernard, George Ipo (Ps), Bernard Buri (Ps), Kissam Tare (Mrs), Sharon Korakali (Miss), for your aid and help. Without your help that were provided, my long time dream of writing a book wouldn't have come to pass. I thank you all for your unforgettable help.

I also want to acknowledge my dear wife Florina Talipan (Mrs) who had tirelessly typed all my drafting. Honey, you've really indeed fulfilled the duty of a wife as it is your purpose of being a partner that is comparable to me (Genesis 2:18-24). Though you are a mother of four kids, you could able to make time available for my book. And it's not only that but you have also contributed ideas and searched Bible references to support my theology in this book. Thank you indeed for your time and commitment!

FOREWORD

It is my pleasure to express my gratitude to Ps. Clement B.Talipan, one of our long time and Senior Pastors of the Assemblies of God Church of Papua New Guinea, to come up with such a book to enlighten the knowledge regarding the Church of God. The Church of God is an institution that really needs to be studied and understood properly by our Christian folks. However, it is a tragedy that each one of us has our own way of interpreting the Bible, and in doing so, we have all kinds of beliefs regarding the matter.

I believe this book will surely answer some of your unanswered questions as to which church is the right church and what must one do to get eternal life. It is very crucial that we must know whether we are saved or not, for no one can be saved without becoming a member of the Church of God. Church of God is only one as we all know but should we say that it is the one that we belong to? How do you know that you are saved? This book will answer some of these very important questions in life.

I would therefore, recommend that it be read thoroughly from the first to the last chapter.

Further more, not all but some books as such are indeed worth reading for the betterment of our lives. I would comment that this book is one of those good books that should not be ignored if it passes through your way. Why not pick one and read? Surely you will never be the same again after reading the book.

Foreword

Instead you will be a happiest person for at least knowing a piece of truth in the Word of God.

Friends; knowing a piece of truth in the Word of God is all we need in order to enter the Kingdom of God as it actually says in John 14:6. Jesus the Word of God that gives life (John 1:1-4) and He is the Truth that leads to heaven. I would further encourage you to read this book, for it contains more of such truth that will surely save your soul!

Rev. Joseph Maru
General Superintendent
of the Assemblies of God
of Papua New Guinea.

20th Feb. 2008.

PREFACE

It is very important to note by the readers of this book, that the following facts are to be read consecutively in order to understand this book. Every book is written to be understood by the reader and thus, the purpose of the book will only be accomplished when the reader reads it comprehensively.

First of all, this is a book of only one subject and it is not a collection of many different topics as you may think it is. Therefore, the different topics found in this book are to be read from the first chapter to the last chapter. Only then, the reader will able to understand this book. Though the book is written in very simple English terms, the reader will find it hard to understand and comprehend the total picture of this book, if he or she prefers to do scan reading. Also, the reader is not encouraged to read any topic by his or her own choice (though he/she is free to choose) but it must be read consecutively from the first chapter to the last chapter. For the exceeding chapter will only be understood, when the preceding chapter is read comprehensively.

For this book contains the very important subject of all, the "Church" which is truly the reason for all that needs to be read thoroughly. This book is not a Bible but honestly speaking; it is a book that has interpretations purely from the Bible only. It is also not dogmatic but is generally opened to be read critically.

Preface

Hence, don't feel hesitate to contact the author on any queries or comments or critiques regarding this book.

This is a study book and it is therefore, necessary to keep a Bible next to the reader to correspond with the Bible texts given. For the Bible is the only solution and the final authority to solve and answer all the unanswered questions.

Finally, this book will only be understood by the help of the Holy Spirit. I therefore encourage the reader to pray and ask for the guidance of the Holy Spirit before making an attempt to read this book.

I also pray that whoever chooses a copy of this book and reads it will never be the same again; only if he or she reads it thoroughly and with understanding.

Anyway, this is just another book amongst many hundreds of thousands of books; even millions on bookshelves around the world. Yet only the fortunate ones will somehow choose to read this book and they will never regret after reading it, but instead will be happy and thankful that they have read the book. Why not you? Grab one and read; for it may cause a u-turn in your life that might prosper you not with chattels or properties but in your spiritual and eternal life. So don't you please ever take your eternal life for granted: Cheers!

Ps. C. Talipan

10/03/08

Introduction

Like any other Christian books, this book is written for any class of people can read for the benefit of their lives. It is an open book that may help the Christians, the non-Christians, the politicians, even the Satanists or the atheists for that matter. Why not pick one and read? My friend, you are the sum total of your own makings in life.

This small book consists of twelve (12) chapters that generally talk about the Church of God with its ingredients. As you read on, you will come across some twelve chapters of different topics but you will also notice that each chapter is related to the main idea, which is the Church.

This is a study book that the reader will only understand the contents of the book, only when it is read thoroughly from the first chapter to the last chapter with a Bible in front of the reader.

The unborn Church of God was really mysterious but thank God, it was indeed the reason for all. The idea of establishing Church on earth was concealed in the mind of God for a long time in the eternity. It was conceived in the heart of God even before the foundation of the world. And it was for the Church that God had to do all that He has done. In His great wisdom, God knew exactly when and how to bring it forth into this world.

When the right and perfectly appointed time ("kairos" in Greek) came, God had to let go the promise of Him sending His Son into this world to save the sinners. That was the fulfillment of God's promises of sending His only Begotten Son into this sinful world as its Redeemer and Saviour. Everything that God had ever planned to do with man was all in the package of the incarnation of Jesus. It is therefore; Jesus is the only answer and the way for man to have access to God.

As Jesus walked on this earth, He carefully followed the design and the plan of the Church and laid its foundation accordingly. He showed us how and where to build the Church. For He alone knew very well about every particle and the reason for the Church. His instructions on how to build the Church were precisely accurate that no man can ever do otherwise. He also pointed out that God the Father is the Architect and He is the Chief Builder of the Church. It is therefore; wise to follow the building plan that was given by Jesus rather than listening to and following all kinds of so-called Church strategies.

Jesus also taught on what Church is all about. He made it very clear that Church is an independent entity that is made up of every born-again Christian from every Christian church. He taught that Church is not one particular person or one particular church or one particular denomination. It is very clear in the Bible that the Church of God is a collective body of every born-again Christian from every Christian church group around the world.

Jesus Christ also pointed to Himself as the Head of the Church. Apostle Paul was very keen in this area and stated for several times in his epistles that Jesus is the Head of the Church.

Apostle Paul in his eagerness in the Church of God, he went into the extreme of taking the human body as a metaphor or an example of the Church.

That was how far he could go to explain the mysteries of the Church. I guess Paul was motivated by some unnecessary in-fighting among the early Christians who really did not know much about the Church of God. In fact they caused divisions among themselves and had different theology altogether about the Church. Each Christian or group had a funny idea of being a Church or a favorite one of God by itself excluding the others. That could have been the reason why Paul had to say that the Church is like a body and the body is of Christ.

Paul went on to say that the body is only one and has many members so as the Church of God. He deliberately took the human body as an example to explain that the Church of God is only one with many members. The one Church does not necessarily mean one particular church group or one church denomination like I said. But it is the collective body of born again believers from all Christian churches around the world.

For God so loved the world that He gave His only Begotten Son. God did not send His Son into this world for one particular person or one particular church group but for the all world. It is therefore, whoever believes in Him and obeys His commandments, no matter how bad his background is or from what church he or she belongs to, that person will be saved. The only condition is that, man has to repent from his sins and come to Jesus Christ that his sins be washed and cleansed by His blood. For without the washing and cleansing of sins by the blood of Jesus, there is no remission of sins. Hence, there is no any other possible way except with Jesus through which man can be saved.

God's love is for all mankind and that alone guarantees that the Church can grow as far as it could, depending on the duration of God's love. We should not be surprised that the Church of God is a growing organism that it will definitely grow as long as this world exists. God's love is of course eternal, but the duration for exercising the love of God on earth will come to its end when the Church will then cease to exist on earth.

It is therefore, when the time is not yet ripe, God is really in a serious business of calling man and woman to do His work. He does not call anybody into His service to do nothing. When He calls a person to serve Him, He has already prepared and allocated spiritual positions of ministries and gifting that are necessary for his or her calling. It is not His character to call anybody just to walk into the field of God, to do anything according to his or her own wishes. There is a purpose behind every calling of God; that it is our responsibility to find out what He has for each one of us.

Consequently, when all ministries and gifting of the Holy Spirit operate diligently in accordance with the perfect will and purpose of God, the Church will then be positioned in her rightful place in this world. The Church of God has a place in this world and so it is in heaven. The Church of God should not be reckoned as another social organization for it is not. But its position should be highly respected and placed above all other man-made organizations, institutions, interest groups, governments, etc.

The Church should have preeminence over all things under the sun. For it will be the Church again will have preeminence over all things in heaven anyway. Church is the only precious property God has. Besides that, my Bible does not show me any other thing in this world; or the world to come that will have preeminence over all the creations of God. No wonder, our title for this book "Church the Reason for All" is correct and unquestionable.

It is therefore, those who are already in the Church, have an obligation to share this great love of God to those who are lost in sin. No matter how bad the sinner is, God still loves him. He is just ready to forgive him, wash him, cleanse him and off course save him.

It was somebody out there who prayed and interceded for us and made direct or indirect contribution for our salvation. It is hard for us to pay any reward for their contribution for our salvation, but in return, we can share this same love of God to others.

Truly Church ought to love; for love is the only element that caused God to do what He did. If it wasn't the love God had for mankind, then I don't have any clue about where the world would have been. Friends, it was a thing called "love" that caused and motivated God to create the entire universe for man and for man alone. It is therefore, the Church ought to love regardless of what; and should not take the love of God for granted!

Chapter 1

The Mysteries of God

God is a God of mysteries. There must be mysteries about God, for God will cease to be God without the mysteries about Him. For Him to remain God forever; there must be mysteries about the infinite God that no human being or even an angel can able to comprehend and understand everything about this God.

We call Him by His attributes (natural/absolute) as Omnipotent; which means, All Powerful, Sovereign, and Almighty. Omnipresent; which means, Ever-present, everywhere at the same time. Omniscient; means, All-knowing about every bit of it from the very beginning to the end and the Answer for every situation in life. Eternal; means, Everlasting and Lives forever and ever. Immutable; means, Can Not and Will Never Change at any time, and the list goes on mean nothing but the mysteries of this great and awesome God. No human intellectual brain-cell can ever able to accommodate and comprehend Him who is loving, full of mercy but also mysterious. For mystery is part of Him that without it, He will cease to be God and all creation will be equalized with Him. He is mysterious that He alone can able to interpret His own mysteries. Joseph was once told about a dream and he said; *"Do not interpretations belong to God"* (Genesis 40:8)? Here Joseph is telling us that only God could able to interpret dreams and mysteries as such.

In Daniel 2:28 it says; *"But there is a God in heaven who reveals secrets."* He is truly a mysterious God that no man can ever elucidate Him.

It says in Job11:7-9 that; *"Can you search out the deep things of God? Can you find out the limits of the Almighty* (vs.7)? *They are higher than heaven-what can you do? Deeper than Sheol-what can you know"* (vs.8)? *"Their measure is longer than the earth, and broader than the sea"* (vs.9).

Apostle Paul said something similar about the mysteries of God in Romans 11:33 and it reads; *"Oh, the depth of the riches both of the wisdom and knowledge of God! How unsearchable are His judgments and His ways past finding out!"*

In the book of Ecclesiastes 3:11 it says; *"He has made everything beautiful in its time. Also He has put eternity in their hearts, except that no one can find out the work that God does from beginning to end."*

"God is the Infinite One. In one sense, He is incomprehensible; how can finite beings comprehend the Infinite, Limitless God?" "If the heaven and heaven of heavens cannot contain thee" (1Kings 8:27), "how can a sentence or paragraph of human words define His Being?"[1]

Though He has given everything to mankind even eternity for that matter, man has felt short of the glory of God (Romans 3:23) that he (man) will never ever become equal with God. He will remain a mysterious God forever and ever.

---

[1] Guy P. Duffied and Nathaniel M. Van Cleave, "Foundations of Pentecostal Theology" (OMF Literature Inc. Manila, Philippines, 2006). pp. 50, 56.

Anyway, before we go on, let's see the definition of the word mystery. According to Oxford Learner's Dictionary, "Mystery" is "something of which the cause or origin is hidden or impossible to explain," or "religious truth or belief that is beyond human understanding."

In that case, this Great God and His attributes are mysterious that no man or an angel can ever study and comprehend the completeness and totality of Him.

It will be a waste of time, effort, energy and other resources that might involve in the process of studying and hoping to know everything about this God. All we have to do is to believe only.

For it is impossible for any one to dig-out and expose the completeness and totality of all His attributes and His personality. Truly, it is beyond human intellectual comprehension and as such, we are commissioned only to believe and have faith in God.

In one incident when there was pain, sorrow, doubt and fear, Jesus said, *"Do not be afraid; only believe"* (Mark 5:36). Here Jesus was saying something very interesting. He was saying to the ruler of the synagogue that he didn't have to know how and when his daughter would come back to life. All he had to do was to believe in God; no matter what.

In that regard, only believing that He is a mysterious God is no exception. The Bible tells us that we must only believe, even if it is not visible and beyond human understanding. Our level of faith should not decline or exceed but be measured with the Word of God.

We don't have to know and understand in full the great and Almighty God, before believing in Him. For the Bible says that; *"Now faith is the substance of things hoped for, the evidence of things not seen"* (Hebrews11:1). The only possible way for us to approach the God of Israel is through faith and there is no short-cut whatsoever. It further says that; *"But without faith it is impossible to please Him, for he who comes to God must believe that He is, and that He is a rewarder of those who diligently seek Him"* (Hebrews 11:6).

Therefore, the mysteries of God that we are going to see here can never be understood by human intellectual brains. We must accept the fact that He is a mysterious God; and it's our duty to believe in Him as far as the Bible is concerned. To be a better student of the Bible, one has to believe Him as He is and trust not in his or her own intellect and reasoning. For the Word of God forbids us from having trust in ourselves. Proverbs 3:5-7 says that; *"Trust in the Lord with all your heart, and lean not on your own understanding* (vs.5). *In all your ways acknowledge Him, and He shall direct your paths* (vs.6). *Do not be wise in your own eyes; fear the Lord and depart from evil"* (vs7).

Anyway, the mysteries of God that I will talk about particularly in this book are the origin of Church, and its contributing elements. Like I said, it is impossible to interpret all the mysteries of God however; we can go as far as that which God wills and permits.

In one situation, the disciples asked Jesus why He had to say things in parables. And this is what Jesus said; *"Because it has been given to you to know the mysteries of the kingdom of heaven, but to them it has not been given"* (Matthew 13:11). The same story is recorded by Apostle Mark, and this is what Mark says; *And he said to them, "To you it has been given to know the mystery of the kingdom of God; but to those who are outside, all things come in parables"* (Mark 4:11).

According to these Bible texts, it is very clear that only the children of God can at least able to know the mysteries of God, while the children of this world can not. The children of this world can not know the mysteries of God, for their minds are blinded by the god of this age (2Corinthians 4:4).

Apostle Paul said similar things regarding the knowledge of the mysteries of God in 1Corinthians 2:6-16. In his explanation he said, the children of God can able to know the mysteries of God by the help of the Holy Spirit, for they have the mind of God. And this is what he says;

"However, we speak wisdom among those who are mature, yet not the wisdom of this age, nor of the rulers of this age, who are coming to nothing" (vs.6). *"But we speak the wisdom of God in a mystery, the hidden wisdom which God ordained before the ages for our glory"* (vs.7). *"Which none of the rulers of this age knew; for had they known, they would not have crucified the Lord of glory"* (vs.8). *"But as it is written: "Eye has not seen, nor ear heard, Nor have entered into the heart of man. The things which God has prepared for those who love Him"* (vs.9). *"But God has revealed them to us through His Spirit. For the Spirit searches all things, yes, the deep things of*

God" (vs.10). "For what man knows the things of a man except the spirit of the man which is in him? Even so no one knows the things of God except the Spirit of God" (vs.11). "Now we have received, not the spirit of the world, but the Spirit who is from God, that we might know the things that have been freely given to us by God" (vs.12). "These things we also speak, not in words which man's wisdom teaches but which the Holy Spirit teaches, comparing spiritual things with spiritual" (vs.13). "But the natural man does not receive the things of the Spirit of God, for they are foolishness to him; nor can he know them, because they are spiritually discerned" (vs.14). "But he who is spiritual judges all things, yet he himself is rightly judged by no one" (vs.15). "For "who has known the mind of the Lord that he may instruct Him?" But we have the mind of Christ" (vs.16).

According to Paul, we the children of God, can at least able to know some amount of the revealed mysteries of God, for we have the mind of Christ, and we are also led by the Spirit of God. I therefore, with the help of the Holy Spirit, will at least try my best to interpret some of these hidden truths.

As we read on, we will see that in everything God was in the business of establishing the very important institution known as Church.

The concept of Church can be viewed or traced from the very beginning. It was in the mind of God before everything else came into existence in God. Truly it was the Church that caused God to do what He did before the time began. Time began in accordance with Geneses 1:1, but God with His mysterious plans already existed outside of time in the eternity. The Bible from Genesis to Revelation is full of narratives that talk about what God did after the time began. However, it also talks about what God did before the time began. What He did and what He had in His mind before the time began, and the invisible things that are yet to be revealed, are what we call the mysteries of God. For man can only study to understand what is already revealed. That which was not revealed before the beginning of time (known as the mystery of God) was the very cause or reason for what He did after the beginning of time. In other words, God only did what He did after the beginning of time for the good of that which was in His mind before the time began.

That alone is sufficient for us to conclude that this great universe and everything else in it were created only for the good of that mysterious plan in His mind, before the time began.

No wonder, the Bible is telling us in Romans 8:19 that; *"For the earnest expectation of the creation eagerly waits for the revealing of the sons of God."* Sons of God refer to those who are saved and are members of this Church that I am at least trying my best to explain concisely; though I am not a theorist.

It further goes on to say through verses 20-22 that the whole creation is frustrating in waiting and suffering as a child birth pain, just for the revealing of this hidden treasure. What a joy for us who are part and parcel of that great hidden reality God had for so long in the eternity, yet it was not concealed.

For God it was not a vision or a dream or a hope. Because what He had in His mind was not half-done or incomplete, but it was hundred percent (100%)

complete in its prefect shape. Therefore, God was not hoping for something in the future but He had a complete and finished work just ready to be presented at the right time. Like Apostle Paul said; *"For we were saved in this hope, but hope that is seen is not hope; for why does one still hope for what he sees"* (Romans 8:24)? We can apply this same principle in this situation; for God already sees things in advance; (for He is the Omniscient God) that will take place in a million years from now.

For us as human, we could say, it was a great plan, or vision, or dream of God. Because we are limited with time and space, we count and plan from the beginning to the end.

We are at the beginning of time and have plans and dreams to achieve at the end of time. And therefore, the things that we are hoping to do at the end of time are known as plans, visions or dreams. In actual fact, we really don't know how big it will be, or how it will look like. All we know is that; we have something in our mind that is only a picture (of whatever it is) or an imagination without the physical substance with its complete shape.

Nevertheless, believe me, with God it is the other way around. God operates from the end to the beginning; so to say. That means God knows everything in full and complete shape from the end to the beginning; in His but great Omniscience knowledge. For God operates primarily from the spiritual world then to the physical world. With God the initial part begins in the spiritual world with its complete shape and finished work. Therefore, the mysterious plan God had before the beginning of time was all in its complete shape and finished work just ready to be presented at the right time.

To make a very long story short, the mysterious plan God had for a long time in the eternity, that was also paramount, was no other than to establish a very important institution known as "Church."

Like we have seen the principles of God in the above phrases, lets say that the Church was a complete and finished work with its particles fitted perfectly well together only in the eyes of God. This mysterious plan of God to establish the Church; could be the primary plan God had before all His other plans.

The authority for my theology is derived from the Bible texts taken from the following books. Ephesians 1:4, 1Peter 1:2, and 2Thessalonians 2:13, where it says; *"Just as He chose us in Him before the foundation of the world, that we should be holy and without blame before Him in love"* (Ephesians 1:4), *"Elect according to the foreknowledge of God the Father, in sanctification of the Spirit, for obedience and sprinkling of the blood of Jesus Christ"* (1Peter1:2) and *"But we are bound to give thanks to God always for you, brethren beloved by the Lord, because God from the beginning chose you for salvation through sanctification by the Spirit and belief in the truth"* (2Thessalonians 2:13).

I also get my indirect authority from 1Peter 1:20, where it says; *"He indeed was foreordained before the foundation of the world, but was manifest in these last times for you."* Can you see that we the members of the Church are indeed chosen and elected in Him; before the foundation of the world? I believe the above authority referred to; is sufficient; for the Bible says in Deuteronomy 19:15 and Matthew 18:16 that more than one witness is sufficient to establish the truth. Hence, it says in both verses that; *"By the mouth of two or three witnesses the matter shall be established."*

I know that it is not easy to understand what I am trying my best to explain here. I pray that the Holy Spirit will enlighten the eyes and minds of the readers of this book, so that whoever reads it will at least understand what the Church is all about and its purpose. The Church is not just another man-made organization as we may think it is, but it is indeed the reason for God to go to such extents of creating the great universe.

We know that everything on earth has a purpose attached to it, and likewise, the whole creation should also have a purpose to it and that is none other than the establishment of the Church. In other words, God created everything else just for the Church. Or let's say; the ultimate reason for the whole creation is to serve the Church. It is the Church that supposed to have preeminence over everything, both in heaven and on earth.

Why Church? Because Church is the Body of Jesus and Jesus is the Head of the Church. And God the Father also had given everything both in heaven and on earth to Jesus, and that Jesus together with the Church which is His Body will have pre-eminence over all things. Jesus indeed transferred all things that were given to Him by the Father to the Church, which is also His Body.

Our Bible references or authority to support this concept are precisely recorded in Ephesians 1:20-23, Colossians 1:15-18 and Philippians 2:9-11. It also says in Romans 8:16-17 that we are the children of God and that we are heirs of Him and joint heirs with Christ Jesus. It simply means whatever was granted to Jesus by God the Father, can also be the property of His other children in Christ Jesus.

No wonder, the Bible continues to say in Romans 8:19 that; *"For the earnest expectation of the creation eagerly waits for the revealing of the sons of God."* You see, the whole creation is not only waiting for Jesus but also for the revealing of the sons of God. It means the whole creation is also subjected to the sons of God in Christ Jesus. Well, who are the sons of God then? The sons of God like I said; are those who are members of the Church; that the whole creation is waiting for their revealing.

This is a mystery of God that no man or an angel had ever understood. People of all generations had wondered why the great universe had come into existence as it is now. Why this and why that had happened the way it happened. The why questions have one common answer and as I said, it is all for the Church. It was for the Church that God created; as He spoke the great universe into existence. And it will be the Church through which God will definitely bring the whole universe back to nothing. And finally it will be the Church again that will have preeminence over everything in New Jerusalem, the glorious Heaven. Oh! What a joy that will be up there, forever and ever! Amen.

But first, God chose the Church through Jesus Christ. Jesus Christ became the centre of the mysterious plans God had for the Church. It was all in Jesus, and Jesus had to play the major role in establishing the Church (Ephesians 1:4-11). In Ephesians 1:4 it says, *"God chose us in Him (Jesus) before the foundation of the world, that we should be holy and without blame before Him in love."*

Here we see that, God chose us before the foundation of the world, or even before the beginning of time in Him (Jesus). But He (God) had to wait until the right time (the kairos time) came (Ephesians 1:10, Galatians 4:2). As the right time came, God did not prolong His plans or promises. By then, He had to send Jesus to fulfill His promises. *"But when the fullness of the time had come, God sent forth His Son, born of a woman, born under the law"* (Galatians 4: 4).

But before that, God was in the business of planning and structuring the Church as to how it would be in the physical world, as well as in the spiritual world. The Church was not yet born into the world but it was there perfectly well in the mind of God. God had given the task to Jesus to purchase the Church, and to wash and cleanse the Church by His blood. He was also given the task to forgive all sins, and to save the Church from this sinful world. Jesus was also given the task to become the Head of the Church and to share His blessings and inheritance with the Church.

To share His inheritance and His Kingship with the Church both here on earth and in heaven, is something very interesting that I will elaborate more in the later chapters. God had all these plans in His mind before the incarnation of Jesus. It was only when Jesus descended; God began to manifest His multitude of mysterious plans one by one.

And even now, God is still in the business of fulfilling and revealing His mysterious plans only through the Church until He will leave nothing unfulfilled or hidden!

Chapter 2

The Fulfillment of God's Mysteries

God did not prolong His promises and plans. When the right and perfect time had come, the hope of glory had to be released; and so God did by sending His only Begotten Son into this sinful world. Let's read again Galatians 4:4; *"But when the fullness of the time had come, God sent forth His son, born of a woman, born under the law."* In John 1:14 it says; *"And the Word became flesh and dwelt among us, and we beheld His glory, the glory as of the only begotten of the Father, full of grace and truth."* In John 3:16 it says; *"For God so loved the world that He gave His only begotten Son, that whoever believes in Him should not perish but have everlasting life."*

The incarnation of Jesus was the time when God became man and began to reveal the mysteries that were hidden in His mind. Colossians 1:26–27 says; *"The mystery which has been hidden from ages and from generations, but now has been revealed to His saints (vs.26)."* *"To them God willed to make know what are the riches of the glory of this mystery among the Gentiles which is Christ in you, the hope of glory"* (vs.27).

God did not send His Son only to save this world from its sinful nature as it says in John 3:16, but also to reveal the hidden mysteries in His mind. Jesus Christ was the fulfillment of God's promises, plans and mysteries. It was all in Jesus Christ and nothing in God's promises, plans and mysteries that He had in His mind to deal with men was held back by God.

The fulfillment of God's mysteries is that, God became a man (the incarnation of Jesus), not only to live among men, but to make His home or dwelling place in the hearts of mankind, which institution is known as ekklesia, the Church (Ephesians 2:22). God becoming man is the "hope of glory," the people in the Old Testament have been waiting for some 4,000 years. "Jesus Christ" was the real substance and was everything. God gave everything to men but only through Jesus Christ. *Jesus said to him, "I am the way, the truth, and the life. No one comes to the father except through Me"* (John 14:6).

For example; eternal life was granted to us but only through Jesus Christ. For it also says in 1John 5:11-12 that; *"And this is the testimony: that God has given us eternal life, and this life is in His Son"* (vs.11). *"He who has the Son has life; he who does not have the Son of God does not have life"* (vs.12).

It's not only life but all other things God has for us are only to be found in Jesus and through Him. For it says in Ephesians 1:17 that; *"That the God of our Lord Jesus Christ, the Father of glory, may give to you the spirit of wisdom and revelation in the knowledge of Him."*

Jesus Christ became the Mediator between God and mankind (1Timothy 2:5, Hebrews 9:15). Through Him, man could able to have access to God, and God could also able to have access to man (John 14:6). Jesus, the Mediator also became the Chief cornerstone as Ephesians 2:20 says and eventually became the Rock Foundation, on which the Church was built (Matthew 16:18).

And the Church that is built on that Rock Foundation is God's dwelling place, according to Ephesians 2:22. Any other church built perfectly well but physically, and only according to man's ideas and philosophies, is not built on the Rock Foundation. And therefore, it is like a house built for the master, but not according to the model and plan ordered by the master. In such cases, the Bible elaborates more that whoever builds his house not on the rock foundation but on sand, will definitely be destroyed for the house is not saved (Matthew 7:24). A safe house is what people want more than just a house. In the same token, a safe church is what God wants of it more than just a church. And a safe church is no other than the Church that Jesus Christ was talking about in Matthew 16:18.

The Church built on the Rock Foundation is the only safest Church that God had, had in His mind. Besides that, any other church built any way else in this world is not recognized by God. If it is the Church of God then, it should be built on the Rock Foundation. For a church that is built on the Rock Foundation will surely survive the testing from this world.

We are living in a fallen world so anything that is not built on the Rock Foundation will definitely fall. In that case, it is wise to follow the instructions given by Jesus Christ (the instructor) for He is the fulfillment of God's promises. In order to know the mysterious plans of God, Jesus Christ is the only right key to open all the treasures in the Kingdom of God.

No wonder Jesus says; *"I am the way, the truth, and the life. No one comes to the Father except through Me"* (John 14:6).

Jesus is not only telling us that He is the gateway to heaven, but He is also telling us something remarkable. *"I am the way"* would mean many things. It doesn't have to be the gateway to heaven only. It would generally mean that He is the master key that opens the doors (whatever door it may be) that man can have easy access to the Father. *"No one comes to the Father except through Me,"* is indeed a challenging one that should not be taken for granted. This is Jesus speaking on one hand, and yet people are looking for gaps to approach the Father without Him on the other hand. If Jesus is the fulfillment of all mysterious plans of God, then it must be Jesus first before anyone can have any access to the Father.

Another piece of truth in this statement is that; Jesus is everything or in other words, all things are in Jesus. All truth is in Jesus as well as all life is in Jesus. All truth means, every single Word that proceeds from the mouth of God, has its meaning and fulfillment in Jesus Christ. That means, no mysterious plan or promise or Word for that matter, can be interpreted outside of Jesus. The full meaning of every single Word can only be found in Jesus. For that reason, Jesus once again referred to Himself as the Word of God (John 1:1-17). Jesus is indeed the Word of God from Genesis 1:1 through Revelation 22:21. The meanings or fulfillments of any plan or promise or prophecy that was proclaimed in between these time intervals, are all in Jesus.

"I am the life" referring not only to the Spiritual life, but physical life as well; has a better place of living in Jesus. When we talk about life in Jesus, some people may argue and say; 'we have everything in the world, what sort of life are you talking about?' That's fine with them but the real substance in life; I think is not there. For life is not only subjected to; or is not a matter of materialism; but righteousness, peace, love and joy in the Holy Ghost (Romans 14:17).

If all the worldly materials filled up in a house but important elements such as righteousness, peace, love and joy are missing; to me it is a house just as good as beautiful grave yards on the outside, but on the inside it is full of dead man's bones (Matthew 23:27). Jesus further warns such people by saying; *"For what profit is it to a man if he gains the all world, and loses his own soul? Or what will a man give in exchange for his soul"* (Matthew 16:26)?

Jesus, the only fulfillment of God's mysteries can not be substituted for any material stuff or any other so-called anointed man of God for that matter. For He was; He is; and He will be the voice of God, for all ages of all times.

God the Father literally confirmed in two separate occasions, that Jesus was truly His Son in whom He was well pleased. Hence, He also ordered that we should listen to Him alone. In Matthew 3:17 God said; *And suddenly a voice came from heaven, saying, "This is my beloved Son, in whom I am well pleased."*

The other occasion was on the mount of transfiguration where God said something really powerful. With due respect for all the prophets, God literally revealed that Jesus Christ is His only Begotten Son; whose deity should not be vicariously shared with other so-called anointed man of God. Man can easily be tempted to listen to or even to deify or worship fellow man, if proper direction is not given. For that very reason, God purposely allowed the precious moment of transfiguration to take place on that cold mountain. This is what had actually happened on that day.

And behold, Moses and Elijah appeared to them, talking with Him (Matthew 17:3). *Then Peter answered and said to Jesus, "Lord, it is good for us to be here; if You wish, let us make here three tabernacles: one for You, one for Moses, and one for Elijah"* (vs.4). *While he was still speaking, behold, a bright cloud overshadowed them; and suddenly a voice came out of the cloud, saying, "This is my beloved Son, in whom I am well pleased. Hear Him"* (vs.5)!

This is indeed a warning that man should only listen to Jesus and not fellow man in terms of superiority. That means the preachers of the Word of God are commissioned only to preach what they hear from God and nothing of their own or from any other fellow man. For Jesus is the fulfillment of God's mysteries that whatever we preach has to be ordained and directed by Him (Jesus). Otherwise our preaching would have no real Spiritual substance and significance.

The fulfillment of God's mysteries can be lined up in the following chronology. The incarnation of Jesus, or the Word becoming flesh (John 1:14), the preaching of the Kingdom of God (Matthew 4:17), the declaration of building His Church (16:18), the demonstration of love on the cross (Romans 5:8), the power of God unto resurrection (Ephesians 1:19-20), the ascension of Jesus (Mark 16:19), the pouring of the Spirit upon on flesh (Acts 2:1-4). These are only few to name, but major areas in which God had revealed His mysteries.

Generally, it's all in Jesus and Jesus was the fulfillment of God's mysteries. Whoever eager to know the interpretation and revealing of the mysteries of God, should prayfully read the narratives of Jesus and all the other New Testament Books. For the New Testament is the fulfillment of the Old Testament. That doesn't mean the Old Testament is all used up that we should only focus on the New Testament. No, that's not the point. The point is; the prophecies about the mysteries of God were all said in the Old Testament that needs to be studied and look for their fulfillments and meanings in the New Testament. Only then, you will understand the whole Bible, even the mysteries of God!

Chapter 3

The Architect and the Chief Builder of the Church

a: The Architect

It is a common understanding that nothing happens by itself and for its own benefits. Scientifically speaking, there's got to be a force behind every thing that happens or there must be one or more objects essentially and necessarily needed to make another object. It is very true that no human ideology or philosophy can ever able to say something otherwise.

In the same token, the Church, a very important institution that has been taken for granted by all levels of people over the ages, is not just any other institution or social organization, as it seems to be. But it has a source that needs to be understood carefully and precisely. We should not take it for granted that, anybody can form any church or ministry for that matter and preach anything against one another. And the church followers also should not move from one church to another without any solid reason with substance.

I see that this is very serious business that we should think twice, when we are prompted to take a step along that line. One very important thing that we should not loss focus, is the author and finisher of our faith, the man Jesus (Hebrews 12:2), and so the Architect and the Chief Builder of the Church. And we should also know the fact that we are not the source of this Church. Actually, we had contributed nothing when the Architect sat down to draw the plan and structure for the Church. It took God's time in the eternity, so to say, and costed Him to design particularly this Church.

As we have seen earlier, even before the beginning of time and before everything else, God gave preference in designing the Church. None of us or even an angel was there instructing God or sharing ideas with Him, in designing and structuring the Church. It was God and God alone through Jesus Christ in the Power of the Holy Spirit that He designed the Church. "Being God, He does not have to consult with, nor ask the opinion of, anyone else." or lets say, "there was none with whom God could consult."[2]

For it says in John1:1-3 that; *"In the beginning was the Word, and the Word was with God, and the Word was God"* (vs.1). *"He was in the beginning with God"* (vs.2). *"All things were made through Him, and without Him nothing was made that was made"* (vs.3). It also says in Colossians1:16-18 that; *"For by Him all things were created that are in heaven and that are on earth, visible and invisible, whether thrones or dominions or principalities or powers. All things were created through Him and for Him"* (vs.16). *"And He is before all things, and in Him all things consist"* (vs.17).

Further more in Hebrews 1:2 it says; *"Has in these last days spoken to us by His Son, whom He has appointed heir of all things, through whom also He made the worlds."* Again in Ephesians 1:4-5 it says; *"Just as He chose us in Him before the foundation of*

---

[2] Ibid, (2006). p. 207.

the world, that we should be holy and without blame before Him in love" (vs.4), "Having predestined us to adoption as sons by Jesus Christ to Himself, according to the good pleasure of His will" (vs.5).

The above references prove that it was God the Architect who designed the Church and even this world through the Word, who is Jesus. That is why the Church is a sole property of the Godhead in which Jesus Christ is also the Head of the Church. "And He is the head of the body, the church, who is the beginning, the first born from the dead, that in all things He may have the preeminence" (Colossians 1:18).

God had designed the Church as to how the Church should be built. As a Planner, He structured first the foundation. He knew the quality materials for the foundation, and so He structured how the materials should be laid and the other components of the building should also be erected. As an expert Planner, He did in such a way that no other planner or builder should come up with contrary ideas to obstruct His plans and purposes of the building.

In the book of Isaiah 28:16 it says; *Therefore thus says the Lord God; "Behold, I lay in Zion a stone for a foundation, A tried stone, a precious cornerstone, a sure foundation; Whoever believes will not act hastily."* I hope you understand that "Zion" speaks of the Church, and tried and precious cornerstone, a sure foundation refers to none other than Jesus Christ.

Apostle Paul knew what he was doing. He said something about him laying a foundation, but the foundation he was talking about was the initial foundation that God prophesied through Prophet

Isaiah. Here is what Paul says; *"According to the grace of God which was given to me, as a wise master builder I have laid the foundation, and another builds on it. But let each one take heed how he builds on it; for no other foundation can anyone lay than that which is laid, which is Jesus Christ"* (1Corinthians 3:10-11).

Paul once again demonstrated to the Ephesians that they were built on the foundations of the Apostles and the Prophets. Here he was again referring to Jesus as being the chief cornerstone, the solid foundation that the Apostles and the Prophets preached about. It reads as; *"Having built on the foundations of the apostles and prophets, Jesus Christ Himself being the chief cornerstone"* (Ephesians 2:20).

Now we see that God as an expert Architect had laid a solid and firm foundation on which we can build our faith without fear and discrimination from others. The Bible is very clear that no so-called man of God should preach something that is motivated by egoism. However, if anyone of us lays another foundation and builds accordingly, the ultimate result of the house will obviously be different than to that of what God's house should look like.

It is very easy to tell the differences between two different plans. Even a layman who does not know and doesn't have any clue about designing house can able to tell the difference as he first notices the houses. It is obvious that different plans will have variety of sizes and angles of the houses concern. The costs of the houses will also be different. And of course, the steadiness and firmness, the stability and the durability of the houses will very much depend on the different foundations and other materials that are used in the buildings. Like Rev. Dr. A.R. Bernard, commented in one of Don Clowers books title; "Spiritual Growth;" saying; "A building is only as good as its foundation. What is true of a building is true of the Christian life."[3]

In like manner, the Church of God and man-made churches will definitely have obvious differences that differentiate one from another depending on different foundations. The reason for this book is that; the reader should understand that this world is full of so many man-made churches that are in contrary to the original Church that was designed and ordained by God Himself. Like I said in the preface and introduction, that if you read this book thoroughly, I hope that the Holy Spirit will enlighten your understanding ability or mental faculty that you will understand the Church of God as it is.

I kindly beg you once again to read (this book) every single word of it, and mark my words; you will never be the same again, particularly in understanding the Church of God with all of its different components.

The Church designed by God and built by Jesus Christ on the Rock Foundation, will ultimately take its rightful position when all other man-made churches will naturally extinct one fine day as the world comes to its end. The Church of God however, will not extinct for its foundation is not of any corruptible material of this natural world. We must be smart enough to spend our resources in building our

---

[3] Don Clowers, "Spiritual Growth" (Book Production by Image Source, Inc. Tulsa, OK, 1995). Cover...page...

churches; for this world and everything thereof will definitely pass away. Matthew 24:35 confirms this and it is final. For it says; *"Heaven and earth will pass away, but My words will by no means pass away."*

It's worth building our churches in accordance with the Word of God, for it is the solid foundation and the only steadfast and safest place we have in this world; for the Word will never pass away. And it is the safest ship in which we should be engaged to in our journey; for this world is sinking in the sea of sin and corruption. Actually, God did not design His Church in a worldly structure but purely on the Word which is Jesus Himself the Rock Foundation.

b: The Chief Builder

A chief builder or an instructor is a person who understands every bit of the plan of a house. He normally instructs others what to do and how to build. He is the next person close to the designer because he can able to read and understand the designer's plans and instructs the other builders what to do. Without the proper instructions from the chief builder, the other builders may build the house but not according to the plan as it should be. So it's priority number one for the other builders to listen very carefully and obey the instructions given by the chief builder and do accordingly. Only then the house is built properly according to the plan. And that will help so much in accomplishing the house in an anticipated time and minimize the cost. And finally, the house will last for many years.

The same can be a good example in the building of the Church of God. As we have seen earlier, the man who has designed the Church is God the Father, and the Chief Builder can be referred to Jesus Christ, the only Begotten Son of God. Like we have seen the structure of a physical building, Jesus Christ is the Chief Builder who is the only person who knows better how to read and understand the plan and structure of the Church.

One good reason for this is that; Jesus Christ was there when God the Father designed the Church and it was only through Him (Jesus) God did what He did (refer back to John 1:1-3, Colossian 1:16-18 and Hebrews 1:2). In that regard, we will see now what Jesus actually did in order to build the Church when He descended from heaven.

But before that, lets go back to see that Jesus was right there next to His Father when God was in the business of designing the Church as He willed before the beginning. According to Ephesians 1:3-4, *"God the Father had blessed us with every spiritual blessing in the heavenly places in Christ"* (vs.3), and not only that but, *"He (God) chose us in Him (Jesus) before the foundation of the world, that we should be holy and without blame before Him in love"* (vs.4). We were not only blessed and chosen; but for Him as well in accordance with Colossians 1:16.

Here we see that those of us who are members of this Church, are dearly chosen by God in Jesus, and for Jesus only. Because we were chosen even before the foundation of the world, Jesus came in order to make sure that none of us is left out in becoming a member of this great institution known as Church.

Even though we were chosen from heaven before the beginning, we are capable of missing the real substance in life and do otherwise.

For that very reason, Jesus had to descend from heaven to establish the foundation of the Church properly according to the master plan drawn by God. For becoming a member of the Church of God is the only possible way for anyone of us to enter the Kingdom of heaven. That is why Jesus said; *"I am the Way, the Truth, and the Life. No one comes to the Father except through Me"* (John 14:6).

In order for us to be successful in our Christian walk and to continue in glorious life in the eternity, we must be very careful in obeying the instructions from the Man who knows the way. I think none of us is smarter than Jesus, so why not we swallow our own pride and do accordingly?

Anyway, the Church was then not yet born and Jesus carefully started off with laying the foundation by saying; *"Repent for the kingdom of heaven is at hand"* (Matthew 4:17). Like I've said earlier, Jesus was the Chief Builder who knew very well the quality materials that should involve in the building of the Church. He therefore said; *"Repent for the kingdom of heaven is at hand."*

To me, a very short and simple word "repent" means a lot more that I should not take it for granted. This is Jesus speaking, before anything else He did in His Ministry. He turned the water into wine (John 2:9), He healed the sick and performed many miracles recorded in (Matthew 8:1-17, 23-34, 9:1-8, 18-35), and etcetera. He fed the hungry ones (Matthew 14:15-21). He raised the dead (John 11: 43 – 44), but before them and above all, He said; *"Repent for the kingdom of heaven is at hand."* This is short and simple but powerful and sufficient foundation for the Church.

For the Church of God needed solid foundation and as such, repenting from sins was essentially necessary and very important element needed particularly for the laying of foundation. Indirectly we can also learn from Hebrews 6:1, which refers to repentance as elementary principle of Christ which is indeed the foundation of faith in God for perfection.

As we read on, we will see in the later chapters that the Church of God will never be built with physical materials like money etc. It will also not be built with human ideas, philosophies, knowledge, techniques, beliefs or doctrines. However, the Church of God is supposed to be built purely on the Word of God. Jesus being the Expert and Chief Builder or the Founder of the Church, showed to us how important a repented heart is very much required in the building of the Church.

If Jesus knew that a repented heart is very much required in the building of the Church, on what grounds a so-called anointed preacher or a church organization can paint another picture by preaching contrary messages? Or what is their scriptural basis by telling the people that they become members of the Church of God automatically, as they participate in church activities without bothering to repent from their sins?

The other time Jesus had a very important conversation with Nicodimus, a ruler of the Jews. In their conversation Jesus said to him; *"Most assuredly, I say to you, unless one is born again, he cannot see the kingdom of God"* (John 3:3). He went on to say; *"Most assuredly, I say to you, unless one is born of water and the Spirit, he cannot enter the kingdom of God"* (vs. 5).

In order to see and enter into the Kingdom of God, one has to be born again by the water and the Spirit of God. To be born again by the water and the Spirit is also very much required in the building of the Church. Truly a born again and a repented heart is all that is needed in the Kingdom building.

Let's elaborate little bit on the water and the Spirit before we go on. The water here speaks of the Word of God. Some say that it could speak of the water baptism. It could be right too but there are few references give support that water can be referred to the Word of God. In Ephesians 5:26 it says; *"That He might sanctify and cleanse her with the washing of water by the word."* Washing of water by the Word shows that the Word can be used or applied as water to sanctify and cleanse the Church.

The other time Jesus said; *"You are already clean because of the word which I have spoken to you"* (John 15:3). Still another time in His intercessory prayer Jesus said; *"Sanctify them by Your truth. Your word is truth"* (John 17:17). The Psalmist was also convinced that the water of the Word could cleanse a man's way. *"How can a young man cleanse his way? By taking heed according to Your word."* (Psalm 119:9). These references clearly show that the Word can wash, cleanse and sanctify as if it has some elements of water, such as hydrogen or oxygen, so to say. That means the water of the Word can produce new life in the power of the Holy Spirit.

Secondly, the Spirit refers to the Holy Spirit, the third person in the Godhead. It is the Holy Spirit, who gives life to those who are spiritually dead. The combination of water, (the Word, which is also the seed) and the Spirit is powerful enough to create new life. It was the Word (Jesus) and the Spirit who were there side by side with God when He created the great universe (Genesis 1:1-2, 26, John1:1-3). And so their combination can surely give new life to a spiritually dead person. It is His priority number one to give new life into the spirit of man, in order to meet the requirement in the building of the Church. For without the new life in the spirit of a man, that person will not be a useful material in the Kingdom building or the building of the Church.

Therefore, Jesus was perfectly right when he said; *"You must be born again by the water (the Word) and the Spirit."* Only then, it is very easy for the man to have access to see and to enter the Kingdom of God. To see and to enter into the Kingdom of God means to become spiritually qualified to be a part and parcel in the building of the Church. It is now a repented heart and a born again spirit of a man, is all that is required as essential and necessary material for the primary laying of the foundation of the Church.

Repenting from sins and being born again seem to be two different things here; but in actual fact it is not. Instead they happen simultaneously in a life of a person. And the two are very essential to one another in the Kingdom building. For the Church of God can not be built with decaying and deteriorating materials such as unclean hearts that are full of evil and spiritually dead.

Jesus goes on to explain the very crucial issue within the Christian circle as to how and where the Church should be built. In this statement of Jesus, He also explained and in the process, he indirectly answered one of the very serious questions as to which church is the right church in this world.

The very simple answer for all these questions is found in Matthew 16:18, as Jesus said; *"And I also say to you that you are Peter, and on this rock I will build My Church, and the gates of Hades shall not prevail against it."*

Let's try and see some remarkable truths in this short statement. The name Peter for instance; in this situation. "Simon," was the given name by his family. But Jesus called him Peter, the rock. Peter is derived from the Greek word "Petros" which means a huge rock. Jesus did not give the new name, just for the sake of giving a name. It was based on the revelation Simon Peter received in verse 16. He said; *"You are the Christ, the Son of the Living God."* Other people were confused and they didn't know who He was. They missed understood Him, and mistaken Him with other prophets (Matthew 16:13-14). The truth about who Jesus was; had not been revealed to them.

So they had no basis on which Jesus could able to found or establish His Church in their lives. The revelation of truth about Jesus Christ in the heart of Simon, really prompted Jesus to call him Peter, the rock, on which he founded His Church. It is only the truth that is in the heart of a person that will attract God and cause Him to establish His Kingdom in that person's heart. How can the man have truth in his heart? It is only by hearing the truth, believing in it, and acting upon the truth.

It is therefore, let's conclude that the Architect or Designer of the Church; God the Father, and the Chief Builder of the Church; Jesus Christ will very much like to see a born again and repented heart, which has a Word of truth for that's what it matters so much in the building of the Church. Without these very, very essential elements in a life of a person, the concern person should not deceive him or herself by thinking that he or she is a heaven bound Christian. For how can he or she participate in the building of the Holy Church; with such a filthy lifestyle?

It will never ever eventuate as we think it would, so it's proper not to be proud of our own understanding (Proverbs 3:5-7, 16:2, 21:2, Jeremiah 9:23-24), but humble ourselves and do it right as the Bible commands before it's too late!

Chapter 4

What is Church?

a: **The Ekklesia or the Universal Church**

The Church is called **ekklesia** in Greek, which means a people group or an assembly of people, the universal Church or Body of Christ (not as an individual) that is 'called out' and is 'saved,' from sin and no longer belongs to this sinful world. Sinful world does not really mean about this physical world with mountains, rivers, valleys, plants, animals, seas etc. These are beautiful creations of God. In fact He created them beautifully and every thing was good in His eyes (Genesis 1:1-31). There was absolutely nothing wrong in the creation of God and so does at this time. All the beautiful creations of God speak for His Awesome Power and Wisdom (Psalms 104:24, 136:5, Proverbs 3:19, Jeremiah 51:15). They are the witnesses of God to prove to us how Powerful and Mighty He is.

It was only when sin entered into the world that things went wrong (Genesis 3:6-19). In that case sinful world does not really mean about the natural creations but indeed it means about the lifestyle in which people live in this world. See what Graham Fitzpatrick says in one of his books. "The word "world" in the Bible is not defined as the physical earth but as the "non-Christian attitudes prevalent among many people in all nations").["][4]

Therefore, the Church or this particular people group is obliged to live totally in obedience in the Word of God and should have nothing to do with the worldly people in regards to their lifestyle as it says in Romans 12:1-2 and 1Peter 1:14-16. The new life that they are engaged to, is a supernatural life that natural or physical laws cannot able to elucidate or explain. It is really a lifestyle that can be easily distinguished from natural to supernatural not on the outside but on the inside.

The word church is also derived from another Greek word called "kuriakon" which means "belonging to the Lord." That means, it is an assembly of people that belongs to the Lord. However, according to Guy P. Duffield and Nathaniel M. Van Cleave, "In post-apostolic times the Greeks used the term kuriakon to designate the church building."[5] Well, now we will see the four components that distinguish this people group from the worldly people.

Firstly, they are a people who are **born again** by the power of the Word and of the Holy Spirit. This is in accordance with John 3:3-8, where it tells us how we can **see** and **enter** into the kingdom of God. It reads in verse 3 that; *"Most assuredly, I say to you, unless one is born again, he can not **see** the kingdom of God."* It also says in verse 5 that; *"Most assuredly,*

---

[4] Graham Fitzpatrick, "How To Recognize God's Voice," (Spiritual Growth Books, Queensland, 1985). p. 37.
[5] Ibid, (2006). p. 419.

*I say to you, unless one is born of water and of the Spirit, he can not **enter** the kingdom of God."*

Like I have said earlier in chapter 3, the water here speaks of the Word and the Spirit refers to the Holy Spirit. How it happens in a life of a person is truly a mystery of God that none of us can able to understand, as it explains more in verses 6-8. Anyway, let's read verses 6-8. *"That which is born of the flesh is flesh, and that which is born of the Spirit is Spirit"* (vs.6). *"Do not marvel that I said to you, You must be born again"* (vs.7). *"The wind blows where it wishes, and you hear the sound of it, but can not tell where it comes from and where it goes. So is everyone who is born of the Spirit"* (vs.8).

You see, man must be **born again** by the power of the Word and the Spirit that will qualify him to be a member of that people group. In this subject matter the Bible is self explanatory that I can't go any further.

Secondly, they are **washed** and **redeemed** by the blood of Jesus Christ. This is in accordance with Matthew 26:28 where it says; *"For this is my blood of the new covenant, which is shed for many for the **remission** of sins."*

The blood of Jesus Christ was shed on the cross of Calvary particularly for the remission of sins. We can apply the blood of Jesus in many other situations as well, but its priority number one is for the remission of sins. Apostle Paul confirms this by saying that; *"In Him we have redemption through His blood, the forgiveness of sins, according to the riches of His grace"* (Ephesians 1:7). In the book of Hebrews 9:22 it says; *"And according to the law almost all things are purified with blood, and without shedding of blood there is no remission."*

The blood does not only redeem us and forgive our sins but it also cleanses and washes us from our sins. In 1John1:7 it says; *"But if we walk in the light as He is in the light, we have fellowship with one another, and the blood of Jesus Christ His Son cleanses us from all sin."* Again in the book of Hebrews 9:14 it says; *"How much more shall the blood of Christ, who through the eternal Spirit offered Himself without spot to God, cleanse your conscience from dead works to serve the living God?"*

This is something that the animal blood could not do in the Old Testament. In the Old Testament the blood of animals could only redeem and cleanse outwardly but could not cleanse and wash away sin on the inside (Hebrews 9:13). In that sense, those who are **cleansed** and **washed** by the blood of Jesus Christ on the inside are members of the Church of God.

Thirdly, this particular people group is a people that are **saved** from this sinful world by the grace of God. It is only through the grace of God that sinners will have access to salvation. The Bible says in John 3:16 that; *"For God so loved the world that He gave His only begotten Son, that whoever believes in Him should not perish but have everlasting life."*

John 3:16 shows how much God loves us as sinners by giving His only Begotten Son to us. There was no other greatest gift God could give in place of Jesus. In Romans 5:8 it says; *"But God demonstrates His own love toward us, in that while we were still sinners, Christ died for us."*

The demonstration of God's love for us is quiet evident in giving away Jesus for the salvation of mankind; that no man can ever ask God for anything better than salvation. Jesus was all that God could give, and that should be enough for a sinner like you and I; that we may be **saved** by the grace of God.

Fourthly, they are a people whose **names are written down in the Lamb's Book of Life**. Revelation 20:15 says; *"And anyone not found written in the Book of Life was cast into the lake of fire."*

Names to be written down in the Lamb's Book of Life, is something that needs to be considered very seriously. For if the name of a person is not found in the Book of Life, that person will definitely be disqualified to enter the Kingdom of God or the New Jerusalem. It's good to have our names enrolled or registered in common rolls in our different church groups, or denominations, or local congregations, but we must become extra ordinary smart people to make sure that our names are written in the Lamb's Book of Life. For whether or not our **names written in the Lamb's Book of Life**, will ultimately determine our eternity.

The above four important components must be a testimony for one to be fully qualified to be a member of the Church of God. If the above set of ingredients is missing in one's life, that person should reconsider it again for there is no short-cut whatsoever for anyone to enter the Kingdom of heaven. You've got to be a member of the Church or else forget about claiming to be a Christian, for there is no such thing as Christian without being a member of the Church of God.

How can one claim to be a Christian without having a mark of ownership by the sealing of the above important components in his life? The Bible is very clear in this area that; if one is not sealed by the Holy Spirit who is also the guarantee of our inheritance, and does not have the Spirit of God, he is not a child of God (Ephesians 1:13-14, and Romans 8:9). It is therefore, we can say that the true Christians are those who have passed the test that qualifies them to be members of the Church of God. And it can be anybody from any Christian church denomination. But it can only be done through the right procedure prescribed in this portion and it is none other than the above four prescribed components.

Some smart guys can still try not to be members of church organizations in this world for some good reasons of their own, and yet they live good Christian lives. This is possible in some sense, but they can't afford to live a Christian life without becoming a member of the Church of God. It is impossible, and it will be a waste of time if one wants to give a try.

Becoming a member of the Church of God is the only possible way for us to be Christians or followers of Christ. The Spiritual significance in this is that; the Church is the Body of Christ in which Jesus Himself is the Head of the Church, and we are His Body (Ephesians1:22-23).

How can one claim to be a Christian or a member of the Body of Christ, when his spirit-man is dead and nothing of Christ is found in him? He is like a man who is biologically different in his DNA; (so to say), to claim that he is a member of a family that he actually does not belong to. He can still claim to be a Christian without becoming a member of any other church organizations, but it's not the same thing with the Church of God.

Here we are trying to distinguish the difference between "ekklesia," the Church of God or the "Universal Church" the catholic (not the Catholic Church) and the other big or small church organizations or denominations. The difference here is; to be a member of the Church of God is something spiritual or invisible, while to be a member of a church organization is physical or visible. It is physical (visible) for it's very easy to identify which church the particular person belongs to, while on the other hand it is spiritual (invisible) because we can't see it with our physical eyes.

For ekklesia, the Church of God is a Spiritual Body, and therefore it is invisible. We can only see the actions and characters of those who are members of this Church on the outside. A member of the Church of God is invisible that only God alone knows. And it's only those things on the inside of a man that qualify him whether or not to be a Christian.

These qualified Christians shouldn't have to be from only one church group or organization. Some believe that those who are members of their church group are the only members of the Church of God. This is ridiculous and it is a fake from the pit of hell. The truth is that; whoever is a born again Christian and has a repented heart, who is washed and cleansed by the blood of Jesus, and his name is written in the Lamb's Book of Life, is truly a member of the Church of God; regardless of which church denomination he belongs to. And it is very true that this kind of Christians can be found in all the Christian church organizations, only if we thoroughly do a good research. "The Universal Church is composed of all genuine Christian believers of all ages, both on earth and in paradise, the total Body of Christ."[6]

It is also true that may be one church organization or a local congregation has more born again Christians than the other; but that does not simply qualify that particular church group to be the only church of God. I don't know about you but to me, it is a very shameful and a frightening thing for one particular church group or a ministry team to profess that it is the only church of God on the face of this earth. These sort of teachings must be one hundred percent (100%) convincible enough to challenge the all world. But I still believe that most of us will never agree with such a doctrine and it will be definitely repugnant stuff to us. Apostle Peter was correct when he said; "God has no favorites." *Then Peter opened his mouth and said: "In truth I perceive that God shows no partiality"* (Acts 10:34). *"But in every nation whoever fears Him and works righteousness is accepted by Him"* (vs.35).

Truly God has no favorite church groups or so-called independent last day ministries. But having said that; still there are some favorite ones of God in this world. May I show you who they are? They are right under your nose. Read verse 35 of Acts chapter 10 again. The favorite ones of God are the ones who fear Him and do righteousness in every nation. That

---

[6] Ibid, (2006). pp. 420, 421.

means they can be from any church in any nation. It will be a waste of time and energy for some few to claim that they are the only favorite ones of God. What a shameful thing to claim such an adoration that is not mandated by God.

b: The Kingdom of Heaven.

The Kingdom of Heaven is a Kingdom not of this world. It is a Kingdom that has a King and a government of its own. It is a Kingdom that does not adopt or apply rules and laws from this sinful world to operate in its systems. It has its own way of doing things and therefore, will never ever compromise with the rules and principles of this world.

The word "kingdom" is derived from Greek word "basileia." It means a king's rule, reign, dominion, or authority. In our case, Jesus Christ is the King with a new government, with new rules and orders and principles with a system completely new altogether.

Jesus was right when He said; *"Repent, for the kingdom of heaven is at hand"* (Matthew 4:17). Before Jesus went on to preach about many other things, He was very careful in addressing the world why He was here for. The very first message He ever preached straight after being in the wilderness, tempted by the devil, was what He ought to preach. He said; *"Repent, for the kingdom of heaven is at hand."*

The people then must repent, not to feel some good about a new invention, a new lifestyle, a new model or anything of that matter. They had to repent because the "Kingdom of heaven;" a Kingdom that has transferred from the Most High Throne of the Almighty God to rest up-on the face of the earth.

It was then established on this earth some more than two thousand years ago. The Kingdom had come with the King with all the blessings to be shared with the people of this world. But before they get a share of those blessings, they must first of all become citizens of that Kingdom. Only those who are citizens of that Kingdom are eligible to participate in those Kingdom blessings. No wonder, Jesus said; *"Repent, for the kingdom of heaven is at hand."* For that is the only possible way through which the people could able to become citizens of this Kingdom.

The Kingdom of God that I am talking about here is spiritual and currently in existence. It is but not the future (eschatological) Kingdom in which Jesus will literally reign in power and glory in righteousness in His Millennial Reign, according to Guy P. Duffield and Nathaniel M. Van Cleave.[7]

The way of repentance goes well together with the birth of the spirit-man in accordance with John 3:3-8. We have already seen how the birth of a spirit-man takes place in a life of a person in the previous segment. The process is some how similar to that of the physical birth. In a physical birth (at the day of the birth), the young infant automatically becomes a member of a family as well as becoming a citizen of a country. The very reason is that; the infant was born into the family and into the country where he was born.

Because the infant is an automatic member of his family, he has all the right of a son to claim what he

---

[7] Ibid, (2006). p. 444.

should from his family first of all, and then his country for he is also an automatic citizen of his country.

Therefore, there is no slight restriction whatsoever for the automatic citizens than the non-citizens. Likewise, those who are born again in their spirit, are born into the Kingdom of heaven. And so they become automatic citizens and heirs together with Jesus in the Kingdom of heaven as soon as they are born in the Spirit; regardless of the location and the person who prayed over them.

It says in 1Corinthians 6:17 that; *"But he who is joined to the Lord is one spirit with Him."* When we are born again, we actually join with Him by becoming the children of God and hence, become automatic citizens of heaven and also become members of the family of God, which is known as the Church of God. All these happen simultaneously, that I can't explain which one comes first. But it is true that they happen at the same time.

Anyway, these people group, who are born again in the Spirit, are surely the automatic citizens of the Kingdom of heaven. Because they are automatic citizens of heaven and have birthrights as sons of the Kingdom, they have the right to claim all the blessings of God as sons of the Kingdom. Therefore, though they are here on earth, they no longer belong to this world as they used to be in the past. But they only live in this world as foreigners to accomplish their purposes as it is recorded in Ephesians 2:12-22.

Here it states that; *"That at that time you were without Christ, being aliens from the commonwealth of Israel and strangers from the covenants of promise, having no hope and without God in the world"* (vs.12). *"But now in Christ Jesus you who once were far off have been brought near by the blood of Christ"* (vs.13). *"For He Himself is our peace, who has made both one, and has broken down the middle wall of separation"* (vs.14), *"Having abolished in His flesh the enmity, that is, the law of commandments contained in ordinances, so as to create in Himself one new man from the two, thus, making peace"* (vs.15), *"And that He might reconcile them both in God in one body through the cross, thereby putting to death the enmity"* (vs.16). *"And He came and preached peace to you who were afar off and to those who were near"* (vs.17). *"For through Him we both have access by one Spirit to the Father"* (vs.18). *"Now, therefore, you are no longer strangers and foreigners, but fellow citizens with the saints and members of the household of God"* (vs.19), *"Having been built on the foundation of the apostles and prophets, Jesus Christ Himself being the chief cornerstone"* (vs.20), *"In whom the whole building, being fitted together, grows into a holy temple in the Lord"* (vs.21), *"In whom you also are being built together for a dwelling place of God in the Spirit"* (vs.22).

The Biblical term for this people group who are citizens of the Kingdom of heaven but foreigners to this world are called "ekklesia," the Church of God; as we've seen earlier. That does not mean the Church of God is here hoping and dreaming about a lifestyle that is yet to come, but it is in fact living in that Kingdom life. For the Kingdom of God is not a legend or a myth, but it is actually a Spiritual lifestyle that is in the hearts of all believers. It is also true that the perfection of the Kingdom lifestyle will be tasted up there in New Jerusalem but it all begins here on earth. Jesus said the Kingdom of heaven has already come and is in you. This is recorded in Luke 17:21 where it says; *"Nor will they say, "See here!" or "See there!" For indeed, the kingdom of God is within you."*

It is interesting to see that the Kingdom of God has not come to reside outside of us but in us. To have the Kingdom of God in us is not another religious myth, but it is a people group who is literally living a standard of life that is completely unique to all other lifestyles in this world. For the Kingdom life is a life that imitate and does almost everything about and in line with the things of the Kingdom of God.

Those who are in it and the Kingdom in them are the ones who talk Kingdom, walk Kingdom and every bit of their lives is dominated by the Kingdom lifestyle. Though they are originally from all the different races around the world, they have one tradition. Despite the little barriers they have among themselves as a result of their different church groups with different theological backgrounds, those who are in the Kingdom are identical.

It is very easy to identify; no matter if he is a Japanese or an English. A Catholic or a Protestant. For the Bible tells us that you are no longer a Jew or a Greek or a slave or a freeman. We are all one in Jesus Christ. Apostle Paul made this very clear in Galatians 3:26-29. This is what it says in verse 28; *"There is neither Jew nor Greek, there is neither slave nor free, there is neither male nor female; for you are all one in Christ Jesus."*

In fact the Kingdom of God consists with a people group, irrespective of different race, culture, tradition, language, etc, and even their different church groups. Because they are members of this one Kingdom of God, the Kingdom lifestyle unifies them not only on the outside but on the inside as well. The first white uniform so to say, which speaks of righteousness, had been dyed in the *"Blood of Jesus; that cleanses and washes them from their iniquities"* (1John 1:7).

In Matthew 26:28, Jesus says; *"For this is My blood of the new covenant, which is shed for many for the remission of sins."* Here Jesus first declared that His blood was shed, not only for some few favorites, but also for many. This refers back to John 3:16; *"For God so loved the world that He gave His only begotten Son, that whoever believes in Him should not perish but have everlasting life."*

Jesus came for the all world and so His blood. Jesus' blood washes and takes away every sin and makes them clean, white as snow. It is then, the white robe that unifies many around the world. John saw this in his revelation in the Island of Patmos. It is recorded in Revelation 7:13-14, where it says; *"Then one of the elders answered saying to me, "Who are these arrayed in white robes, and where did they come from"* (vs.13)? *"And I said to him, "Sir, you know." So he said to me, "These are the ones who come out of the great tribulation, and washed their robes and made them white in the blood of the Lamb"* (vs.14).

The seal of the Holy Spirit also unifies them. Paul tells the Corinthians and the Ephesians that the Holy Spirit is the seal of ownership, and that He is the guarantee that we are His children and members of the Kingdom of God. *"Who also has sealed us and given us the Spirit in our hearts as a guarantee"* (2Corinthians 1:22). *"In Him you also trusted, after you heard the word of truth, the gospel of your salvation; in whom also, having believed, you were sealed with the Holy Spirit of promise"* (Ephesians 1:13), *"Who is the guarantee of our inheritance until the redemption of the purchased possession, to the praise of His glory"* (vs.14).

The Kingdom of God is a Kingdom comprised of new people. There is a law in the Kingdom of God that any person with old fashion can not effectively live in it. There is no such thing as fifty, fifty in the Kingdom of God. You've got to be either in the Kingdom or outside the Kingdom. You've got to be either black or white. Or you've got to be either sheep or goat. Even if we are all mixed-up and live together, and have fellowship together in one church, thinking that we are all Christians, wait until one fine day the sheep will be separated from the goats.

"All the nations will be gathered before Him, and He will separate them one from another, as a shepherd divides his sheep from the goats" (Matthew 25:32). *"And He will set the sheep on His right hand, but the goats on the left"* (vs.33). *"Then the King will say to those on His right hand, "Come, you blessed of My Father, inherit the kingdom prepared for you from the foundation of the world"* (vs.34).

Isn't this very clear that the Kingdom of God belongs only to the sheep and not the goats? Then how comes both sheep and goats all live together in one place? Well, it's only the Kingdom on earth that is mistaken by religious myth in which we are all mixed-up but it will never continue in heaven anyway.

Really, the goats are not members of the Kingdom of God, but just because we commonly share the planet called earth together, it only seems like we are all together in one place.

In the eyes of God, spiritually we are a separate and peculiar people. In the eyes of this world, on the other hand, the sheep and the goats look alike by sharing some similarities and can be together in one church. This is possible because in Matthew 13:24-43, Jesus said; they can be together in one place. But it is a sad thing that when the Day of Judgment comes, Matthew 25:32-34 will come to reality. The sheep will be separated from the goats. What a day that will be; a day full of tears of joy for the sheep, and also a day full of tears of pain, agony and turmoil, sorrow and suffering for the goats.

Let's see what Peter said about this people group. *"But you are a chosen generation, a royal priesthood, a holy nation, His own special people, that you may proclaim the praises of Him who called you out of darkness into His marvelous light"* (1Peter 2:9); *"Who once were not a people but are now the people of God, who had not obtained mercy but now have obtained mercy"* (vs.10).

I pray that our eyes be opened to see that we are a chosen generation, a royal priesthood, a holy nation, and His own special and peculiar people.

Only when the knowledge of this truth is registered and sank into our system, we will begin to respect the Kingdom, serve the Kingdom, and help build the Kingdom and not our own little empires. However, if one is found doing opposite things, he should be questioned to find out whether he is doing it deliberately or in ignorance.

I believe those who are doing it deliberately are not servants of God, but angels of the light on the outside but on the inside, they are indeed wolves in our mist only to destroy the Church. The ones who are doing it in ignorance are servants of God who only need correction and direction, from those who are matured in the things of God.

Finally, it is the Kingdom of God that we should serve and be participants in the Kingdom activities.

c: The Church Organizations

The church organizations whether big or small are people groups that organize themselves and come together for one common tenet (doctrine or belief). Each organization has its own basis that becomes the foundation for their standing in God. One way or the other, almost every individual member believes that the church organization he belongs to could be the best and is the only true church which knows the way better than the others. In the process, others are prompted by new revelations or visions and even doctrines that are only charisma to leave their old church organizations and join up with new groups. The trend in forming new and reform groups here and there seems to continue forever till the end comes.

However, the only exception is the move of the Holy Spirit. That is when the Spirit of God changes a person, and gives new life according to John 3:3-8 and 2Corinthians 5:17. Only then, the changed person will have a good reason to look for a better place where he can be fed properly in the Word of God.

Other times the religious church leaders would not accept the ones who are led by the Holy Spirit and have fresh touch from on High. This would again lead to have different faction in the church that might gradually cause division in the church. Anything other than these two very important reasons should not and never be accepted by God. For the idea of forming new groups every now and then and moving from one group to another, will definitely not help to build the Church of God as it is desired by Him. It will only produce its own kind like rebellious and antichrist-like children.

Yet people are very anxious in this prohibited area. I think there is a spirit behind forming new groups every now and then, and moving from one church to another. Apostle Paul discouraged the very movement in its initial stage. However, some people are little bit smarter than Apostle Paul; and they deliberately ignore what he said in 1Corinthians 3:1-9. *"For you are still carnal. For where there are envy, strife, and divisions among you, are you not carnal and behaving like mere men"* (vs.3)? *For when one says, "I am of Paul," and another, "I am of Apollos," are you not carnal"* (vs.4)?

It is very obvious that when one forms his or her own group, he or she seems to have something new and better that the other group does not have it. In doing so, the Bible, the Word of God is the only book on the face of this earth that has countless of interpretations.

One says this and the other says that. It is very true and nothing is secret that each one of us is bound to any one of these tenets. Some of us, we know that Jesus is the source or author and finisher of our faith (Hebrews 12:2), yet we are tangled with our little doctrines. We are firmly bound into our little ways of serving and worshiping our God. Even as I am writing this, I am also convinced and I could not deny the fact that I am also one of them. I would rather say what a tragedy we are engaged to, whether we know it or not.

Unlike any other metaphors of the Church, "church organizations" are hardly found in the Bible. In fact Apostle Paul who was then led by the Spirit of God really discouraged the idea of forming different factions in the Church, the Body of Christ (1Corithians 3:1-9). No where in the Bible, can one draw his Biblical authority to support his argument that its God's perfect will that we have different church organizations. No, I don't think so, because the Word of God does not support it. I think it's God's permissive will that the like-minded should get themselves organized, not to compete with other Christian brothers and sisters but to help build the Body of Christ through different methods as the Lord leads.

In fact the Church of God is not an organization but it is a growing organism. It has its own way of growing from stage to stage in the Word of God through the help of the Holy Spirit. The growing from infant stage to maturity stage and its expansion and extension, depends so much on what kind of food it takes. It is obvious that the combination of the Word and the Spirit in a clean vessel is what it naturally requires for its growth. However, over the years, people tend to apply different methods as they see fit to build the Church. Because every man is a unique being, his way of interpreting things unnecessarily varies from one another.

It is therefore, different people have different interpretations from the Bible that some agree with them and others not. In the process, those who agree with them go together in one direction and the others take the opposite direction. In doing so, such movements ultimately result in forming different groups with different doctrines and beliefs. I don't think God is interested in this group or that group but all He wants to see is the unity in the Body of Christ.

May be one group has like-minded of a hand while the other group has like-minded of a leg. It is therefore; one good thing about them is that, each group will perform diversities of activities from one another. But it is the same God who works all in all (1Corinthians 12:6).

I would therefore, conclude that it is not altogether bad to have many different church groups, but one must be very careful in what he does, for God will not judge him for having different groups; but different actions and behaviours as a result of their different motives and intentions. It is what we do that will determine our destiny than our location or our name. It doesn't matter; whether you belong to group A or group B but that which matters the most is what really you are.

The little knowledge that I have from the Bible, is a problem for my own standing in God. It is a problem to me, because I at least know what I should do; but I don't do that which I should do. Like Apostle Paul said in Romans 7:14-20 that; what he wills not to do, is what he does and what he wills to do, is what he does not do.

In many situations as a Pastor, and a Leader serving our God for more than thirty-three (33) years now, I have noticed something that really frightens me. I don't know about others but what I have noticed over the years is that; only a less percentage of our church members are there to obey the Bible as it is. Most of us have our own little sideline agendas to cater for, in the name of the service for our God.

We have more respect for our little doctrines and our beliefs; even in our leaders or founders of our churches than the Bible itself. With due respect for our doctrines and our leaders or founders, we should not loss focus on the author and finisher of our faith (Hebrews 12:2), Jesus Christ. Mark my words, if the trend of putting our trust in our own little strength, whatever it is and loss focus on Jesus continues, then we are getting closer to destruction.

The Word of God is very clear that we should not have anybody or anything else in the place of God and put our trust in it. But if we do, then it becomes our little god and we are violating the decrees of God.

Let's read Exodus 20:1-5. *And God spoke all these words, saying* (vs.1). *"I am the Lord your God, who brought you out of the land of Egypt, out of the house of bondage"* (vs.2). *"You shall have no other gods before Me"* (vs.3). *"You shall not make for yourself a carved image-any likeness of anything that is in heaven above, or that is in the earth beneath, or that is in the water under the earth"* (vs.4); *"You shall not bow down to them nor serve them. For I, the Lord your God, am a jealous God, visiting the iniquity of the fathers upon the children to the third and fourth generations of those who hate Me"* (vs.5).

Anyway, I don't know how you understand the church organizations but to me, like I've said; they are people groups who come together for one common tenet. The reason for many new church groups coming up every now and then is obvious. It could be that each group sees something differently from different angle and perspective to one another. And of course some other little sideline agendas are also attached in these strings. It is not absolutely wrong to do so, but we must be very careful in what we are doing. I believe our doctrines or beliefs are only methods through which we can serve our God, but the methods whatever they are, must agree with and in the light of the Word of God.

To my understanding, all Christian church organizations are founded on a single revelation or a Word of God. Some of these are truly God given and others are not. These revelations or visions or Words or whatever they are, are their basis on which they build their church organizations. Because these revelations or Words happen to be their foundations, they emphasize a little bit more on them.

Sometimes in the process the real meaning of the Word, for instance; is not clearly exposed or preached but covered-up with human ideas and philosophies. They forget the fact that the true foundation is none other than Jesus Christ; the original and the only solid Rock Foundation for the Church; according to the book of Isaiah 28:16, 1Corinthians 3:10-11, and Matthew 16:18. *"And I also say to you that you are Peter, and on this rock I will build My church, and the gates of Hades shall not prevail against it."*

The Rock Foundation is not Apostle Peter, as some claim that he is. Peter in Greek as I've stated earlier, is Petros, which means a rock; and the rock as we know that it refers to Jesus Himself. Peter only carries a name that means a rock; but he is not the actual rock. For he is just a simple and mere human being like you and I. Peter has no Spiritual qualities such as Godly deity and attributes that could qualify him to become the foundation for the Church of God.

How can a mere man becomes the foundation for the Church of God? For goodness sake; I can't swallow it; for its bitterness is like a stinking egg of a poisonous snake. It doesn't matter if it is Apostle Peter or anybody else or whatever it is that competes with Jesus, is a direct counterfeit doctrine from the pit of hell.

Most Christians are tempted to believe that the Apostles and the Prophets are the foundations of the Church of God; in which Apostle Peter is no exception that he must be the foundation for the Church according to Matthew 16:18. The more convincing Bible text is found in Ephesians 2:20, where it says; *"Having been built on the foundation of the apostles and prophets, Jesus Christ Himself being the chief cornerstone."*

"Having been built on the foundation of the apostles and prophets" doesn't necessarily mean that they in person become the foundation. In fact they have laid a foundation using separate material apart from themselves. I believe the material apart from themselves is no other than the Word of God that they preached, which is Jesus who is also the Rock. No wonder, it says; "the foundation **of** the apostles and prophets." It does not say, the apostles and prophets **are** the foundation; as it is clearly stated with the position of Jesus. Jesus' position in this situation is that; "Jesus Christ Himself being the chief cornerstone." Here we see that Jesus is the subject of the foundation, where as the Apostles are the objects of the foundation. The 21st and 22nd verses of Ephesians chapter 2 precisely declare that we are built and fitted together with Jesus Christ who is the Rock foundation; where as with the Apostles and Prophets, the Bible is silent.

The Apostles and the Prophets are only the ministers of the Gospel (Ephesians 4:11-12). They are in fact gifted to lay foundation in the work of God with His Word, who is Jesus (1Corithians 3:10-11) that others can build on it but not the Apostles themselves. They (the Apostles and Prophets) were not and will never be the foundation themselves; so it's proper not to propagate a theory/theology that has not enough support from the Word of God.

In fact Jesus meant to build His Church on the confessed revelation by Apostle Peter found in Matthew 16:16. Well, what was the confessed revelation then? *Simon Peter answered and said, "You are the Christ, the Son of the living God."* "You are the Christ, the Son of the living God," was the revelation, isn't it? If we all agree with the revelation of Peter, then the revelation was all about Jesus Christ, and it has nothing to do with Peter himself. Peter was only an instrument to what Jesus was trying to accomplish on earth. I think it's proper not to argue with the revealed truth by firmly defensive in our ignorance.

Yet, the more we do it, the more we will be led astray from the truth. Please read again Chapter 3 from page 26 through the rest of the pages of this book for more clarification on the foundation of the Church.

There has been a tendency over the years that so-called church leaders and others are carried away by believing in their own little tenets, thinking that they are the only favourite ones of God.

We must know the fact that there are no favourite ones among the children of God. *Then Peter opened his mouth and said: "In truth I perceive that God shows no partiality"* (Acts 10:34). *"But in every nation whoever fears Him and works righteousness is accepted by Him"* (vs. 35).

All of us are children of God, and therefore, His love for us is measured in John 3:16. *"For God so loved the world that He gave His only begotten Son, that whoever believes in Him should not perish but have everlasting life."*

Here we see that the "love" of God is not limited to one or few individuals only. The size and the weight of God's love for mankind are immeasurable. I pray that those who are led by the deceiving spirits to believe that they are the only favorite ones of God, be convinced by the Spirit of God that their eyes are enlighten to see how big and great the love of God is for us. I mean, this is something incredible for anyone of us to lay judgment on others and claim to be the only loved ones of God. In doing so, we are taking His place of judgment, which we are forbidden not to do so. *"Judge not, that you be not judged"* (Matthew 7:1). *"For with what judgment you judge, you will be judged; and with the measure you use, it will be measured back to you"* (vs. 2).

How dare can a simple creation of God do something that supposed to be done by God Himself? Self righteousness and thinking of oneself is better than others could be one of the major vanities and reasons that have caused them to come up with their own little groups. Sometimes it is very hard to distinguish, and getting confused whether to listen to this one or to that one in whatever they say. Everyone seems to be the best, and in the process, the venerable people of God who are also vulnerable in the things of God are confused and deceived.

As we are busy fighting for our own little groups, we forget the fact that we are all members of one body, the Body of Christ that can not be divided into many in accordance with 1Corinthians12:12, 20, 27 and Ephesians 4:4. All these Bible texts talk about one body, which is the Body of Christ that symbolizes the one Church of God.

The one Church of God that I am referring to; is not this anticipated worldwide phenomenon or scenario that will operate in total contrary to the Word of God; in accordance with the orders directed by the beast that the book of Revelation talks about in chapter 13. If this scenario truly comes to pass, then it will be the obvious counterfeit for the real one. It will actually take place after the rapture for only a duration of last three and half (3½) years found in Revelation 13:1-18. A mixture of human philosophy and a bit of truth should not desecrate the full gospel, let alone the one Church of God.

Fighting for our own little personal interests has overwhelmingly blinded our eyes that we can't able to see the very basics in our Christian belief. In 2Corinthians 4:4, the Bible says; *"Whose minds the god of this age has blinded, who do not believe, lest the light of the gospel of the glory of Christ, who is the image of God, should shine on them."*

If we find it hard to know these basics, I suggest that we should at all cost re-check our standing in God. I mean, to know and understand the basics such as one Body or one Church, one Spirit, one hope, one Lord, one faith, one baptism, one God, and of course one heaven according to Ephesians 4:4-5, are elementary stuff that we really need not a Bible philosopher to elucidate them to us.

The Bible that we have is very plain, straight-forward, explicitly and precisely written in simple terms; particularly in the areas of the basics. I don't think a good and a loving Father would make that issue so complicated for His little ignorant children to understand. Just imagine; why would He ever do that, knowing the fact that we are indeed some bunch of ignorant and incompetent people who are also vulnerable in the spiritual matters?

Another feature about the church organizations is that, they are in-fact man-made little church groups. They are man-made because truly they are. We can distinguish the man-made churches from the Church of God in the following categories.

They are man-made because first of all, they are one way or the other founded by either a man or a woman or a group of believers. Secondly, they are man-made because all of them (except Judaism) whether big or small, old or new were started after the Church of God founded by Jesus Christ through the Power of the Holy Spirit in the day of Pentecost. Thirdly, they are man-made because they consist of so-called Christians who are not truly born again in the Spirit, who have not truly repented from their sins, and who are not truly free from their sinful nature. Yet they profess to be Christians of whatever church they belong to. Fourthly, they are man-made because the fellowship of non and truly born again Christians in sharing communion together, sharing the Word of God together, and do almost everything together, thinking that they are all members of the Church of God, is not the way the Bible encourages. They are man-made church organizations because the groups are mixture of either true or non- Christians and thus; are good religious people only.

In the Church of God on the other hand, there can't be both true and non- Christians living together, for it is a Spiritual Body. This is impossible and will never ever eventuate; no matter how best we try to squeeze ourselves into one place. For this is what the Bible says in 2Corinthians 6:14-16: *"Do not be unequally yoked together with unbelievers. For what fellowship has righteousness with lawlessness? And what communion has light with darkness"* (vs.14)? *"And what accord has Christ with Belial? Or what part has a believer with an unbeliever"* (vs.15)? *And what agreement has the temple of God with idols? For you are the temple of the living God"* (vs.16).

Finally our actions, whatever they are, show explicitly and clearly well that our church organizations are truly man-made.

Well, what do we really mean by church organizations? And what is the actual difference between the church organizations and the Church of God? The answers for such questions are as follows.

Church organizations are mixture of saved and unsaved people groups. They have common beliefs in one or more tenets or doctrines. And they have registered themselves to be members of whatever church organization that they belong to.

The Church of God on the other hand, is a Spiritual and invisible Church that by no means, can it accommodate unsaved souls. It is a Church consists of only saved souls from all Christian churches around the world. Like I've stated earlier, the Church of God is an invisible Church that will never be identified physically as we normally do with church organizations.

Church organizations are people groups that bring finances and other resources together for the side-line physical developments; such as church buildings, Bible schools, other educational institutions and schools, health centers and so on. And of course their uniforms (the name tags) that they wear are obvious such as Catholics, Lutherans, Baptists, Seventh Day Adventist, Assemblies of God, Four Squares, Apostolics, etc. I call these name-tags our uniforms, because by these names we are easily identified as to which church organization we belong to.

Really it was not the case during the Bible days. "During New Testament times no groups of Christians arose with separate name identities similar to modern denominations. Therefore, the word "church" did not come to be appended to the names of leaders or doctrinal tenets, as in Lutheran church or Baptist church, to identify distinct ecclesiastical organizations."[8]

I am not trying to influence anybody by saying all these; that he or she may run away from his or her church group and run into the Church of God. No, you can't do that physically because the Church of God is invisible; yet it can be done spiritually.

Our church organizations or groups are in fact bodies in which we have our fellowship with one another, only in this world; which is also right and acceptable. The writer of Hebrews encourages us not to forsake the assembling of ourselves together (Hebrews 10:25). Nevertheless, it is very important that we must become members of the Church of God with the help and support that we draw from other fellow Christian brothers and sisters through the Word of God. For becoming members of the church organizations alone, is not good enough and it is not beneficial for our spiritual lives and our eternity.

---

[8] Ibid, (2006). p. 423.

d: The Church Building and the Church Service.

The church building and the church service are both known as church. Like we have seen earlier, the church organization or denomination is also called church. The word church or let's say the name church, was first heard by the Apostles when Jesus declared for the first time that He will build His Church on the rock foundation (Matthew 16:18). As we know, it was originally derived from the Greek word "ekklesia." Ekklesia, like we have seen earlier, is not a building, a service, or an organization or a denomination. It is also not an ordinary gathering, but it is in fact a people group or an assembly of people embodied together to worship God. It is also not a single person. One single Christian can't be the Church. A single Christian is only a temple of God where He dwells through the Holy Spirit (1Corinthians 3:16-17, 1Corinthians 6:19, 2Corinthians 6:16).

Paul says in the above Bible references that you are a **temple** of God; referring to each one individually. He did not say; you are the **temples** of God. Because he knew that when addressing a group of believers in plural term, the right term to use was, the "Church of God;" not temples of God. Therefore, individually, we are a temple of God but collectively, we are a Church of God. Lets see what Paul says in 1Corinthians 12:27. *"Now you are the body of Christ, and members individually.* Doesn't it make sense to us that individually, we are only members and not the Church; and collectively, we are a Body of Christ, which speaks of the Church of God? You will see more clarification on this subject matter in chapter 7.

For ekklesia in Greek, is not a singular term, but it is a plural term. Therefore, Church is indeed a people group or an assembly of people and it should not refer to individual Christians. Then, why do we have church buildings, church services and church organizations? What do they really contribute towards the ekklesia, the Church? I have already explained why many church organizations are here for; however, in this segment we will see the reason for a church building and the church service that we turn-up for regular gatherings.

d (1)   The Church Building

Church Building is a building that has been dedicated particularly for church services. It is a place where people gather together to perform Christian activities such as praise and worship, pray meetings, personal devotions, and of course to hear the preaching of the Word of God. No matter how expensive or cheap it is, a church building is only a building, just like any other buildings that we have. The only difference is that it has been dedicated to serve the above purposes. It only becomes special when we feel the presence of God in the midst of these activities.

Without the above Christian activities performed in the church building, the building amounts to nothing but it is only a collection of physical materials of whatever qualities they are. The qualities of materials can be either cheap or expensive; but what it really matters is the achievements of purposes of the building. Some church buildings around the world are very excessively expensive. But the actual purposes of the buildings are not achieved in full as anticipated. Still other church buildings are very cheap but more achievements of purposes of the buildings.

Where would you want to be if a choice is given to us to choose? I don't know where you would like to be but for me, I would rather choose a place where all (not only some) the necessary Christian activities are performed to the fullest; whether it is done in an expensive building or a cheap building. And of course the vitally important thing above all is to feel the presence of God and to meet Him. God must be first of all there in a church building, (irrespective of the quality of the building) in order for us to feel His presence. Truly without the person, his presence is not inevitable, so as with God.

According to Guy P. Duffield and Nathaniel M. Van Cleave, "The Greek word ekklesia which is translated "church" always has reference to people; it never has reference to a building." "Inasmuch as no church buildings were built until the third century, no word was coined to refer to one. When church buildings were built, a different word (kuriake), meaning "the Lord's house," was used to refer to them. On the other hand, the use of one word to describe both the building and the congregation is a natural development. Calling the building a church is a figure of speech called "metonomy" (the container put for the contents)."[9]

---

[9] Ibid, (2006). pp. 422, 423.

By now I think you at least know the purposes of the church building. It is whatever the Christians do in the church building that matters the most; than the building itself. In that case, let's conclude that church building is only a place where we gather to worship our God, but it is not the only place where we should worship Him.

Our God can be worshiped from inside our house, office, garden, in the car, in the plane, in the ship, in the bush and everywhere. But listen to this very carefully. That doesn't mean that we do away with church buildings and worship God anywhere as we wish. The Bible discourages us from doing it intentionally for bad motives (Hebrews10:25), but for reasonable purposes, I think it is accepted; for God is everywhere.

The Bible tells us that; our *"God does not dwell in the church building."* Paul made this clear in the book of Acts 17:24; where it says; *"God, who made the world and everything in it, since He is Lord of heaven and earth, does not dwell in temples made with hands."* But even before Paul said this, Stephen in his address to the Council by saying something similar in Acts 7:47-50 where it says; *"But Solomon built Him a house* (vs.47). *"However, the Most High does not dwell in temples made with hands, as the prophet says"* (vs.48): *"Heaven is My Throne, and earth is My footstool. What house will you build for Me? Says the Lord, Or what is the place of My rest"* (vs. 49)? *"Has My hand not made all these things"* (vs.50)?

Stephen quoted this portion of scriptures from the book of Isaiah 66:1-2. Here God was speaking through Prophet Isaiah to show what was vitally important than to that which was of less importance. First of all, God declares that He does not dwell in temples made with human hands, and on the other hand, He also declares where He desires to dwell in. In the last part of verse 2 of Isaiah 66; God says; *"But on this one will I look; On him who is poor and of a contrite spirit, And who trembles at My word."*

The Word of God is precisely telling us how God feels about the temples built by human hands as well as the temples made by Him. The temples built by human hands are important but not very important as it is with the temples made by Himself. The temples made by Himself are the individual Christians as we've seen earlier; in accordance with 1Corinthians 3:16-17, 6:19, and 2Corinthians 6:16.

Another thing we can also learn from this portion of scriptures is that; God is against the idea of man building churches or temples, thinking that by doing so, they would invite God to come and dwell in them. I want to make it very clear here that; God actually is not against the idea of building churches or temples. However, He is against the concept of thinking that God would come and dwell in our good buildings. He is also against the idea of thinking that He would be honored more if we spend more time, effort, energy and of course more money in building our churches or temples or whatever it is.

Having said that; let me also make it clear that we badly need buildings to meet our needs and our requirements. Whatever size of a church building must meet the necessary requirement of that area, or that church group or that particular congregation. And of course it must be done in accordance with a divine direction.

I have seen people building churches and some are still on the run looking for places to build more churches. Like I said, church buildings should only cater for the needs and requirements of the area first of all, and then the concern church group, and of course the congregation itself.

In some areas, there are enough church buildings. But yet people want more and eventually there are more church buildings with a volume of capacities that does not match with the total population of the area. In other words, the aggregate volume of capacities they have in the church buildings is more than the number of people they have in the area. What a shameful thing to have so many buildings but not enough people to fit into those buildings. This is not so much so in a densely populated area but particularly in places with less population.

When I see places as such, the message that I get is the ignorance of people regarding church buildings. It is a sad thing to have so many different church groups at one particular place. By doing that, they are creating two problems, one for themselves and the other for God. Their problem is that; they are very busy trying to fill-up the unreasonable capacity that they have created in their church buildings. In the process, they end-up stealing sheep from one church into another. As it continues; pain, suffering, division, hatred, unforgiveness, envy, jealousy and so on are inevitable.

The problem for God is that; His only one Church, the Body of Christ has been divided into many different parts. To make it worse, each different part is trying to survive without the help and support from the other parts. This is against the Spiritual law and the system set by God; for a part that is not joint together with the other parts in the Body of Christ, can not survive by itself. It is seemingly possible but it is only a trick by the physical sense. In actual fact; spiritually it is impossible.

For the Bible tells us in 1Corinthians 12:21-22 that; *"And the eye cannot say to the hand, "I have no need of you;" nor again the head to the feet, "I have no need of you" (vs.21). "No, much rather, those members of the body which seem to be weaker are necessary" (vs.22).*

Some times some Christians think they can, but they can not, for it is a fake from the pit of hell. It doesn't matter whether we know it or not; one way or the other, we depend so much on each other for the growth of our spiritual lives. It's very true because we are members of one Body, commonly sharing the life giving blood together. However, yet most Christians practically think that each one of them is an independent believer. In some sense it is right but when it comes to the Church, the Body of Christ, the concept of independent mentality is foreign to the Spiritual system set by God. This is indeed a problem for God, because it is causing spiritual pain in the Body of Christ.

It is a painful thing for God because Church is the Body of Christ. How would one can't feel pain if his body is torn into many pieces? Feeling pain in situation as such, is very obvious and it is inevitable. It is exactly the same thing with Jesus; for the Church

of God is His Body. It says in Ephesians 1:22-23 that;
"And He put all things under His feet, and gave Him to be the head over all things to the church" (vs.21),

Which is His body, the fullness of Him who fills all in all" (vs.23).

Because it is the Body of Christ, God can feel pain as He did when the Church was first persecuted at the time of the Apostles. Paul, who was then Saul, was on his run to persecute the Church and Jesus stopped him from his evil actions and said; *"Saul, Saul, why are you persecuting Me"* (Acts 9:4)*? And he said, "Who are you, Lord?" Then the Lord said, "I am Jesus, whom you are persecuting. It is hard for you to kick against the goads"* (vs.5).

The Bible also tells us that we should not grieve the Holy Spirit as we fight each other for unnecessary things; which are not worth fighting for, while serving God in His Kingdom. We are encouraged by God to be kind to one another and forgive one another. But He discourages us not to have bitterness, wrath, anger, clamor, evil speaking and other such evil manners (Ephesians 4:29-32).

It is also true that some church organizations or church groups are not led by the Holy Spirit. Those people involve in such movements are two types of people groups.

The first ones are so-called Christian workers yet not ordained and directed by God in what they are doing. May be they are called to support the ministries or churches that are already established. Sometimes they are called to do something else but they might have misunderstood what God was actually speaking to them in terms of involvement in ministry, or other support ministries. They instead do something that does not please God, because it's not what God wants them to do.

The second people groups are the ones who talk like Christians, act like Christians and do almost everything like Christians, but in actual fact they are not. This kind of people are not led by the Holy Spirit but are led by the spirit of antichrist. And so, they are obviously known as false prophets (Matthew 7:15, Mark 13:22, 2Peter 2:1, and 1John 4:1-3). False prophets don't have to be declared publicly and known as false prophets. They can be among the so-called Christian brothers and sisters in a church.

Church buildings consist of such people are tools well prepared to attack the Church of God by the enemy. We are reminded to be watchful of people as such and allow them not into our churches. When you identify one you should not call him a Christian brother and greed him for he is not.

To conclude, there's nothing wrong in building physical churches; for that's where we come together for our fellowship. But the motive behind building churches and the activities perform in the church building matters the most.

d (2)   The Church Service

The church service is a gathering of Christians coming together in one place to worship God. It is a requirement that the Christians should not abandon the habit of coming together in one place to worship their God. Again in the book of Hebrews 10:25 it says that; *"Not forsaking the assembling of ourselves together, as is the manner of some, but exhorting one another, and so much the more as you see the Day approaching."*

This scripture is urging us not to forsake the assembling of ourselves together for two reasons. The first one is that to exhort one another in the things of God through the breaking of the Bread of Life; the Word of God.

Normally as human beings, it is not our habit to go anyway to do anything. We know the reason for our going and our doing. We are not like any other animals that live their lifestyle in an ad hoc basis. We have plans and purposes that drive our movements.

Likewise, going to church service should be for a purpose and that purpose must be accomplished. Beside anything else, there must be exhortation among the Christians especially in the spiritual matters. It is not good enough for Christians to assemble together just to socialize for the physical matters. Nowadays, there is a trend becoming more active in the name of the church service everywhere is to discuss, to share and to socialize, all for physical matters.

Some go to church service to meet their boyfriends or girlfriends. Others go there to meet their business partners. Still others go there to meet their friends for some other personal things. In some churches, there are people who go to church service to be judgmental or to criticize the Pastor, or whoever for their performances in the church. Others go there just to kill time, and make funs with friends in their leisure times, for church gatherings happen to be some wonderful places on earth. People have all kinds of reasons for going to church services.

Finally, I guess, the most frightening one is the religious habit of going to church service. In some churches, eighty to ninety percent (80-90%) of the members are just good religious people who go there regularly just because it has been their place for their life time. May be once upon a time they had engaged in religious ceremonies in which they were ritually sealed to be members of that particular church, that they find it hard to stay away from it and leave for other places.

Anyway, let's go back to Hebrews 10:25 to see what it really tells us as Christians to do. It says, *"Not forsaking the assembling of ourselves together, as is the manner of some, but exhorting one another, and so much the more as you see the Day approaching."*

Like I've noted earlier, the two reasons according to this verse, must be the cause/reason for us going to the church service. First of all we must go there to exhort one another. To exhort means to advise or teach somebody very strongly or earnestly on whatever subject it matters. In our case, we must go to church service in order to exhort one another for one very important reason. We should not exhort one another aimlessly just for the sake of exhorting.

Secondly, the reason for exhorting is no other than for the Coming of our Lord Jesus Christ. This is reason number two for us going to the church service.

God allows us to use ample time on other issues of life on planet earth, but He also urges us not to give-up with the time of assembling together as others are doing.

In our same key verse, we also see that; some are beginning to abandon their habit of assembling together. There are two kinds of people who are doing this. The first people groups are the ones who forsake their faith in Christ completely and turn back into the world. The second people groups are the ones who forsake their fellowship with other Christian brothers and sisters and they go out try to form their own little groups with the likes of themselves.

Having such experiences in our churches, what shall we do then? Shall we leave them alone and bother not to do anything about it? Or should anybody get up and say or do something that might contribute any positive measure towards combating the evil practice? I believe, Hebrews 10:25 is one of the New Testament commandments that through it, our God is commanding us not to forsake our habit of assembling together, but to exhort one another for the Coming of the Lord.

Another feature I want to show here is that, we are only commanded to exhort one another. Our church services are supposed to be gatherings of exhorting, encouraging, lifting, blessing, healing, helping and more of that. Unfortunately, in some churches, people go for services only to be hurt by their Pastors or Priests or whoever the Preacher is there to feed them. As leaders, we are also commanded in John 21:15-17 that we should feed and tend our sheep with the Word of God, rather than whipping them with our little sharp mouths. We are commanded to love people and help build the Church of God (John 15:12-15; 1John 4:7-8).

Many times, pulpits have been used for personal glorification and have become places for sticking others. Pulpits are regarded as holy grounds where God comes down to meet with His people through the preaching of the Word. It's only through the preaching of the Word, whether it is from a pulpit or any other place that He comes down and not through other human wisdom or knowledge. Some Preachers are wasting their time preaching something that does not come from God (Jeremiah 23:25-32). Thus, their preaching and involvement in the church activities would not attract the presence of God either. It is therefore wise to take the pulpit with substance from the Word in order to feed the sheep.

For God will only come down to where He is preached even in His own name. Jesus said the other day that He will come and be with us in our midst. It happens regardless of how big or small we are in numbers, only if we gather together in His name. In Matthew 18:20 Jesus says; *"For where two or three are gathered together in my name, I am there in the midst of them."*

Jesus promised to be in the midst of an assembly that is gathered in His name, not in the name of a man, or an organization or a doctrine. He is also not worried about the number of people. So long as an assembly gathered in His name, (even if the number is less than five), for His glory and for His purpose, He will definitely be there in their midst. Because according to His promise, the maximum number is three and the minimum is two.

Further more, Jesus must be the centre of everything that we do. Any gathering without Jesus is more like a funeral service or any other social gathering. For without Jesus, we can't accomplish anything in our lives (John 15:4-5). It has got to be Jesus Christ in our midst or else do something worthwhile for the physical life on earth; rather than becoming a hypocrite in the eyes of God.

Finally, let's conclude this segment by saying that a church service is not any other social gathering of this world that any Tom, Dick and Harry to come and do anything among the people of God. They are not prohibited to attend the services but their attendance must be fruitful. For a church service is a spiritual gathering that the people of God (Church of God) are assembling to meet God.

It is an extra ordinary gathering on planet earth to talk about and discuss the greatest issue in the history of humanity, even life and death for that matter. Unlike any other gathering from the top executive level down to the grass root level, the gathering in the name of the Lord Jesus Christ is far above any other gathering. Because that's where the God Almighty comes down to meet with His people. Hence, it should not be taken for granted, as if it has no value and less significance only to find solutions for temporary matters of this world.

I don't care how big and profound world summit or convention that attracts the attention of the all world to come together for discussion. It is very sad that man will never find real rest in his soul, though the end results from world summit or convention will of course bring some solutions to human problems but are only temporary. Jesus says; *"Come to Me, all you who labor and are heavy laden, and I will give you rest* (Matthew 11:28)." *"Take My yoke upon you and learn from Me, for I am gentle and lowly in heart, and you will find rest for your souls (vs.29)." "For My joke is easy and My burden is light (vs.30)."*

May I tell you what? The only smart people of this world will come to Jesus to seek solutions for their problems and real rest for their souls. In that sense, coming together for a service for fellowship, is one of these greatest avenues in this world where a man can find real solutions and rest for his soul. There is, therefore no other better place like a church service in this world, for that's where a man can able to at least feel the gleams of the awesome presence of the Almighty God!

Chapter 5

The Head of the Church

The Bible declares very clearly that Jesus Christ is the Head of the Church. It says in Ephesians 1:22-23 that; *"And He (God) put all things under His (Jesus) feet, and gave Him (Jesus) to be the head over all things to the church"* (vs.22). It further says in Ephesians 5:23 that; *"For the husband is head of the wife, as also Christ is the head of the church; and He is the savior of the body."* In Colossians 1:18, Apostle Paul says the same thing again. *"And He (Jesus) is the head of the body, the church, who is the beginning, the firstborn from the dead, that in all things He may have the pre-eminence."*

The legitimate position of a head in any organization is very important. In a government or any business organization, the head is the person who has the ultimate power than the delegation of powers to the inferior ranks according to their status. Not all the time but sometimes when it is required, in some organizations the head has all the powers. The inferior ranks and the other members down the line look up to the head for direction and solution. They have full trust for the man, and they are eager to comply with any orders and directions given by the head. For it is the only healthiest way for the progressiveness and successfulness of the organization.

The functions of the physical body operate in the same manner. The head supplies all the necessary information to the other parts of the body. In order for perfect and sound operation, other parts of the body, such as a leg or a hand with no complication whatsoever, flow smoothly as the direction is given from the head. Only then, the whole body will function well for the betterment and survival of the body.

Likewise, Jesus Christ is the Head of the Church and we as members of the Church are parts of the Body of Christ. We are built and joint together, spiritually speaking, with the Body of Christ. Each individual Christian is not a loose particle but a member of the Body of Christ; as the Bible says in 1Corinthians 12:12, 14, 18, 20, and 27. *"Now you are the body of Christ, and members individually"* (vs.27). And it also says in Ephesians 5:30 that; *"For we are members of His body, of His flesh and of His bones."* Paul also says in Romans 12:4-5 that; *"For as we have many members in one body, but all the members do not have the same function." "So we, being many, are one body in Christ, and individually members of one another."*

Because we are the members of the Body of Christ, we are bound to operate in accordance with the directions given by the Head, Jesus Christ.

Now we should have no doubt believing that Jesus is in fact the Head of His Body, the Church, and we are members of His Body. In that sense, as members of the Body, we should by no means live our own lives and act outside the directions given by the Head. Every bit of our action must be directed by the Head for the glory of God and for the good of the whole Body. No matter what, this must be the rule for the betterment and progressiveness of the Body of Christ. For it is a firm norm that no one can ever neutralize the system to compromise with the rules and orders of this world.

If one feels strong in his heart to do otherwise, it will be against the norms of the Spirit and there-by breaking the rules that govern the Body of Christ. One would still argue and say that; 'it is easy for the physical body and its functions in this manner, for the parts thereof, have no other options but are naturally fixed only to comply with the orders directed by the head. Where as with the Body of Christ, the members thereof, are indeed different individuals who have freedom of choice or will power and as such, there are many options to which they can be attracted.'

This is true in some sense, but what God is requiring from us is a firm decision made from the freedom of choice or will power, of an individual to serve God. God does not want to see robots lining up in a human factory to worship Him without their choice. All He wants is a worship freely and desirably offered to Him from a genuine and willing heart. That's why the Spirit of God does not force people to worship God, but only directs and speaks to the heart of a person that he or she may freely worship and serve Him with a willing heart.

The Head Jesus, as I've stated, does not force a person and controls the spirit-man; as it does on the other hand, by the head of a physical body and its organic system. He (Jesus) only directs the spirit of man that man himself may choose to follow His instructions from a willing heart. The service or praise and worship that is offered in such a manner is genuine and that's what God is looking for; for He is not a God of dictatorship but a God of peace and love.

Jesus once told the Samaritan woman on the subject of worshiping God. The very facts about how and where to worship God are pronounced here at this well that no theological college on earth can prove it wrong. This is what He said in John 4:19-24. *The woman said to Him, "Sir, I perceive that You are a prophet"* (vs.19). *"Our fathers worshiped on this mountain, and you Jews say that in Jerusalem is the place where one ought to worship"* (vs.20). *Jesus said to her, "Woman, believe Me, the hour is coming when you will neither on this mountain, nor in Jerusalem, worship the Father"* (vs.21). *"You worship what you do not know; we know what we worship, for salvation is of the Jews"* (vs.22). *"But the hour is coming, and now is, when the true worshipers will worship the Father in spirit and truth; for the Father is seeking such to worship Him"* (vs.23). *"God is Spirit, and those who worship Him must worship in spirit and truth"* (vs.24).

Isn't this very clear that worship must come from a willing heart? The Samaritan woman had an old fashion of worshiping God. She was very consciously conscious of worshiping God from a certain location, which was not the issue any more. Jesus told the woman what it really matters in worshiping God.

Worshiping God either on the mountain or in Jerusalem has no Spiritual significance and as such, the place from which the worship is offered, must be substituted for the better. Jesus showed us from where and how best we can offer our worship to God. He said, true worship must come from the heart or the spirit of man, and it must be in truth. Worship that is offered from a willing heart of man and in truth is what God is looking for.

Anyway, how can it literally take place in a man's life? The vessel must be born again, washed and cleansed by the blood of Jesus, and is totally subject to the Head; who is Jesus Christ.

Being the Head of the Body, Jesus does make sure that every part should function properly as it should. Every part of the physical body and its operation depends so much on one central control room to get its strength and direction from. Likewise, every individual member of the Body of Christ depends so much on Jesus the Head. For it is the Head that supplies strength and direction for all the members of the Body.

Drs. Guy P. Duffield and Nathaniel M. V. Cleave stated similar point in the relation of the bodily parts to the Head. "There are many members of the Body of Christ; but there is but one Head, the Lord Jesus Christ. The members can not function properly without full submission to the Head who provides direction to the whole Body."[10]

The other definition of head means a chief or most prominent person who has the highest position and takes the lead in a group. It is normal that all the other members down the line depend so much on the head for command and direction. That means they must follow every command from the head no matter how hard it may be. It is exactly the same thing with Jesus in the Church of God. Jesus knows it better than anybody else, so it is proper and wise to comply with

---

[10] Ibid, (2006). p. 440.

whatever the command and order or direction that is given by the Head.

Only when we the members of the Body of Christ, follow every command and direction given by Jesus, the Church of God will definitely grow into the Spiritual measure and stature where it ultimately supposed to be. As Apostle Paul when teaching the Ephesians, he said something similar in the area of distributing of ministries. He said; *"It is Jesus Himself who gives ministries to certain people of His wishes that they might equip the saints for the work of ministry, and for the edifying of the body of Christ, that we might all come to the unity of the faith and of the knowledge of the Son of God, to a perfect man, to the measure of the stature of the fullness of Christ"* (Ephesians 4:11-13).

You see, that's one of the main reasons of distributing the ministries. And it is the order from the Head. It is not His desire to see any of these ministries to come up with their own little self-centered motives. All He wants is unity in the Body and it's the responsibility of each ministry to work on it.

The other time Jesus said; *"You can't do much without Me,"* or *"without Me you can do nothing"* (John 15:5). That means, for us to be successful in whatever we do in the service of God, we must comply with the orders and directions given by the Head. The Bible is full of commandments of Jesus that we need to obey. They are in fact the orders and directions from the Head that should not be overlooked and taken for granted as some religious rituals of old fashion. These are fresh manna from heaven and of course from the throne of the Head of the Church. Let's crown Him King of kings and the Lord of lords who is the Head of the Church of God for ever and ever more!

Chapter 6

Church, the Body and Body is of Christ

The Church is known as the Body, and the Body is of Christ. The Church is divinely ordained in such a way that any simple human being like you and I can able to understand it comprehensively. In fact it is a spiritual institution as we have seen earlier. The metaphor or example used for this institution is something that one can naturally understand even without having to be a trained and learned person.

Anyway, the metaphor used here is of a human body. It was purposely ordained in the manner as such, for that could be the only possible and easiest way for us to understand not only the spiritual but sophisticated theory as such.

As the human body is taken as an example of the Church, the Lord is trying to tell us the functions of all the different parts or members of the Body of Christ. Because of the classical example given as such, the only and the simple way to understand the Church and its functions, is by studying the functions of the different parts of the human body. The general idea God is trying to tell us in this manner is that, all different parts of a body are in fact many but are members of only one body. Because they are members of only one body and are connected to each other, one cannot survive by itself. For instance, a hand or a leg cannot survive by itself without getting its support from other parts of the body.

In order for a part to survive and successfully accomplish its purpose and meaning in life without any complication, it must be connected to the whole body from whence its help comes from. In the same token, all the different members of the Body of Christ must realize that their survival and successful accomplishments are a result of direct or indirect support drawn from the fellow members of the Body of Christ.

If the Church is referred to as a Body, and the Body is of Christ, why can't we take time to sit down and study the spiritual significance that it is trying to tell us? I am convinced so much so to write this book using simple terms that whoever reads it will begin to do something differently before he says good-bye to this world. Like I have stated earlier in the previous paragraphs, the Church of God, though it is a Spiritual Body, it is written and explained in such a way that even an uneducated person can able to at least understand it.

Man like Smith Wegglesworth and many others are testimonies that it does not require very high qualification to understand the Body of Christ. I really don't know why, but people with basic education don't understand the plain truth that has been revealed to us in a very simplest way. I begin to wonder, how people can continue to ignore the truth when it is clearly revealed in such a way and manner as it is with this subject matter.

Jesus made everything simple by using examples that are not complicated to understand. To me, it is very easy to understand the Church of God with all of its ingredients, not because I've got so much anointing from the Spirit of God. But because it has been explained, using a metaphor or an example as such, which is very simple even for a Sunday school kid can able to understand it. I mean, it's very simple because when you really do a systematic study in the functions of your own body, you can able to understand the Church of God as it is; even without high qualification or a Bible School credential.

The Church of God is physically an institution as we know but spiritually speaking, it is a Body, and the Body is of Jesus Christ. When I first began to study the Bible some thirty-three (33) years ago, I was convinced enough to understand the Church, as I first heard the word "body," but referring only to Church. And as a new convert, a very challenging one was not just any other "body" but the "body" of Christ. If it is a Body, and the Body is of Christ, for goodness sake, to me it is a Body of a living person. I believe Jesus Christ is a living God and is also a living person just like me, for I am created in His own image and in His likeness (Genesis 1:26-27).

If I were created in His image and in His likeness, the attributes that I have could have been derived from Him, the source. And therefore, I believe He has feelings in His Spiritual Body as I do. In that case, the pain and the suffering are inevitable; both in the physical and the Spiritual bodies, when a foreign element such as a disease or a stress is contracting into their systems.

To avoid as such, I must carefully study the functions and the routines of my own physical body, for the same principle applies to the Spiritual Body. For example, if a finger has a connection to my hand, and if it is a part of my whole body, then the whole body will suffer, if it has a sore or anything like that.

The same will apply to the Body of Christ; if a least one is suffering like Apostle Paul says in 1Corinthians 12:26. *"And if one member suffers, all the members suffer with it; or if one member is honored, all the members rejoice with it."*

A physical body is a collective of many parts fitted together, so it is with the Body of Christ, the Church of God. Therefore, no matter how small or a least member in the Body of Christ is very much needed in the Body. Sometimes a least part in the physical body is looked after and treated properly. The same principle should be applied to any one who has no standing in the society and even in the Church.

The least ones in the Church are very important for they are also members of the Body of Christ. They have functions and roles to play in the Body, which are sometimes known by the public but quite often, their services rendered to the Body of Christ are only known by God. Most of us will be surprised when some of these least ones are crowned on that Day of Judgment.

Dr. Frederick F. Bruce commented the following on the subject matter.[11] "No member is less a part of the body than any other member: all are necessary. Variety of organs, limbs and functions is of the essence of bodily life. No organ could establish a monopoly in the body by taking over the functions of the others. A body consisting of a single organ would be a monstrosity."[12]

I know very well about my own body, especially in the area of its functions. One thing I know about

---

[11] Frederick Fyvie Bruce, "The New Century Bible Commentary:" (Grand Rapids, MI: Mm. B. Eerdmans Publishing Company, 1978). p…?
[12] Ibid, (2006). p. 440.

my body is that; it is a complete and perfect body. My body is fed well and looked after properly which is my everyday duty for its completeness and perfection, so to avoid outside influences that might cause destruction to my body. I see that my body is complete and perfect because all (not only some) of its parts are naturally inbuilt and has a system of its own to operate. I also know that I can't form my own body as to how the body should function and where to put all the different parts in their respective positions. All I have to do is to feed this body and look after it in whatever way I should in my capacity.

Another thing I have also noticed is that; I am limited only to service the body from on the outside but on the inside, it is taken care of by the system itself. I see that the more careful I am on the outside, the healthiest the body would be on the inside. Let me repeat again by saying that; all I have to do is to feed my body with the right food and look after it carefully on the outside, that on the inside it will be taken care of by the inbuilt system itself.

It's all the same thing with the Body of Christ whether we like it or not. What a wonderful and remarkable Spiritual significance we can learn from here. As leaders of the Church, Jesus told us to feed and look after the sheep (John 21:15-17). We are not commissioned to build the Body, the Church. We are only commissioned to preach and feed the sheep with the Word of God. The building of the Church or the Body of Christ is a Spiritual matter that it will be taken care of by the Spirit of God and of course Jesus Himself.

For Jesus said, *"I will build my Church"* (Matthew 16:18). It is Jesus who builds the Church and as leaders or fellow Christian bothers and sisters, we are told to feed, look after, take care, and to cherish the sheep. And of course to love one another, forgive one another, pray for one another, share with one another and the list goes on.

When we humble ourselves and simply do what we are commissioned to do, the growth of the Church will be taken care of by the inbuilt Spiritual system that we really don't understand. Again, it is one of the mysteries that no intellectual mind can explain in a human language.

According to my observation over the years, we fail miserably in these areas. What we do is completely opposite to what the Bible is requiring of us. There is too much infighting, jealousy, division, unforgiveness, hatred, criticism, envy, self-righteousness, boastfulness, pride, self-exaltation and many more, are spiritual epidemic. This spiritual disease is literally eating away the Spiritual strength, which is in fact the cause of our slow progressiveness in the Body of Christ.

How can we expect to grow healthy and stronger in our Spiritual lives, when we are bombarded with spiritual epidemic? It is very sad to see that we are a sick generation, yet hoping and dreaming for big things and good times to come our way, without really bothering to live a healthy life according to the Bible. If we don't live according to the Bible as we should, we should also forget about having big dreams and hoping for good times and even calling ourselves Christians with unnecessary attachments with titles. For there is no such thing as Christians without obeying the Bible and live accordingly. Christians are followers of Christ. And are people who are members of the Body of Christ. They are members of the Kingdom of God on earth, who are obliged to obey the laws of that Kingdom.

The Bible is very clear in Galatians 5:19-21, that those who practice such things will not inherit the Kingdom of God. *"Now the works of the flesh are evident, which are: adultery, fornication, uncleanness, lewdness"* (vs.19), *"Idolatry, sorcery, hatred, contentions, jealousies, outbursts of wrath, selfish ambitions, dissensions, heresies"* (vs.20), *"Envy, murders, drunkenness, revelries, and the like; of which I tell you beforehand, just as I also told you in time past, that those who practice such things will not inherit the kingdom of God"*(vs.21).

To inherit the Kingdom of God doesn't only mean the Spiritual home in heaven but it also talks about the Kingdom life here on earth. Before we really taste and experience the life in heaven after we retire from this world, we should also experience it here on earth. It doesn't have to be exactly like in heaven, but we should at least feel the gleams of its taste. But this is not happing (not all, but in some parts of the world), though we are in the Church for many years. Simply because we have failed miserably in the areas like the book of Galatians is talking about. I know, and I know it for sure that, only when we are free from nothing but sin, we will surely experience this life here on earth. And we will find it hard to harm and destroy our fellow members in the Body of Christ and even the people of this world.

Because we are members of one Body, how dare we destroy our own Body? No person with a good sense of mind can ever do that. Only a fool or a mad-man may destroy his own body. It is therefore, whoever destroys the Body of Christ, is indeed a fool or a mad-man.

We are a Body; consists of members from all Christian churches around the world. We are a Kingdom people, sharing common interest, but passing through this world to our eternal home.

You should not be confused by the terms the "Kingdom of God" and the "Church of God." The Kingdom of God particularly on earth is the same thing known as the Church of God. The only difference is that, when you see it from the perspective of Jesus' Kingship, the King Jesus and His people are a people of power to rule and reign. On the other hand, when you see it from the perspective of Jesus' Lordship, you see Him as Lord and Saviour of the Church. You will see more about it in the next chapter.

Anyway, the terms and the metaphors like the Kingdom of God, the people of God, the house or building of God, the field of God, the nation of God, the holy priests, and etc; generally, all mean the same thing. One way or the other, they are simple metaphors of the Church of God, the Body of Christ; unless the words are ambiguously used or unless otherwise noted.

Finally, the Church is the Body, and the Body is of Christ. That it should not be divided and split into many, but be solid in the unity of all the members for that's what God desires!

Chapter 7

One Body means One Church

a: One Body but Many Members

In this segment we will see that the body is only one but many members (1Corinthians 12:12). Like we have seen in chapter 6, the human body has been taken as an example of the Church. For that reason, I will elaborate more on the human body in this chapter. For the body that the Bible talks about; speaks of the Church. It says in Ephesians 1:22-23 that; *"And He put all things under His feet, and gave Him to be the head over all things to the church," which is His body, the fullness of Him who fills all in all."* Before we see the features of the One Church of God, let's see some important facts about the human body first; because by doing that, we'll have a clear idea about the one Church of God.

A body is one with many members or parts collectively fitted together that makes a whole body (1Corinthians12:12). The word body can't be a single part of the body but it consists of many different parts as it says in (1Corinthians12:14). A single part is only a part that has its own distinctive position in the body (1Corinthians12:18). Let's refer back to what Dr. Frederick F, Bruce said, quoted by Guy P. Duffield and Nathaniel M. Van Cleave.[13] "No member is less a part of the body than any other member: all are necessary. Variety of organs, limbs and functions is of the essence of

---

[13]Ibid, (1978). p...?

bodily life. No organ could establish a monopoly in the body by taking over the functions of the others. A body consisting of a single organ would be a monstrosity."[14]

Each part has its own distinctive name as well. And it's not only that but each part has distinctive function in the body. It is very interesting to study the different functions of the human body; for all its sophisticated parts, both internal and external; operate in harmony (1Corinthians12:25). The body is made in such a way that none of the parts operate for its own interests and benefits. Any thing that a part does benefits first of all the whole body; and even its own share is shared together with the other parts but not as an individual.

When one single part operates its function, its course of action, though it is done independently, it does not operate in isolation. In fact it depends so much on other parts for it draws its strength from them (1Corinthians12:21). Each part has its own distinctive ability, but its ability will mean nothing to itself, if it does not draw its strength from the other parts. Therefore, one part is very important to a body as well as the other parts. For each part depends so much on each other. One can never operate by itself, for they are connected to each other. It is impossible to do, even if one attempts to give a try.

Another thing is the position where each part is located is highly respected by each other systematically. Each one's position is firmed and stationed in its own respective area. None of them has any bad feelings or envy towards another for its

---

[14] Ibid, (2006). p. 440.

position or even its ability. Each one of them is fully satisfied with where it is stationed and what it does. None of them wishes that it be another. All of them accept the fact that they are made to be what they are and really consistent in their positions and what they are made to do.

If they ever speak, you will never hear words such as envy, jealousy, hatred, unforgiveness, boastful, pride, selfishness, contention, dissension and the like of it, in their vernacular. These kinds of words are foreign to them. They are not part of their system and in their vernacular. However, you will notice that words such as love, joy, peace, happiness, gladness, goodness, cheerfulness, kindness, gentleness, respect, faithfulness, self-control, admiration, care, compassion, appreciation, longsuffering, honesty, forgiveness, and the like of it, would be their everyday language. They speak one language for they are one in one body. Therefore, if one (a leg for instance) suffers, all the other parts suffer together with the one that is hurt (1Corinthians. 12:26).

As we know, the body is not only one part, but it is made up of many different parts (1Corinthians12:14). For example, a leg or a hand or any other individual part can't be the body. A body is a collective of many parts or all the parts of the body.

Therefore, one single member/part can not claim to be the whole body; or the only one that is making up the body and claim the body as its own. It will be a funny thing for one particular part to claim as such. For *"If the whole body were an eye, where would be the hearing? If the whole were hearing, where would be the smelling"* (1Corinthians.12:17)?

In the same token, one single church group or one particular ministry cannot claim to be the only church of God or the only body of Christ.

When the Bible is very precisely clear as such, there is no logic in making such claims and it will be a waste of time if one ever feels as such. Let's see again the quotation of Drs. Guy P. Duffield and Nathaniel M. Van Cleave. "No organ could establish a monopoly in the body by taking over the functions of the others. A body consisting of a single organ would be a monstrosity."[15]

b: One Church but Many Congregations

As the physical body is one with many different parts, it is exactly the same thing with the Church of God (1Corinthians 12:12). For the Church of God is only one, called the ekklesia with so many members/ congregations. Paul's reason for taking the human body as an example of the Church is obvious. He wants us to study the human body and its parts or members of the body and their functions; only to tell us that the Church of God is just as it is with the body. It is simple as that and straight-forward.

Only if we can sit down and take time to do a careful and systematic study about the human body, our minds will be widely broaden by the light of the Word to really understand and know the characteristic of the Church. The Church or Body of Christ is a Spiritual and sophisticated institution that can only be understood by studying the physical body with its

---

[15] Ibid, (2006). p. 440.

different parts, as to how they operate in the body in their respective functions.

I don't think Paul was out of His mind to take the human body as an example of the Church, just for the sake of filling the gap. He really wants us to know how the Church should operate; as it does in the physical body.

If one could not give time to study the physical body and its system of operation, I would rather suggest that; that person should also give up studying the Bible in order to know particularly about the Church of God. Because it is an invisible and Spiritual institution; and thus really complicated subject that you just can't understand it properly as it is; without studying the simple metaphors/examples that are provided for your sake. Truly Apostle Paul was led by the Spirit of God to explain the Church of God as such, that we should be proud of him and give time to read the Bible and understand it.

Anyway, in the previous segment, we have studied a bit about the human body. If you have learnt something from that segment, I am sure you will definitely understand the only one Church of God with its so many different members. In this portion of our reading, we will now see the Church of God with its different members as well as their operations.

First of all, the Church of God is only one; (whether you like it or not) with so many big and small congregations around the world. I appeal to you that you read the verses in 1Corinthians12:12, 20 and 27 carefully and prayfully. Here is what the Bible says in these verses. *"For as the body is one and has many members, but all the members of that one body, being many, are one body, so also is Christ"* (vs.12). *"But now indeed there are many members, yet one body"* (vs.20). *"Now you are the body of Christ, and members individually"* (vs.27).

Doesn't the body is only one with many members? It is the same thing with the Body of Christ. I don't care who tells you what; for the Body of Christ or the Church of God is only one with many big and small congregations.

Let's also read the following verses regarding one body. In Romans 12:4-5, 1Corinthians 10:17, and Ephesians 4:4-6 have something interesting for us. *"For as we have many members in one body, but all the members do not have the same function"* (Romans 12:4). *"So we being many, are one body in Christ, and individually members of one another"* (vs.5). *"For we all partake of that one bread* (1Corinthians10:17). *"There is one body and one Spirit, just as you were called in one hope of your calling"*(Ephesians 4:4); *"One Lord, one faith, one baptism"* (vs.5); *"One God and Father of all, who is above all, and through all, and in you all"* (vs.6).

Having seen the above Bible references, there is no point in arguing the idea of only one Church of God. This theology has nothing to do with the propagating teaching on one church, one government and one money. I am very sorry that the books of Daniel chapter two and Revelation chapter thirteen have been misinterpreted. It is a scenario that has become a theory of its own that it needs separate explanation that I don't want to touch here. For it is also a sophisticated theory that some believe it might take place before the Coming of the Lord, (the rapture) while others believe that it might take place after the Coming of the Lord. In contrast to these, there are still others believe that it might not come to pass. It is a prediction that is yet to be proven as it takes place.

But for one Church of God that I am talking about here is already in existence. Whether you know it or not, if you are a born again and blood washed Christian, you and I are already in this one Church of God, irrespective of our differences in our different church denominations.

Let's correspond what we have learnt in the previous segment about one body with one Church. According to Ephesians 1:22-23, the body truly speaks of the Church. Because the physical body has been taken as an example of the Church, let's find out how many bodies are there. In accordance with 1Corinthians 12:12 and 20, the body is only one. If the body is only one, then the Church could also be one. I mean when you really do a systematic study in 1Corinthians 12:12-27, you will notice that it only talks about one body.

When plain truth is revealed in such a manner, how can one hide behind a denominational scene and paint another picture by saying something contrary to the revealed truth? One body stands for one Church, the ekklesia, is not debatable. No matter who says what, with what sort of revelation he gets, is only a fake from the pit of hell. It's not only this one but any other revealed truth found in the Bible, should not be twisted by so-called anointed last day prophets or apostles or whatever their title is.

One single part or member such as a hand or a leg can not be the whole body according to 1Corinthians12:14. Likewise, one single church denomination, or one church group, or one local congregation, or one ministry team or one single Christian can not and will never ever be the only Church of God.

We've seen it in a physical body situation that, it takes all the parts or members to form the body and it is exactly the same thing with the Church of God. It definitely takes a people group or an assembly of people to form the Church of God. Like I have explained earlier in the above portions, ekklesia the Greek word simply means, a collective body with the involvement of many people.

Though the members of the body are many, they operate together in harmony (12:25). You will hardly see anyone of them (either the eye or the nose) get up and say something offensive to one another. They speak only one language, for they are one in one body and their cooperation and unity is undivided. In the same manner, though we are so many different church groups, we must learn to be one with others. Jesus even prayed that we should be one as Him and His Father are one (John 17:21).

Another important feature is that, each part does its distinctive operation for the good of others. We as members of the Body of Christ should not forget the fact that; anything that has been entrusted to us, a gift or a ministry or whatever it is, must be used for the good of others. We are told to do so in 1Corinthians 12:7 with the gifts that have been entrusted to us. Let's see what it says in this verse. *"But the manifestation of the Spirit is given to each one for the profit of all."*

The nine gifts of the Holy Spirit and any other gift from God should not be exercised for self-gain and exaltation, but they must be used for the good and for the profit of all. The five-fold ministries recorded in Ephesians 4:11-13 are also not given, so that we may exercise them for our own benefits but they are also given; *"For the equipping of the saints for the work of ministry, for the edifying of the body of Christ"* (vs.12), *"Till we all come to the unity of the faith and of the knowledge of the Son of God, to a perfect man, to the measure of the stature of the fullness of Christ"* (vs.13).

You see; the gifts, or ministries, or revelation, or whatever a gift or blessing is given from above, must be executed for the good and benefit of other members of the Body of Christ. Everything thereof has a purpose behind and hence, it must be utilized for the purpose for which it was given.

According to 1Corinthians 12:18, *"But now God has set the members, each one of them, in the body just as He pleased."* God has positioned each member of the body in its respective position and that's where it remains stationed for the rest of its life. Likewise, we the members of the Body of Christ have been called and placed in our respective areas or positions, that we too must be stationed there to fulfill our calls.

Unless we have fulfilled our first call and removed by God Himself to another ministry or position, by any means we should not try to do it ourselves. If we move from one ministry to another or from one position with title to another without the direction from God, we are only causing problem in the system. When we become the problem in the Body of Christ, things won't flow, as they should. In a situation as such, we fight to get into the position or the ministry that had not been ordained for us. It is also true that God can change things around according to His own plans and purposes, but let it be God and not man.

Have you ever heard of paradigm-shift taking place around the world these days? A paradigm-shift or a spiritual-shift, or whatever shift it may be, it must be a shift ordered by God. Only then, we will be free from problems but be a blessing to the Church. For the blessings and prosperity are purposely entrusted to one, not only for the concern individual but also for the benefit of all.

In the physical body, each member has a high respect for one another. The simple reason is that one can not do the work of another. It's not only that, but they depend so much on each other for each one draws its strength from one another like it says in 12:21-25.

Likewise, we the members of the Body of Christ should have respect for one another. We should understand the fact that each one of us is a unique member in the Body of Christ. That means there are things that you can do, that others can't do. On the other hand, there are things that others can do, that you can't do. It's not only that but each one of us draws our strength from one another. As Christians, we draw our strength from each other that I guess most of you don't know.

Some of you may disagree with me and say that; 'I do my own Bible study, conduct my own pray meetings, run my own Christian affairs and live my own Christian life.' It's very true in some sense but spiritually speaking, if you are a born again Christian, one way or the other, you are connected and joint together with other born again Christian brothers and sisters. Those brothers and sisters can be from your own local congregation, in your church organization, and even with other members of other church groups or other denominations.

The Bible tells us that those of us who are members of the Body of Christ are connected and joint together with other members whether we like it or not. I mean, this is obvious; how can you dare to be an independent part when you are a member of the Body? It is impossible. In fact there are some things that we depend so much on others that we don't know, because it's all spiritual.

However, if you still disagree with me and say that; 'you are an independent person of your own, or your group is an independent group altogether,' in some sense you are right because physically and mentally you are indeed an independent person. But when it comes to the Spiritual Body of Christ the Church, you are no longer an independent person but a part that is connected to that Body.

Further more, if you would never accept that either, then I think you are not a member of the Body of Christ and so you are not of Christ. That means you are not a Christian at all. For the only thing that qualifies someone to be a member of any social organization or body, is by some kind of a link and connection between the two.

To confirm this, you have got to read again 1Corinthians 12:12-27, Ephesians 2:19-21 and 1Peter 2:5. In this portion of scriptures, you will see that we are connected and joint together, because we are built to the house of God, which is the Church of God. That's why whether we like it or not, spiritually speaking, we need each other so badly, for we depend so much on each other, for our Spiritual growth and betterment.

It is also true that we are segregated because of our different races, beliefs, doctrines, creed etc; however, it shouldn't be our excuse. Even some of us have gone into the extreme of secluding ourselves both physically and mentally from other members of the Body of Christ. This is just a waste of time; for if you are a born again Christian, you are an automatic member of the Body of Christ; whether you like it or not. And so you are bound to the Spiritual laws of that Body. Therefore, though we congregate in many different places under many different name tags, we are all in one Body the one Church of God!

Chapter 8

God's Love for Mankind

God's love for mankind is not merited and therefore it is unconditional. His love did not base on anything good that we did. He just loved us, the all of human race regardless of our sins. Because of His immeasurable love, He did something that no man can ever do without any condition at all. His love is not limited to any one particular people group or race or any one particular generation. His love could have been limited only to His chosen people of Israel but it wasn't the case. God's love is extended to every mankind on the face of the earth. His love does not know about any racial or denominational boundaries.

According to Dr.William Evans; "God loved not the Jew only, but also the Gentile; not a part of the world of man, but every man in it, irrespective of his moral character." "The love of God is broader than the measure of man's mind. God desires the salvation of all men (1Timothy 2:4)."[16]

God's love was literally poured once and for all (Hebrews10:10), when Jesus made a holy sacrifice by His own body. Once and for all means, God's love was for the people at the time of the pouring of His love till the end of time. Whoever lives in between this time interval is under this great love of God. It does not matter God with what one does, for God's love does not measure with any sin, no matter what it

---

[16] William Evans, "Great Doctrines of the Bible," (OMF Literature Inc. Manila, Philippines, 1987). p. 36.

is. For God's love for man does not base on anything that man does whether good or bad.

His love for mankind is expressed in John 3:16, as it states; *"For God so loved the world that He gave His only begotten Son, that whoever believes in Him should not perished but have everlasting life."*

We will discuss the last part of this verse in the latter portion, but in this segment, I will elaborate more on the first part of the verse. The first part of the verse reads as *"For God so loved the world that He gave His only begotten Son."*

God loved the world so much that He had to give Jesus, whom He also loved more than any angle to redeem man, by His (Jesus) blood. God actually loved both man and His only Begotten Son Jesus Christ before the foundation of the world (Ephesians1:4, John17:24). Unfortunately, the man whom God loved failed into sin that He (God) had to exchange love for love by giving Jesus whom He also loved. You see that's how expensive a human soul is; that only Jesus could able to purchase it by His blood. Or in other words, God loved man so much that He had to redeem him (man) by His only Begotten Son whom He also loves.

Dr.W.Evans describes how God loves Jesus in the following manner. "Matthew 3:17-"This is my beloved Son, in whom I am well pleased." Also Matthew 17:5 and Luke 20:13. Jesus Christ shares the love of the Father in a unique sense, just as He is His Son in a unique sense. He is especially "My chosen." "The One in whom my soul delighteth," "My beloved Son"-literally: the Son of mine, the beloved."[17]

---

[17] Ibid, (1987). p. 35.

One of the moral attributes of God, and I guess the most prominent of all is love. For the Bible says in 1John 4:8 and 16 that; "God is love." God who is love was fully in Jesus or in other words, God's love was all in Jesus. Therefore, when God gave Jesus, He actually shared His love with us. The love of God was sent to us in a form of a man. There was no difference between the love of God and the person Jesus. The level of God's love for us was demonstrated in His Son Jesus. *"But God demonstrates His own love toward us, in that while we were still sinners, Christ died for us* (Romans 5:8).

You see, Jesus, the second person in the Godhead, had in Him (Jesus) the whole of God. In other words, it was God Himself descended from Heaven to save the all world, through the person Jesus in a form of a man. The Son Jesus took the front line by descending from heaven; yet God was in Him (Jesus) through His (God's) love in the power of the Holy Spirit. Therefore, the cost of saving the world was not cheap with any other created material but it was God, the Creator Himself. The formula in which we can work out the love of God for us should be something like this; God the Father and His love plus (+) Jesus Christ the demonstration of love and His willingness equals (=) **love.** That's how great and big the love of God is for us.

The love of God did not evolve into its maturity stage as man felt into sin. Or the love of God is not a developed theology that it got its full shape and its completion or perfection when Jesus died on the cross. No, it's not. The incarnation of Jesus and His death on the cross of Calvary was only a demonstration of this great love. It was a complete and perfect love that originated in the heart of God the Father, even before the foundation of the world (Ephesians 1:4, 5, 11, 1Peter 1:2, 20, 2Timothy 1:9-10, Romans 16:25, Colossians 1:26).

If God loved us even before the foundation of the world, what else could able to take us away from this great and unconditional love of God? No, nothing. Nothing from above the earth, or nothing from on the earth, or nothing from beneath the earth. For God's love for us is more powerful that nothing can undo and nullify what God did even His love.

"Love is the expression of His personality corresponding to His nature. It is the nature of God to love. He dwells always in the atmosphere of love. Just how to define or describe the love of God may be difficult if not impossible."[18]

Apostle Paul made this clear when he wrote to the Romans in chapter 8:33-35, through 38-39 that; *"Who shall separate us from the love of Christ? Shall tribulation, or distress, or persecution, or famine, or nakedness, or peril, or sword"* (vs.35)? *"For I am persuaded that neither death nor life, nor angles nor principalities nor powers, nor things present nor things to come"* (vs.38), *"Nor height nor death, nor any other created thing, shall be able to separate us from the love of God which is in Christ Jesus our Lord"* (vs.39).

If you can sit down and meditate in what Paul was trying to tell us about the love of God, you will surely discover that Paul went out of words to explain the great love of God for us. Paul might have been

---

[18] Ibid, (1987). p. 35.

convinced so much so that what he said was; how deep and extremely he could express the love of God.

You can see the spirit behind Paul as he tried his best to express God's love. This kind of love is called "agape" in Greek. It is a love that one has for another regardless of what. It is a kind of love that causes one to sacrifice his own life for another, even if it means to die; he is sold out for it. And that's what exactly happened, when Jesus gave away His life even to die on the cross for us. God loved us so much that He gave away Jesus who then laid down His own life for us (John 3:16, 10:11, 15, 15:12-13, 1John 3:10, Philippians 2:8). There is no greater love than to lay down His own life for us (John 15:13).

"Love is more than compassion; it hides not itself as compassion may do, but displays itself actively in behalf of its object. The cross of Calvary is the highest expression of the love of God for sinful man. He gave not only a Son, but His only Son, His well-beloved."[19]

If one thinks, that he is smart enough to question the love of God, I suggest that he should also question the death of Jesus, for that's how far God can reach in showing His love for us. And the death of Jesus was not just any other normal or natural death. It was a death that carried or took all the pain and agony that should have been felt by every mankind that would be born on the face of the earth, after His death. The pain that Jesus felt on His body was a pain that supposed to be felt by all of us as a result of our sins (Isaiah 53.1-12).

Jesus' death for the all world was the first and last of its kind, that it is truly a history that could never be

---

[19] Ibid, (1987). p. 36.

repeated or followed by any man in the history of mankind. That's how great the love of God is for us.

"Election" and "Salvation" are Two Different Things.

Election and Salvation are two different things, for Paul says they are. In the process of his words of encouragement to young Timothy, he tells the reason for his endurance as he goes through all the sufferings that he encounters. This is what he says; *"Therefore I endure all things for the sake of the **elect**, that they also may obtain the **salvation** which is in Christ Jesus with eternal glory"* (2Timothy 2:10).

In this verse, you can see that election is different from salvation. Paul says that he endures all things for the sake of the elect, that they also may obtain the salvation, which is in Christ Jesus. According to Paul, though we are elected, chosen or predestined to spend eternity with God in heaven, it's another thing to obtain salvation in Christ Jesus. I'll explain the definition and the difference of election and salvation in the following segments.

a: Election of God

In this topic we will see the definition of election and salvation of God. But firstly, election of God can be referred to predestination of God, in accordance with the agape love of God for mankind. I think most of you are aware that words such as 'election,' 'chosen' and 'predestination' in the Bible mean the same thing. These words fall under one big word called, "agape" love of God.

Because God loved us so much, He went into the extreme of using such words to express His agape love for us. And like I said, He did not love us only by words, but He also acted upon His own words by laying down His life for us. For He says in His words, that He will never abandon His own words. *"My covenant I will not break, Nor alter the word that has gone out of My lips"* (Psalms 89:34).

So the Bible says that; we were chosen by God from the very beginning even before the foundation of the world (Ephesians 1:4; 2Thessalonians 2:13). It says in 1Peter 1:1-2 that; *"We were elected by God according to the foreknowledge of God the Father."* God did not only choose us or elect us but He also predestined us in accordance with His foreknowledge of us. Apostle Paul also made this clear in Roman 8:29-30, where it says; *"For whom He foreknew, he also predestined to be conformed to the image of His Son, that He might be the first born among many brethren"* (vs. 29) *"Moreover, whom He predestined, these He also called; whom He called, these He also justified; and whom He justified, these He also glorified"* (vs. 30).

When you really do a systematic study in this area, you will be surprised to see that no man that had ever lived on this planet earth was purposely born to suffer in hell. But instead every man was purposely born to enjoy the wonderful eternal life in heaven. There is no where in the Bible that will prove that man was one way or the other, created purposely for condemnation in hell, as it is with life in heaven. "The

Bible does not teach selection, but election. Nowhere does the Bible teach that some are predestined to be damned. This would be unnecessary inasmuch as all are sinners and on their way to eternal condemnation."[20]

We have countless of Bible texts; almost the whole Bible talks about man forsaking sin and turn to God to get life. I hardly find even one single Bible text that encourages the idea or concept of 'predestination' and 'limited atonement.' My Bible from Genesis to Revelation tells me that the fallen man has no other option but to turn back to God that he may be saved. And I also see that the call of God for mankind is not a specific call for those who are already chosen and elected. It is a general call from God to the fallen world that whoever attends to it, will be saved.

I am very sorry to see that those who believe and follow in the Calvinistic theory of a limited atonement, have not even one single authority from the Word of God. I suppose their own stubborn imagination is only a speculation that has no basis in the Word of God. We have a lot of Biblical authority to support our theory, but the following texts are only a few to support our point of argument.

*"All we like sheep have gone astray; We have turned, every one, to his own way; And the Lord has laid on Him the iniquity of **us all**"* (Isaiah 53:6). *"Go into **all the world** and preach the gospel to **every creature**"* (Mark 16:15). ***"He who believes and is baptized will be saved;*** *but he who does not believe will be condemned"* (vs.17). *"Behold! The Lamb of God, who takes away the **sin of the world"*** (John

---

[20] Ibid, (2006). p. 208.

1:29)! *"For **God so loved** the **world** that **He gave His only begotten Son**, that **whoever believes in Him should not perish but have everlasting life"*** (John 3:16). *For God did not send His Son into the world to **condemn** the **world**, but that the **world** through Him might be **saved"*** (vs.17). *"Who gave Himself a ransom for **all**, to be testified in due time"* (1Timothy 2:6). *"And He Himself is the propitiation for our sins, **and not for ours only but also for the whole world"*** (1John 2:2). *"But there were also false prophets among the people, even as there will be false teachers among you, who will secretly bring in destructive heresies, even denying the Lord who **bought them**, and bring on themselves swift destruction"* (2Peter 2:1).

*"The Lord is not slack concerning His promise, as some men count slackness; but is longsuffering toward us, **not willing that any should perish, but that all should come to repentance"*** (2Peter 3:9).

*"But we see Jesus, who was made a little lower than the angles, for the suffering of death crowned with glory and honor, that He, by the grace of God, might taste death for **everyone"*** (Hebrews 2:9).

The above Bible texts and others not quoted here precisely declare that Jesus died for the all world. Even those who are bound to destruction, have been bought by Jesus with His blood according to 2Peter 2:1. Hence, there is no point in arguing, only to defend a false theory that has no ground in the Word of God.

The Bible says in Psalms 139:13-18 that; *"For You formed my inward parts; You covered me in my mother's womb"* (vs.13). *"I will praise You, for I am fearfully and wonderfully made; Marvelous are Your works, And that my soul knows very well"* (vs.14). *"My frame was not hidden from You, When I was made in secret, And skillfully wrought in the lowest parts of the earth"* (vs.15). *"Your eyes saw my substance, being yet unformed. And in your book they all were written, The days fashioned for me, When as yet there were none of them"* (vs.16). *"How precious also are Your thoughts to me, O God! How great is the sum of them"* (vs.17)! *"If I should count them, they would be more in number than the sand; When I awake, I am still with You"* (vs.18).

According to these texts, the Psalmist is telling us that we were fearfully and wonderfully made in the secret place of our mother's wombs. Here we see that God had so much concern for man, that His thoughts about man were precious (vs.17). If His thoughts about an individual are precious, even before the beginning of time or from the very beginning, then how can a God who is love and full of mercy create such a precious ignorant infant just to suffer in hell? I don't think so.

One might still challenge me by saying that; 'truly there are people who are chosen and predestined to spend eternity in heaven than others.' They might say; no matter what they do, those who are chosen and predestined for hell will still end-up in hell. "This extreme position is based on the so-called doctrines of 'unconditional election.' It has sometimes been presented in such an extreme manner as to make it sound as though those who are elected will certainly be saved, regardless of their response to the Gospel, and their manner of living. Contrarily, those who are chosen to be lost are said to perish eternally, regardless of any endeavor to come to God through faith in Christ."[21]

Friends, can I tell you what? This is the very thing that the devil wants the unbelieving folks to think. It is a great lie from the pit of hell. Please don't you ever yield to such a lie. It's only a matter of genuinely saying no to sin and Satan and make a u-turn in your life and come back to God, for He is indeed a loving Father.

It is very; very true that God does not create some for heaven and others for hell. The only person who says that He (God) does that is; His arch-enemy by the name of Satan; incase you don't know his name. If you think you are smart; then be smart and say no to hell and claim heaven for it is indeed your eternal home. The smart people are the people who don't give-up and do things right, even if the all world falls apart. Why not you be one of them; if you are an ignorant person, who thinks that you can't make it to heaven?

Well, listen to this; in His great wisdom; God had decided to share His life with man that man should exercise his freedom of choice to choose. That's something very precious that words can not express the power of choosing.

For there is no greediness in God, He had gone into such extent of sharing the power; the power of choice to choose life. It was God who had created man and provided eternal life for man, but man was given the power to choose his own destination to spend his eternity. That was God's plan and so He

---

[21] Ibid, (2006). p. 206.

made everything possible that man should enjoy this wonderful life in heaven.

Man is the product of Himself in His Great Agape Love (Genesis 1:26-27). It is therefore; God created the great universe both the heavens and earth just for man. On-top of that, He wanted man to fully enjoy life. In order for man to enjoy life to the fullest, man should not be controlled by any outside force. He should have a total freedom of choice to choose what to do. If not, he will only be like a robot that will be controlled by outside force and will have nothing much to enjoy about. That's why man was given freedom of choice or will power to choose. For that reason, God does not bother to intervene and touch the will power of man.

If God hadn't ever done that, He would have turned to be a greedy and selfish God. No, He is not. The sharing of His power to choose from good and bad proves the real condition of His heart that He is a God of love and fairness. If not, men would have been like robots lining up in a human factory to praise and worship God and honour Him; but such honour would not have been genuine. Then, I think we know that anything from us that is not genuine, will obviously not go down well with God. In that sense God created man that man would choose to do what he wants to do and enjoy life.

It is also true that according to Romans 8:29-30, God had foreknowledge of every man. He knew who would choose life and who would not. Then one would ask; 'why not He created only the ones who would choose life and ignore the rest'? Again, He would not have been fair by creating only the ones who would worship Him. That would have again counted down to robots lining up to offer honour that would not have been genuine. God is a righteous God and all He wants is honour that is offered to Him genuinely from a willing heart.

He does not want to get any praise and honour by force. Because, using force to get something really indicates how less powerful, less significance and less worthiness or importance of a person. And I think we know that obviously, such character is not of God and He will never try to force anybody to do anything in contrast to his willing heart.

Further more, it doesn't mean that man's eternal destination is based on the foreknowledge of God. May be it is the last thing God had ever have in His Deity. "It is not a man's non-election that leads to eternal ruin; it is his sin and failure to accept Jesus Christ. Every man is free to accept Christ as his personal Savior, if he wills. Not only is he invited, he is urged to do so."[22]

In fact God in His great love had given freedom of choice to every man at the first instance. God has given every man the measure of faith (Romans 12:3) which is indeed the power to choose life. He didn't give the will power only to those who could choose life. No; not at all. In other words, every man is granted life, but its man's own choice that he chooses otherwise.

One may still argue and say; 'God still would have done or structured something better that every man should get life and none be lost. Had He run out of effective measure to make sure that every one is saved'? I think what God has done is far better than

---

[22] Ibid, (2006). p. 208.

any structure that one may suggest. I even want to admit that I have nothing more to bring to the surface. I am only a man and thus, I've exhausted myself and come to my limitation, particularly in this area.

I think it's proper not to unnecessarily dig out the unrevealed mysteries of God. Let God be God and man be man; no matter who we are even with our intellectual brains.

By the way, I want to conclude that every man is potentially given enough power to say no to sin and turn back to God. Not one single man will have that courage to argue in the Great Judgment; that he lacked the potential to choose life. God's judgment will be perfectly righteous that no man will succeed in his argument.

However, if one seems to be the master of his philosophy, his theory must be one hundred percent plus (100% +) convincible enough to challenge not only man but also God.

But listen very carefully to this unanswered crucial question that is asked by many. 'If God had purposely created every mankind to spend his eternity in heaven with Him, how comes millions end-up in hell?' I'll try my best to answer this question in segment "B" of this subject. I'll explain whether it's God's fault or man's own fault that man ends-up in hell. I hope it will be another interesting topic for you to know.

The Bible is a book consists of letters that were written to certain people but that's what we are applying, as it is the Word of God to all of us. Because the Word of God is fresh as it was at the time of its initial stage. Therefore, we are also the chosen and elect ones of God.

I want to touch something very important here that needs to be read very carefully with understanding. If we believe that God's love is only for a few who are chosen, elected, and are predestined for eternity, than we are wrong. If that is the case then, this Bible that we are reading, using and applying in our situation, must be thrown away and we must pray that we should have a new Bible. For this Bible in fact was written for those people who were there at the time when it was written.

In Actual fact, they were letters addressed to those concerned people that we read about their narratives in this Bible; even the Israelites for that matter as well as few Gentiles. For this Bible was written directly to and for them (especially the Israelites) so they supposed to be the prominent ones to be chosen or elected and predestined for salvation. Then we should also say that we have been wasting our time, for we are not part and parcel of that great blessing of God.

Nevertheless, I think we all agree that it is not the case. One way or the other, we know that we are part and parcel of this great blessing of God known as salvation. We, the other Gentile world are the Spiritual descendants of Abraham for we are joint heirs with Jesus Christ. In fact Paul was addressing some Gentile people and said; we are joint heirs with Christ, and it is recorded in the following books.

In Romans 8:17 it says; *"And if children, then heirs – heirs of God and joint heirs with Christ, if indeed we suffer with Him, that we may also be glorified together."* It also says in Galatians 3:29 that;

"And if you are Christ's, then you are Abraham's seed, and heirs according to the promise." It further says in Ephesians 3:6 that; *"That the Gentiles should be fellow heirs, of the same body, and partakers of His promise in Christ through the gospel."*

You see, the Gentiles have access in sharing God's blessings together with the chosen Nation of Israel. Only because we have faith in God, we have the same right and privilege to inherit the blessings of God as the Israelites do. However, we don't have to follow the same Jews rules such as circumcision etc. For Abraham was called the father of many nations, not basing on circumcision but on faith. He was called the father of many nations before his circumcision. You will confirm this when you read Romans 4:1-25.

But for our case, let's see verses 9-11. *"Does this blessedness then come upon the circumcised only, or upon the uncircumcised also? For we say that faith was accounted to Abraham for righteousness"* (vs.9). *"How then was it accounted? While he was circumcised, or uncircumcised? Not while circumcised, but while uncircumcised"* (vs.10*). "And he received the sign of circumcision, a seal of the righteousness of the faith which he had while still uncircumcised, that he might be the father of all those who believe, though they are uncircumcised, that righteousness might be imputed to them also"* (vs.11).

With this confirmation, we see that salvation is not only for a few whom are already predestined but it is a great blessing for those who have faith in Christ.

Like we've seen earlier, *"For God so loved the world that He gave His only begotten Son"* (John 3:16). God didn't send Jesus for only a few but for the all world. Every one of us, no matter in which race or religion or creed we belong to; all of us are bound by John 3:16. Dr. William Evans says; quoting Ephesians 5:25-27. "Christ also loved the Church, and gave Himself for it." "Not for any one particular denomination; not for any one organization within any four walls; but for all those whom He calls to Himself and who follow Him here."[23]

I believe that John chapter 3 verse 16 covers the Muslims or the Islamic people, the Indus, the Buddhists, the Jews, the Catholics, the Protestants, the Reformers, the Pentecostals, the Independents, the Confucians, the Taoists, the Shintoists, the Agnostics or the Humanists, the Atheists, the Communists, and even the Satanists and others.

'For God so loved the world;' simply means, He loved every human soul that had ever lived on this planet earth. In the Old Testament dispensation, God gave laws that people had to follow every single law in order to get life. That was the method of demonstrating God's love for the people in the Old Testament. It is therefore, those who did not obey the laws of God, even by nature, will be judged accordingly (Romans 2:12-16).

In the New Testament dispensation, God really poured out and demonstrated His love for every mankind (not only few who are chosen) by sending Jesus, that whoever believes in Him should not perish but have ever lasting life.

---

[23] Ibid, (1987). p. 64.

The phrase 'whoever believes in Him,' gives me an idea that Jesus Christ did not come only for the chosen ones. Jesus was indeed a free gift for the public. No matter who the person is, or where he comes from, only if he could repent from his sins and believe in His name, that person will be saved according to John 3:16. This, I believe is the election of God for every mankind; not for only few who are chosen.

John 3:16 is the outpouring of God's heart to every mankind. I think God's stand or position in this situation with mankind is clear. Our God the Creator is a God full of mercy and love. I don't believe in these lies which say that; God has created some for heaven and others for hell. If God had ever done that, then we would say that He is not fair and is unjust. No, He is not. He is fair and just and He is love. In fact the Bible says in 1John 4:8 and 16 that He is love. Love is not an outside element that has been adapted by God or has been evolved into His Deity. No, it is not. Love is God and God is love. Therefore, it is really impossible to distinguish God from love or love from God.

In that sense, we can say that John 3:16 is final authority that God laid Himself down for every human soul. Simply because God didn't create anyone that he should perished. That is indeed the election of God for every human soul. However, the reason why so many people end-up in hell will be looked at in segment "B" in this subject as I've noted.

Anyway, there is an exclusive election for the Israelites only in which we are not part of it. The exclusive election of the Israelites only, is stated in the following Bible texts but yet in the future.

Isaiah also cries out concerning Israel: "Though the number of the children of Israel be as the sand of the sea, The remnant will be saved" (Romans 9:27). *I say then, has God cast away His people? Certainly not! For I also am Israel, of the seed of Abraham, of the tribe of Benjamin* (11:1). *God has not cast away His people whom He foreknew. Or do you not know what the Scripture says of Elijah, how he pleads with God against Israel, saying* (vs.2), *"Lord, they have killed Your prophets and torn down Your alters, and I alone am left, and they seek my life"* (vs.3)? *But what does the divine response say to him? "I have reserved for Myself seven thousand men who have not bowed the knee to Baal"* (vs.4). *Even so then, at this present time there is a remnant according to the election of grace* (vs.5). *"And they also, if they do not continue in unbelief, will be grafted in, for God is able to graft them in again"* (vs.23). *"For if you were cut out of the olive tree which is wild by nature, and were grafted contrary to nature into a cultivated olive tree, how much more will these, who are natural branches, be grafted into their own olive tree"* (vs.24)? *"For I do not desire, brethren, that you should be ignorant of this mystery, lest you should be wise in your own opinion, that blindness in part has happened to Israel until the fullness of the Gentiles has come in"* (vs.25). *"And so all Israel will be saved, as it is written: "The Deliverer will come out of Zion, And He will turn away ungodliness from Jacob"* (vs.26); *"For this is My covenant with them, When I take away their sins"* (vs.27). *"Concerning the gospel they are enemies for your sake, but concerning the election they are beloved for the sake of the fathers"* (vs.28). *"For the gifts and the calling of God are irrevocable"* (vs.29).

The above texts talk about the exclusive election of the Israelites only; not basing on faith but on election (see above Bible authorities again and Hosea 6:1-3, 14:1-7, Amos 9:8-15).

But in this election that we are talking about, is an inclusive election that covers all human race, no matter who they are. So long as they breathe and live on planet earth, God still loves them. Or in other words, election means; the love of God for all human race on the face of this earth.

Jesus once declared this in Matthew 9: 12-13 saying; *"Those who are well have no need of a physician, but those who are sick"* (vs.12). *"But go and learn what this means: I desire mercy and not sacrifice; For I did not come to call the righteous, but sinners, to repentance"* (vs.13).

Which sinners does He talk about? Does it mean many or a few? Who are they? Where are they? Can anyone identify the particular group of sinners that Jesus talks about? I hardly see the specific group of sinners that Jesus came for. All I see is a world full of sinners. It doesn't have to be the whites or the blacks; or the yellows or the reds. Anybody who is a sinner is eligible and is a right candidate for this atonement.

The Word of God is very clear that Jesus came to save the sinners, no matter what sort of sin the sinner commits. Whether it is adultery or lust, worship of idols or Satan, big or small, anything that is not right is sin (1John 5:17) and that's what Jesus came for. If God Himself declares that He came for the sinners, who are we to lay judgment on the sinners; saying that you fall under this category or that category of atonement.

Further more let's see the definition of these controversial words- elect, choose and predestine. But first let's see the definition of the term elect. According to Oxford Advanced Learner's Dictionary, elect has two meanings but in our case it means; "choose" or "decide." Well, lets ignore choose and see the definition on decide. 'Decide' means to make up one's mind. If that is the case then, God had decided that mankind be saved from their sins. It does not necessarily mean that God had to decide or elect for His favorites. For God does not have any favorites (Acts 10:34-35, Romans 2:9-11).

Now let's see the definition of 'choose.' Choose also means to 'decide' or 'select' or 'prefer' between A and/from B. Here I also see that God does not necessarily select or prefer some human souls from others. If He ever has to do that; then the souls that are His preference, should have more value than the others. However, this shouldn't be the case because every soul is equal and is costly (Psalms 49:8, Mathew 16:26).

The definition of 'predestine' is to 'fix something precisely' or 'decide.' Let's ignore 'decide' and see more clarification on 'fix something precisely.' For God to fix precisely concerning a human soul is I believe the most important thing that God ever does. I also believe that unlike any other creations of God, man whom He created in His own image and likeness (Genesis 1:26-27) is forever the love of His heart (Song of Solomon 2:10, 13, John 3:16). Even when a life is formed in the matrix of the mother's womb, the loving God is always there forming, shaping, and structuring every part of the being (Psalms 139:13-18). There are of course some mistakes caused not by God but by the biological parents in the formation of a life in the matrix of the mother's womb, which I prefer not to talk about here. But with the Bible authorities here, I now see that for God to precisely predestine a human soul just for hell; is something that my system will never ever swallow. Just imagine; how can a good and a loving God who is also full of mercy can ever do that? Hence, it is proper not to draw conclusion only on speculations.

Those of us who are saved now should also know that we were once sinners like the unsaved ones. It's not our duty to judge, but instead to share the love of God to them. We should not lay judgment on the unsaved ones, for our judgement has nothing good in it but only condemnation. When we as fellow men lay judgment on others, it does not help them to know Christ their Saviour, but it only causes differences among us. Even if we preach a good message, they will hardly swallow it down for we have already created barriers in between them and us and have become their enemies.

The right thing for us to do is only to preach and share the love of God to them like Jesus did. When we preach the love of God to them, the sinners will do only two things, whether to accept the love of God or to reject it. When they accept it, they'll be saved just like us but when they reject it, they will definitely be condemned, even by their own evil actions and not believing in Him. John 3:17 says that; *"For God did not send His Son into the world to condemn the world, but that the world through Him might be saved."*

The only thing that condemns a sinner is not by Jesus the Saviour, nor we the preachers of the Saviour's salvation message, but it is the action of the sinner himself. It is confirmed in John 3:18-19 where it says; *"He who believes in Him is not condemned; but he who does not believe is condemned already, because he has not believed in the name of the only begotten Son of God"* (vs.18). *"And this is the condemnation, that the light has come into the world, and men loved darkness rather than light, because their deeds were evil"* (vs.19).

You see, it's very clear; so let the sinner be condemned by his own sinful actions and not us. Why getting involve in responsibility that should not be ours? Our responsibility is to preach the love of God and let the sinner be responsible for his own life.

Lets see John 3:18 and 19 again. It says in verse 18 that; *"He who believes in Him is not condemned; but he who does not believe is condemned already."* Why is he condemned already? And who really condemns him? Is it Jesus? No, it shouldn't be Jesus. Because it says in verse 17 that; *"For God did not send His Son into the world to condemn the world, but that the world through Him might be saved."*

Or is it us, the preachers of the gospel? No, it shouldn't be us either. Even if we do condemn, our condemnation will have no effects, for we have no authority to condemn others. You know, to condemn means to pass judgement on others and I think none of us has such authority to execute judgement. Yet if we do, we will instead condemn ourselves, according to Romans 2:1. *"Therefore you are inexcusable, O man, whoever you are who judge, for whatever you judge another you condemn yourself; for you who judge practice the same.*

Anyway, let's go back to our question; 'why is the sinner condemned already?' The answer is found in the last part of verse 18, where it says; *"because he has not believed in the name of the only begotten Son of God."*

Not believing in the name of the only Begotten Son of God is the only reason why a sinner is condemned. Now we see that it's not God or man who condemns, but it is the action of the sinner himself that condemns him. God the loving Father has elected and chosen us that we should live together with Him in heaven, but it's the choice of the sinner himself that he ends-up in hell. "It is not a man's non-election that leads to eternal ruin; it is his sin and failure to accept Jesus Christ. Every man is free to accept Christ as his personal Savior, if he wills."[24]

When this understanding is fresh in your mind, without any delay, we'll go straight to the next segment in which we will talk about the salvation of mankind.

b: Salvation of Mankind is Based on Man's Own Will Power.

In this segment, I will now talk about Salvation. But before that, like I said in the previous segment, election and salvation are two different things. We've

---

[24] Ibid, (2006). p. 208.

seen that election of God is not for some few who were chosen or elected, or predestined, but it is indeed a free gift for every mankind regardless of what he does or what race he belongs to. We've also seen that God has chosen and predestined all us even before the foundation of the world. To fulfil this mysterious plan of God, He sent Jesus not to condemn the world but only to save the world. *"For God did not send His Son into the world to condemn the world, but that the world through Him might be saved"* (John 3:17).

That was to fulfil the election of God, not only for some few but for the all world. The election was a choice of God to save the all world, but the salvation of mankind depends so much on the choice of man and is not free altogether as it is with the election of God. It is a result of freedom of choice man has. I will elucidate this in detail as we go on, but the point is this. God wants all of us to be with Him in heaven but it is our own choice whether or not to accept it. For those who accept it, are given the power to become God's Children, according to John 1:12.

"But as many as received Him, to them He gave the right to become children of God, to those who believe in His name." On the other hand, those who don't accept Him are already condemned (John 3:18-19). The Israelites who did not receive Him were already condemned even though they were His own chosen people according to their election (1:11).

Unlike any other important topic in the Bible, I believe this topic on "Salvation of mankind" is very, very important. It is very important because directly or indirectly the whole Bible from Genesis to Revelation means only one thing and that is the salvation of mankind. Or in other words, the whole Bible's summary could be that; man must be saved from his sinful life to serve and worship God even in the eternity forever and ever.

Man must be saved, irrespective of what, for that's what man was made for. In Ecclesiastes 12:13 it says; *"Let us hear the conclusion of the whole matter: Fear God and keep His commandments; for this is man's all."*

To fear God the creator and keep His commandments will definitely result in salvation of man's life. Man is an eternal being (Genesis 2:7) and therefore, he has a long, long way to go. Here is a little hint, just for your information! When I say "man," it includes both male-man as well as female-man, or it means both man and woman like Dr. Myles Munroe says. And so, if you are a male-man or a female-man, or whatever man you are, please don't forget the fact that you are an eternal being and your eternal life must be saved, before you get involved in your busiest life schedules. You will be a smart man to do so, if you can only give a fraction of your time thinking about your eternity. For man's eternity is all that matters, whether you know it or not.

Because man is an eternal being, he will definitely spend his eternal life in the eternity, whether it is in heaven or in hell. To spend eternal life in any of these two eternal destinations, the choice had been given to man that only man himself will decide for his own destiny. As I've noted, in according to His choice, God had decided that we should spend our eternity with Him in heaven but then again, we also must decide according to our own choice whether to end up in heaven or in hell. The power to decide and choose had been voluntarily given to mankind by God, even from the Garden of Eden.

In Genesis 2:16-17, it says; *"And the Lord God commanded the man saying, "Of every tree of the garden you may freely eat"* (vs.16); *"but of the tree of the knowledge of good and evil you shall not eat, for in the day that you eat of it you shall surely die"* (vs.17).

Here God was telling the man what he should do and what he should not do. When you tell somebody what he should do and what he should not do, you are actually telling the man to decide whether to do that which you tell him to do, or to do that which you tell him not to do. God showed the man what was good for him and that which was not good for him.

If the man was not given the freedom of choice to choose, then God would not have said what He said. He would have created the man and caused the man to do only right. The man would have been totally controlled by God to make sure that he did nothing wrong. And God would have caused every bit of his action, and man would have become a creature that had nothing to get credit for what he did. Man would have simply become like a robot controlled by outside force or remote control and he would have nothing to enjoy about. Just imagine what a boring life it would have been.

In His great wisdom, God created man together with all his attributes to enjoy life. Beside all other creations of God, He created man in a very special way. There is nothing in all the creations of God is comparable with man; not even the angels for that matter.

Let's read Psalms 139:14 again and see what it says; *"I will praise you, for I am fearfully and wonderfully made."* Man was created fearfully and wonderfully by God in such a way that he (man) should have a special place in His Kingdom. He was purposely created for such a position from where he should rule and reign together with Him (Jesus) in His Kingdom both here on earth and the world to come.

It says in Genesis 1:26 that man was created in His image and His likeness to have dominion over all the earth and everything thereof. Paul says in 2Timothy 2:12 that; *"If we endure, we shall also reign with Him."* In Revelation 20:4-6 it says that man will reign with Jesus Christ for a thousand years on earth during the millennium period. And it's not only that but man will continue to reign with Jesus in heaven forever and ever.

John also saw this in his revelation. *"There shall be no night there: They need no lamp nor light of the sun, for the Lord God gives them light. And they shall reign for ever and ever"* (Revelation 22:5).

You see for God to share responsibility with man especially to rule and reign over all of His creations, is something that even the angels wish to have.

This is what King David says in Psalms 8:4-6. *"What is man that You are mindful of him, And the son of man that you visit him"* (vs.4)? *"For you have made him a little lower than the angels, And You have crowned him with glory and honour"* (vs.5). *"You have made him to have dominion over the works of your hand; You have put all things under his feet"* (vs.6).

Angels know that man is little lower than them (angels) for a temporary period on earth. And when that temporary life on earth is over, the world that is yet to come will be under the subjection of man. *"For He has not put the world to come, of which we speak, in subjection to angles"* (Hebrews 2:5). *"You have put all things in subjection under his (man's) feet"* (vs.8). With this and many other things that God does with man are things which angels desire to look into (1Peter 1:12). Because angels were made only to serve both God and man, for they are only ministering spirits. *"Are they not all ministering spirits sent forth to minister for those who will inherit salvation"* (Hebrews 1:14)?

But man was made to rule and reign together with God both in this world and the world to come (Ephesians1:20, 2:6, Revelation 3:21; 4:4, Matthew 19:28). These scriptures indicate to us that only man will be granted to sit with God on His throne. And I think we know that whoever is seated on the throne of God will obviously become little kings to rule and reign together with the King of kings and the Lord of lords forever and ever.

Another thing that disqualifies the angels to be seated together with Jesus in His throne is that, they haven't passed the test in the process of life as man has gone through in this sinful world.

Anyway, in order for man to get into such a high and blessed position, there is a process in which man must go through to be qualified enough to be seated together with Jesus in His throne. And the process begins with the freedom of choice man has. Man must first of all choose to be there and it's a gradual process that involves many things.

Man's will power or freedom of choice is a very crucial attribute God has granted to mankind. For it all begins with the freedom of choice whether it is for good or bad. This principle is not only for the spiritual life but it's also for the physical life as well. Man's destination is determined by what he chooses to do in accordance with the freedom of choice. It is a process in both physical and spiritual lives that man chooses to live the way he wants to live.

Therefore, the freedom of choice or man's will power is the only area where God will never ever intervene. Man has been given the freedom of choice to choose for what he desires to be (Genesis 2:16-17).

In Deuteronomy 30:11-15, and 19, God precisely declared that no human soul will have any excuse whatsoever on that great judgment day. Lets read what He said; *"For this commandment which I command you today is not too mysterious for you, nor is it far off"* (vs.11). *"It is not in heaven, that you should say, who will ascend into heaven for us and bring it to us, that we may hear it and do it"* (vs.12)? *"Nor is it beyond the sea, that you should say, who will go over the sea for us and bring it to us, that we may hear it and do it"* (vs.13). *"But the word is very near you, in your mouth and in your heart, that you may do it"* (vs.14). *"See, I have set before you today life and good, death and evil"* (vs.15). *"I call heaven and earth as witnesses today against you, that I have set before you life and death, blessing and cursing;*

therefore, choose life, that both you and your descendants may live" (vs.19).

I see something that is very challenging in verse 14 that I also want to elaborate little bit more. Let's see verse 14 again. *"But the word is very near you, in your mouth and in your heart, that you may do it."*

Freedom of choice has got to have a basis on which one decides. You just can't simply decide for the sake of deciding without any reason. There's got to be an object that becomes the reason for your decision. Therefore, in our case, there is a word very near us, in our mouth and in our heart, which is the ultimate reason for our decision. The word that is very near us, in our mouth, and in our heart is either a word that will produce neither life nor death.

We've got to be very smart enough to listen to it very carefully and think twice before we act upon it. Because after acting upon the word, which ever it may be, the next step for us is to reap what we've just sowed in our own field. For the Bible tells us in Galatians 6:7 that; *"Do not be deceived, God is not mocked; for whatever a man sows, that he will also reap."*

Now we've seen that freedom of choice plays a major role in man's destination. Like we've seen in the preceding segments that God wants us to spend our eternity with Him in heaven, but it's our choice whether to go with Him to spend our eternity in heaven or to go with Satan to spend our eternity in hell.

Above everything else that you may think of, God has wonderfully elected us and chosen us to spend our eternity with Him in heaven but **salvation has**

certain conditions that we must comply with. Eternal life is a free gift, but salvation is not free. I would therefore, with due respect for the various church doctrines that we have in our churches, let me show to you some important conditions in the following paragraphs.

Eternal life is in Jesus in accordance with John 3:16 and 1John 5:11-12. Therefore, the first condition is that; whoever goes to Jesus will definitely be given eternal life. But listen to this very carefully. The problem is not getting life from Jesus but the process in which we go to Him to get life. You just can't go to Jesus anyhow according to your own human wisdom and ideas to get eternal life. Who says that eternal life is free that anybody can go to Jesus anyhow to get life? There are certain conditions laid down by God that we ought to follow step by step in order to get this free gift called; eternal life.

God wouldn't bother to set conditions one after the other, but He is forced to do so because of our evil deeds. The all of humanity is a fallen generation that God has to find ways and means to save mankind by setting conditions.

I don't know how you understand the Bible, but to me, it's all conditions from Genesis to Revelation that I must follow one by one. I know that life is free, and heaven is also free, but that does not guarantee me to live outside the Bible and just go to heaven and get eternal life when I die. This is assuredly impossible; but if it happens to be a theology, in which some of you are engaged with, I would rather suggest that you run away from it as you would do to a rattle-snake.

Anyway, in the following paragraphs like I said, I will show you few conditions as to how you can follow in order to get eternal life or to spend eternity in heaven.

Firstly, the word "salvation" means 'saving of soul from sin and its consequences;' in according to Oxford Advanced Learner's Dictionary. Unless otherwise noted, the meaning of the word is obvious that you simply can not claim heaven, without the soul is saved from sin. Heaven will automatically reject an unsaved soul that has attachments of worldly things; such as sin. I want to emphasize it more deeply here whether you like it or not, for it matters life and death.

Man must first of all be saved from sin and it's consequences before salvation becomes evident. If that's the case then how can a sinner be saved? In order for one to be saved, he must first of all hear salvation message. Hearing a salvation message is the first thing ever a sinner must do. For man can not experience salvation, without a salvation message.

The Bible says in Romans 10:17 that; "*So then faith comes by hearing, and hearing by the word of God.*" When hearing the Word of salvation, faith begins to build up in the sinner's heart. As the faith builds up, the course of action takes place. But before we go on with the course of action, let's talk more about hearing the Word of salvation.

Hearing the Word of salvation is very important because it produces faith. Therefore, it is very important for a sinner to give attention to whatever the messages he hears. We have all kinds of messages in this world, as well as in the Church. Man is made to change and adapt into any climax of life. Therefore, when man hears something new to him and if he feels like to adapt into it, he makes a decision and there he goes.

Later if he hears another message more powerful or sweetest than the former, he might decide again to change his life for the better. That's exactly what the Word of faith does to a sinner as he hears the Word. Therefore, we as preachers of the gospel are playing a very important role in man's life; as we preach the Word of salvation. What we are actually telling the man to do is to change the cause of his lifestyle and adapt into a new system of lifestyle altogether.

We as preachers of the gospel should know what we are preaching about. If we preach anything other than the Word of God, we shouldn't expect any amount of Godly life in those people's lives. Those who respond to our message will definitely be like the kind of message that we preach. Or in other words, we will bear our own kind in the lives of those people. The principle of sowing and reaping will be evident in those people's lives in their every day walk. "You'll always reap what you sow (Galatians 6:7)", is one of the existing laws in the Bible that no other law can ever supersede it or can it be repealed for the better. Whatever law in the Bible has been purified seven (7) times that it will never ever be altered or repealed; so it's better for us to humble ourselves and comply with it.

Anyway, I would further like to repeat myself for your sake. For the sinners to take course of action in their lives, it is our duty to preach appropriate messages to them. If we preach something about repentance and salvation, sinners will surely repent from their sins and be saved; as a result of our message. But if we preach anything other than the salvation message like I said; we should not expect those people to act like the children of God. How can they become children of God without repentance and being born again? This is condition number one that man must obey and comply with.

Jesus knew it very well; so He made sure that man must first of all repent in order to see and enter into the Kingdom of God. He said; *"Repent, for the kingdom of heaven is at hand"* (Matthew 4:17).

The Kingdom of heaven was coming but a heart without repentance could not see it. It was priority number one that for a sinner to see the Kingdom of God, all he had to do was to repent. The 'ifs' and 'buts' were irrelevant when it came to repentance that matters the most. It was a must for a sinner to repent in order to see and enter the Kingdom of God; and there was no other option. In other words, He made sure that people must repent for there was no other possible and better way than repentance.

He further elaborated it by saying that you must be born again. In John 3:3-8, Jesus said; *"Most assuredly, I say to you, unless one is born again, he cannot see the kingdom of God"* (vs.3). *"Most assuredly, I say to you, unless one is born of water and the Spirit, he can not enter the kingdom of God"* (vs.5).

Again, condition number one like I've stated above, man must go to Jesus only through repentance from his sins and must be born again by the power of the water (the Word) and the Spirit. Only then, the spirit man who is dead as a result of sin according to Genesis 2:17, Romans 5:12; and 6:23, will be resurrected and revived back to life; that it will have eyes to see the Kingdom and legs to walk or enter into the Kingdom of God. Without this new experience in life, the man will still be spiritually dead. And you know, any dead person has no life to live neither physically on earth nor spiritually in heaven.

We see that the freedom of choice or man's will power; can overrule and undo the decision made by God that man should spend his eternity with Him in heaven. And so if condition number one is followed, man will be saved and his salvation will be secured. However, if he fails to comply with this very important condition, he will surely miss heaven.

Another condition is found in John 3:16, 18, and 19. I've already touched a little bit on it in the previous segment, but for this purpose, let's see it again. In these verses, both the love of God for mankind and the condition thereof are stated in the same verses. If you want to be a best Bible Student in your life, please don't show favoritism in one topic or one side of it and jump into conclusion without bothering to see it from the other angle. This is one of the biggest mistakes that people make when they read Bible and of course take subsequent action that is not fully beneficial.

In the above three verses, we see that God declares His great and immeasurable love for mankind as well as the conditions that follow. Let's see them verse by verse again.

"For God so loved the world that He gave His only begotten Son, that whoever believes in Him should not perish but have everlasting life" (vs.16).

It's very clear that the first part of this verse declares the love of God, and the second part declares the condition that should be complied, in order to make the first part a reality in one's life. Or in other words, the first part of John 3:16 will be evident, only when the second part of the verse is executed.

For God so loved the world that He gave His only Begotten Son that we may spend eternity with Him in heaven, but this will eventuate; only when we believe in Him (Jesus). But if we don't believe in His only Begotten Son, then there is no other option but to be perished; though we were loved by God at the first place.

The Bible is self-explanatory, but the problem is that we don't read it with understanding. Of course, there are areas in the Bible that need to be given more time and explanation from others, but some of these basics are explicitly and precisely written that we really don't need any Bible scholars or teachers to elucidate them to us.

Verse 18 of John 3 is another one. It reads; *"He who believes in Him is not condemned; but he who does not believe is condemned already, because he has not believed in the name of the only begotten son of God."*

It's all the same thing here in this verse, and straight-forward. He who believes in Him is not condemned; but he who does not believe is condemned already. Why? Simply, because he has not believed in the name of the only Begotten Son of

God. And so as verse 19 like I said in the other segment; that it is not God or other persons like the preachers of the gospel who condemn the man. A man is condemned only by his own ignorance in not believing in the Son of God and his own evil actions. This is what verse 19 says; *"And this is the condemnation, that the light has come into the world, and men loved darkness rather than light, because their deeds were evil."*

This verse is also self-explanatory. The light has already come but the people loved darkness more than the light. Why? Because, their deeds were evil. That's why they are condemned even though they were once predestined to spend eternity with God in heaven.

1John 5:11-12 is still another one. The condition set here in verse 12 is similar to that we've seen already in the above texts. Here it talks about man having Jesus in his life. Well, let's read verses 11 and 12 of 1John 5. *"And this is the testimony: that God has given us eternal life, and this life is in His Son"* (vs.11). *"He who has the son has life; he who does not have the Son of God does not have life"* (vs.12).

You see, the first part of verse 11 tells us that God has already given us eternal life. But listen to this very carefully. God did not give eternal life straight to us without any mediator in between Him and us. The second part of verse 11 also says that; the life that He (God) has already given to us is in Jesus Christ His Son.

It's like an item that has been paid already, just ready to be picked up, but it is still on the grocery shelf. Unless the owner claims it, it will still be there even though it has been already paid for by the purchaser. The item is one hundred percent (100%) belongs to the person to whom it was purchased. It does not belong to the grocery owner anymore. The problem here is not with the grocery owner or the item. But the problem is with the person to whom the item has been paid for. May be he is not aware of the item that has been paid for him by somebody, or he has not enough time to go and pick it up, or else he deliberately ignores it for he has something better somewhere.

Likewise, according to verse 11, God has given eternal life to us but it is still with Jesus. Therefore, in order to get this life, verse 12 tells us how to get it. Let's see verse 12 again. *"He who has the Son has life; he who does not have the Son of God does not have life."*

Can you now see how you can get this life that has been granted to you by God your Father? You just can't get eternal life without Jesus, though it is yours. In order for you to get this life, which is one hundred percent yours, it is a must that you have to have Jesus in your heart. Because verse 12 tells us that; *"He who has the Son has life."*

However, if we ignore Jesus and do not allow Him to have His residence in our hearts, there is no short-cut, whatsoever to claim eternal life from God the Father. For the last part of verse 12 says; *"He who does not have the Son of God does not have life."*

Again it's like the item that has been paid for but it is still on the grocery shelf. Unless the owner of the item takes time to walk to the store to claim it, the item will never be literally his, though it has been paid for him. What's wrong in walking to the store or getting in touch with the grocery owner? The grocery owner is the person who is keeping the item for the person to whom it has been paid for.

The only possible way I see here is that the item owner should not ignore the grocery owner. Why? Simply because the grocery owner has the key to open the store, that the item owner will have easy access to claim his property.

The illustration here is very simple but I mean to repeat it couple of times; so to make it very simple for some smart guys who think they can make it to heaven without Jesus, the source of life.

I want to repeat myself here for your sake. I said, in the previous segment that not only few but the all world was predestined that we should get eternal life but the condition here is that; we should have to have Jesus in our hearts, in order to spend eternity with God in heaven. For, there is no life without Jesus who is the source of life.

John 14:6 is I guess one of those favorite Bible verses for most of us. It also tells us plainly that there is no short-cut to the Father. Let's read John 14:6 first. *"Jesus said to him, I am the way, the truth, and the life. No one comes to the Father except through Me."*

Isn't this plainly written? God does not forbid anyone to go to Him, but whoever wants to go to Him must do so only through Jesus. Jesus is the only way to the Father and there is no other way besides Him. Before we discuss more on this verse, let's say if anyone wants to go to the Father, the condition here is that; he has to go through Jesus only. It shouldn't be any other man, or an angel or a saint.

I want to say something here that I guess it will surprise most of you. I hope we all have a common knowledge about the Triune God or God the Trinity. There are three persons in the Godhead; God the Father, God the Son and God the Holy Spirit, yet their composition makes only One God. In one particular occasion the all three were present. It happened when Jesus was baptized in the Jordan.

Let's see the all three in action, operated distinctively in that particular occasion. The story about Jesus' baptism is recorded in Matthew 3:13-17, but for our case let's read verses 16 and 17 only. *"When He had been baptized, Jesus came up immediately from the water; and behold, the heavens were opened to Him, and He saw the Spirit of God descending like a dove and alighting upon Him"* (vs.16). *"And suddenly a voice came from heaven, saying, "This is My beloved Son, in whom I am well pleased"* (vs.17).

Listen to this very carefully. Though they are one, the course of action applied in this particular occasion shows their distinctiveness. First of all, Jesus the Son, the second person in the Godhead, received water baptism (vs.16, first part). Secondly, the Holy Spirit, the third person in the Godhead, descended like a dove alighting upon Him (Jesus) (vs.16, second part). Thirdly, God the Father, the first person in the Godhead, was speaking out His pleasure from heaven on what Jesus was doing. All three in action distinctively in one particular occasion, shows to us what use to be their normal practice in the spiritual realm.

But then again operating distinctively does not bring many different end results but to achieve only one common interest. Though they operate distinctively, their unity and cooperation is undivided. They do one thing to achieve one common goal but each one of them has a part to play distinctively. Or in other words, they do one thing distinctively but in togetherness to achieve one common goal.

Therefore, the duty that supposed to be performed by the Father will never be done by the Son or the Spirit. It is the same thing with the Son and the Holy Spirit. Any duty that has been granted to the Son by the Father will always be done by the Son, and so as the Holy Spirit.

In that case, we should know each of their personalities distinctively. Not all the time and I don't think it is a must; but in some occasions, when we pray or preach or try to address them, we should not mix them up in their personalities and even in their personal names in the Godhead. For example, God the Father Jehovah/Yahweh is not God the Son Jesus Christ and God the Son is not God the Holy Spirit, though they are absolutely complete in oneness.

No wonder Jesus said; *"And I will pray the Father, and He will give you another Helper, that He may abide with you forever – the Spirit of truth, whom the world cannot receive"* (John 14:16-17).

Can't you see their distinctive duties in these verses? Here Jesus says; He (Jesus) will pray to the Father and He (the Father) will give you another helper (the Holy Spirit). What Jesus is actually saying here is that; His (Jesus') duty is to pray to the Father, and the Father's duty is to give the Holy Spirit to us and the Holy Spirit's duty is to abide in us forever. We can't mix them up in their distinctive positions and pray something like this. O! Holy Spirit, I pray to you that on behalf of me, please pray to the Son that the Son will send the Father to me who will abide with me forever.

Does that make any sense to your knowledge in line with the Word of God? I don't think so. The way we should pray in this particular area is something like this. O! Jesus, I pray to you that on my behalf, please pray to the Father that the Father will send the Holy Spirit to me in your name that He (the Holy Spirit) will abide with me forever. How about that one? It sounds like what John 14:16-17, and 26 says.

Jesus went on to say more on this in chapter 16 of John. In verses 13-15, this is what He says; *"However, when He, the Spirit of truth, has come, He will guide you into all truth; for He will not speak on His own authority, but whatever He hears He will speak; and He will tell you things to come"* (vs.13). *"He will glorify Me, for He will take of what is Mine and declare it to you"* (vs.14). *"All things that the Father has, are Mine. Therefore I said that He will take of Mine and declare it to you"* (vs.15).

Can't you see the distinctive positions of the three again? Here Jesus says the Holy Spirit will not speak anything of His own authority, but He will only speak what He hears from Him and the Father.

And He further says that all things the Father has are His. You see, Jesus did not say, the Holy Spirit will come and say anything to you according to His wishes, because He is the third person in the Godhead (vs.13). And He (the Holy Spirit) will bring to you anything that He owns or possesses (vs.15). I see that they are very well organized and have respect for one another even for their respective positions. I think I've said enough on this and to make a very long story short, let's go back to our point of discussion.

Our point that has taken us into this very lengthy discussion is a condition set in John 14:6. In John 14:6, we read that; no one goes to the Father except through Jesus for He is the only way to the Father. We've learnt in our lengthy discussion, that no man can make friendship with God and try to go to Him (God, the Father) without bothering to go through Jesus. No matter how much hard work we do to please the Father, if we ignore Jesus, our good works will be done in vain.

This is not so much so of a Christian world, but it is indeed a real problem for a Muslim world. For the Islamic belief says that there is no need of a mediator (obviously Jesus Christ) in between God and man, except Muhammad the prophet. They believe only in God and to them, Jesus Christ the Son of God has nothing much to contribute in their salvation.

Truly it will be a problem for the Muslims because they deliberately deny the Son and in doing so, the Father is also denied. This is confirmed in 1John 2:22-23. *"Who is a liar but he who denies that Jesus is the Christ? He is antichrist who denies the Father and the Son"* (vs.22). *"Whoever denies the Son does not have the Father either; he who acknowledges the Son has the Father also"* (vs.23).

Muslims believe in God the creator but they hardly believe in His Son Jesus Christ who is the Saviour of the world. To them, Jesus is just another prophet who does not have any Godly deity that can save others. On one hand they believe in God but on the other hand they disregard what this same God has provided for their good.

It's like a good friend of a man who wants to spend all the time in the world with the father but completely ignores and hates his only son. The poor friend does not know that the son has all the keys for the store-houses of the father. The poor friend also doesn't know that after long hours of conversation, the father will ultimately direct him to the son for his needs. A man with a good sense of mind will first of all greet the son as much as he would do to the father.

I am afraid that sometimes the spirit of Islamic belief can creep into the Christian churches and deceive the Christians. When such things slowly begin to win grounds in the Christian world, some Christians may say; 'what a waste of time talking about this; when I love God I love Jesus as well; things are fine with me; I am okay; so long as I am a member of a Christian church, I don't have to worry.'

Fair enough, but listen. I've seen many people profess to be Christians but their actions speak louder than their words; that their actions speak completely different language altogether. Jesus says; "*If you love me, keep my commandments*" (John14:15). What commandments? You read the whole Bible and you will notice that it is full of God's commandments. Some are big and others are small. Some are old and others are new; yet they are all commandments of

Jesus. Jesus says again; *"He who has my commandments and keeps them, it is he who loves Me. And he who loves Me will be loved by My Father, and I will love him and manifest Myself to him"* (vs.21).

Please don't be carried away with these so many discussions. You should know that we are still in our topic on conditions. I mean these are some of the conditions that are laid down for us to execute in order to spend eternity with God in heaven.

Here is one more condition; that if we want to be loved by the Father and even Jesus, the condition is; we should have the commandments and keep them. Not only having the commandments, but keeping them as well. To keep the commandments means to observe them, to obey them, and to live our everyday life according to the Word.

I don't want to be judgmental here but I must also be honest, that I see most of us Christians are truly not living the life that the Bible is charging us to live. We are a bunch of hypocrites preaching one thing and doing the other. Sometimes I use to wonder whether we have only one Bible or many Bibles in our respective churches. It seems like each individual Christian or each church organization has its own Bible. We preach against one another. Each group seems to know better than the other. Infightings within the Christian churches are silent; but they are the worst civil wars among the Christian world. But listen; it's God's desire that we should be the light and salt of the world (Matthew 5:13-16).

When are we gonna pull up our socks and be man enough to live the life that the Bible is charging us to live? I don't know what sort of Bible you have but the one that I have, tells me to forgive one another, and to love one another, to be humble, to have concern for others and pray for them, be one with fellow Christian brothers and sisters, be honest to one another, not to cause division in the church, help other people and the list goes on. These are some of the basics in our Christian life. The things that seem to have less significance are truly the essence in life. Therefore, without the essence in life, you can not live the full life, as you should.

How can we claim to be Christians when real substance of a Christian is not evident? Jesus once said; "*Not everyone who says to Me, Lord, Lord; shall enter the kingdom of heaven, but he who does the will of My Father in Heaven.*" (Matthew 7:21). It's not good enough by saying that; "I am a Christian," calling Him Lord, Lord, while in actual fact you haven't done even a fraction of God's will.

Well, what is God's will then? God's will is no other than to obey the Bible and live accordingly. I believe that is God's paramount will for every mankind.

The Bible is full of enough challenging messages for us Christians, so we better clean our own back-yards first before we jump up and down thinking that we are the only children of God. Jesus tells us in Matthew 7:3-5 that we should first of all remove the plank from our own eyes and then, we will be in a better position to see clearly to remove the speck from the other people's eyes. He also says in Matthew 3:9 that God is able to raise up children to Abraham from the stones; if we do not bear fruits worthy of repentance. This is in fact a statement that was directed to the Israelites who claimed that they have Abraham as their father, but they failed miserably in doing the will of God.

It is therefore, if we are not careful to follow the will of God, He can also reject us as He does to the Israelites. For if God can reject His own chosen people of Israel, we being the wild olive tree who were grafted into the natural olive tree, He may not spare us either, according to Romans 11:17-24.

Mark 16:16 is another crucial subject that also has a condition that needs to comply in order, as it is directed. This is what it says; *"He who believes and is baptized will be saved; but he who does not believe will be condemned."*

In this verse, there are two conditions. The two conditions are spelt in verbs, which are doing words. The two verbs are 'believe' and 'baptize.' In order for one to be saved, the first thing he must do is to believe and the second thing that should follow is the act of water baptism. Again, these two conditions should be executed in order as it is directed. For example, the latter should not come first and the former also should not come second. However, if it does, it will not work out well to achieve its goal; even salvation for that matter.

I think most of you know that the Bible is a book that needs to be followed as it is. No matter how smart we are, the Bible does not permit anyone of us to correct its mistakes, if you think there are some. It does not allow us to interpret it in a way as we see fit to us. It does not permit us to take away any bit of it that seems irrelevant to our situation, and add our own to suit our situation. No matter how it sounds to us, or how we feel, we are commanded to interpret and preach it as it is.

In Revelation 22:18-19 it says; *"For I testify to everyone who hears the words of the prophecy of this book: If anyone adds to these things, God will add to him the plagues that are written in this book"* (vs.18). *"And if anyone takes away from the words of the book of this prophecy, God shall take away his part from the Book of Life, from the holy city, and from the things which are written in this book"* (vs.19).

It also says in Proverbs 30:6; *"Do not add to His words, Lest He rebuke you, and you be found a liar."* It further says in Deuteronomy 4:2 that; *"You shall not add to the word which I command you, nor take from it, that you may keep the commandments of the Lord your God which I command you."* Further more it says in chapter 12:32 of Deuteronomy again that; *"Whatever I command you, be careful to observe it; you shall not add to it nor take away from it."*

When all these Bible references, charging us not to add or take away any dot from the Bible, or to execute the latter in place of the former, who are we to ignore the Bible and preach otherwise? I think it's very, very important to obey the Bible as it is; than to be consciously conscious with the man made rules and doctrines.

With due respect for our respective church rules and doctrines, we must not forget the fact that ultimately, God will be our judge. And His judgment will be perfect and final in accordance with every single Word in the Bible (Acts 17:31, Psalm 9:8,

96:13, 98:9). The Words are but perfect conditions that should be followed as it is directed in the Bible.

We should bear in mind that we will be judged individually according to our deeds and not as a church or as a group (Revelation 20:12-13; 22:12). Therefore, in situation as such, each one should make his own decision for his own soul.

In Mark 16:16, we learn that a man can not be saved just because God has predestined him; that he should have eternal life. No, he can't; though God has predestined him. He's got to comply with the condition set by the same God. First of all, he's got to believe and be baptized. Like I said, these two verbs, *"believe and baptize"* are doing words. God wants us to do something in order to be saved. And when we do it, we must think properly and do it right, and in order as it is directed by the Bible. The Bible is right and perfect, for it is purified seven times (Psalms 12:6) and can't be questioned and twisted around.

In this condition, we see that believe comes first before water baptism. One has got to believe first before he gets baptized. Believing and confessing must go hand in hand prior to water baptism. In Romans 10:9 it says; *"That if you confess with your mouth the Lord Jesus and believe in your heart that God has raised Him from the dead, you will be saved."*

Believing in God must be the reason for one's baptism. You should not go and get baptized in a church without knowing the reason for your baptism. Water baptism is a token of leaving the old world and joining into the Kingdom of God. The idea of water baptism was derived from a Jews ritual tradition, that when a Gentile is converted or wants to be a naturalized Jews or to follow the Jews rules, it is by Jews custom that he must be circumcised and be baptized.

Only then the Gentile has the right to take part in the Jews activities. The decision to be converted and to be a naturalized Jews or to observe Jews customs was more important than the circumcision or baptism, which was only a token of this preceding decision. Likewise, the decision to follow Christ and to believe in His Word is paramount important than to be baptized.

In other words, as circumcision and water baptism that were essentially required only as a token of the Gentiles' conversion to comply with the Jews rules, the water baptism of today should not precede the decision to follow Christ. In that sense, if a water baptism had occurred in one's life without the substance, (repentance and the preceding decision to follow Christ), then it only means nothing to God.

A baptismal candidate must first of all believe in the Triune God and should have repented from his sins and turned away from the world to follow Christ. If this experience hadn't happened in the baptismal candidate's life, he is not qualified and not eligible candidate to be baptized. For in His Great Commission, Jesus said; *"Go therefore, and make disciples of all the nations, baptizing them in the name of the Father and of the Son and of the Holy Spirit"* (Matthew 28:19), *"Teaching them to observe all things that I have commanded you; and lo, I am with you always, even to the end of the age"* (vs.20).

Going into all the world and making disciples (or followers of Christ) is priority number one and then water baptism should follow. And of course it does not stop there but teaching them to observe all (not only few that are suitable to them) things that we are commanded to observe.

However, if it did not happen in the way or procedure the Bible instructs, but had occurred in a reverse manner, for heaven sake, it be rescinded and must be done properly in a sequential order. In a situation as such, Apostle Paul had to re-baptize some twelve (12) Christians from Ephesus who had the first baptism by John the Baptist.

When Paul went to Ephesus, he found out that the twelve were baptized by John the Baptist, yet they did not know or had heard about the Holy Spirit. So Paul had to explain to them properly that John's baptism was a baptism of repentance and believing in Christ Jesus. Upon hearing what Paul said, they got up and were baptized again by Paul the second time. The story is recorded in Acts 19:1-7.

It is very obvious that essential elements like repentance and believing in Christ were absent or missing in those twelve people's first baptism. That's why Paul had to re-baptize them again. This history can be repeated again in our time, only if our first baptism had gone wrong somewhere along the line. Otherwise, the Bible says that; there's only one baptism (Ephesians 4:5). One would argue and say that the first baptism was John's baptism and so they had to baptize again in Jesus' baptism. There's no such thing as John's baptism and Jesus' baptism.

Like I said earlier, if you study and know the reason for baptism; both John's and Jesus' baptisms had only one reason. And the reason was no other than for repentance and believing in God. You can't distinguish John's baptism from Jesus' baptism just for want of prove for your ignorance. For the baptism of John was in the package of John's message about the Kingdom of God. And we know that John's message was the same message that Jesus preached. Both John and Jesus' messages found in Matthew 3:2 and 4:17 were in fact preached in different times and different places but they preached only one and same message; that the people must *"Repent, for the kingdom of heaven is at hand."*

The only difference is the preceding message that John preached in advance before the great commission to prepare the way for the Lord. If John's baptism and his preaching were of no significance, Jesus would not have baptized in John's Ministry and he would have also preached a different message than John's. But it was not the case in their time; so it shouldn't be a case for us as well, in our time.

Therefore, it is a condition that man must repent and believe first and be baptized in order to be saved. To be frankly honest with you, I have seen people getting baptized while still living in sin. I don't want to be too judgemental here but I think it's proper to do it right, even if it means to reverse the all thing, then why not; when we have enough time on planet earth.

'Believing first before baptism' also has enough authority to annul the baptism of little infants who know nothing about believing in God. The Bible has not even one record of baptism that involved the little infants.

One more condition in the area of water baptism is the order of names that we should apply. In the great commission, Jesus showed us how to apply the names of the three persons in the Godhead. *"Go therefore, and make disciples of all the nations, baptizing them in the name of the **Father** and of the **Son** and of the **Holy Spirit"*** (Matthew 28:19).

Baptizing them in the name of God the Father, (Jehovah) and God the Son, (Jesus Christ) and God the Holy Spirit, is the 'order' directed by Jesus Christ. Because the word 'name' is singular, that does not necessarily mean that the three have only one name. But it actually means the individual and distinctive name of the three in the Godhead. If the name of Jesus is the name for the all three as some think it is, then Jesus should have also made it clear, but He didn't.

In many situations, Jesus said; *"in **my** name"* (John 14:13-14, 26, 15:16, 16:24, Mark 16:17, Matthew 18:20, 24:5, Mark 9:41). He did not say; in **our** name. That simply means, the name "Jesus" is an individual and personal name of the Son and it's not the name of the Father or the Holy Spirit; though the name of Jesus can be used or applied to represent the all three in some situations or occasions. If one still does not agree with me, then you are saying that Jesus was selfish and greedy when He said; "in **my** name," if the name was meant for the all three. In contrast to this, even some Bible Scholars say that Jesus is the name of the Father, the Son, and the Holy Ghost, which I completely disagree with their theology.[25]

With this kind of theology, they promote the idea of baptizing in the name of Jesus only. They draw their authority from three Bible references from the Book of Acts (8:16, 10:48, and 19:5). I think the Author of the Book of Acts by way of writing, stating that they were baptized unto Jesus. That doesn't necessarily mean that they got baptized in the name of Jesus only; for Jesus Christ is not the name of the Father or the Holy Ghost but it is indeed the name of the Son of God (Matthew 1:21, 16:16, 20, Luke 1:31, Acts 8:37, 9:20, 1John5:13, Philippians 2:9-11).

It is only a presumption without any Biblical authority and they assume that those baptisms were held in the name of Jesus only. No wonder, with due respect, our learned Bible Scholars find it hard to make a solid and scriptural bridge between the great commission (Matthew 28:19); and the Book of Acts (8:16, 10:48, 19:5); to affirm their theology.

Upon this understanding, I want to say that the condition here is the order of the names specified in the great commission should be complied; rather than believing in assumptions that have not enough support and authority from the Word.

Finally, baptism must be by immersion and not by sprinkling. The baptisms that occurred during the Bible days were all done by immersion. Not even one single baptism of that time occurred in a ceremony of sprinkling of waters in a church. The significance in

---

[25] ....? "The Holy Bible" in the King James Version, Thomas Nelson Publishers, Nashville, 1977, prefix notes on the Doctrines of the Bible, p. 6.

these two methods is more important than the methods themselves. Therefore, immersion speaks better than sprinkling. For immersion speaks of both the Word of God and the soil of the earth. When one is baptized, he is fully covered by the water of the Word and is also fully buried of his sinful nature under the soil of the earth (Romans 6:3-4).

Actually the word baptism comes from a Greek word called 'baptizo' which means to go under water or by immersion. I believe most Bible Scholars know it very well that baptism by immersion is the proper way, but they can't speak out for they are enslaved with their churches' very strong doctrines. Anyway, when we see it from a worldly point of view, there is not much difference between the two. Generally, it is only an act of one's commitment to follow the Lord; whether through sprinkling of water or through immersion.

However, the Spiritual significance in immersion that we don't really understand it in full, could be the substance that matters the most. Therefore, I think it is not what we understand that matters but what we believe in the Word of God that matters the most. We don't have to understand everything in full in order to obey the commandments of God. All we have to do is to only believe and obey, even if it looks funny and does not go down well with us.

God prefers obedience more than sacrifice or let's say; obedience is better than sacrifice as 1Samuel 15:22 records. Here in this story, we see from a worldly point of view that, there is not much difference whether to kill the animals and King Agag in their own land, or in the enemy's Territory.

King Saul and his men didn't spare the lives of the animals and the King of Amalekites that they should live. They were captured only to be killed in the enemy's Territory. But that was not the command of God. God's command was that the people and the animals alike should be utterly destroyed in their own land (vs:3).

Not all the time but sometimes God says specifically in some situations than in general. Therefore, God did not accept the fact that they were purposely captured to be killed even in the enemy's Territory; for they disobeyed Him. All He preferred was obedience at the most than any sacrifice that seemed right with King Saul. In our case, this same God prefers obedience from us in His commandments than to stick to our man-made rules and doctrines that seem right only in our eyes.

One more example is the healing of a man born blind found in John 9:1-7. Unlike any other blind man that Jesus healed; just by speaking a word or by laying of hands found in Matthew 9:27-30, 20:29-34, and Mark 10:46-52, this poor blind man was given more trouble by Jesus. He was commanded by the Lord to go and wash in the pool of Siloam, after Jesus covered his blind eyes with clay.

Why would Jesus had to give more trouble to this poor blind man by rubbing wet clay on his blind eyes, and sending him to the pool to wash? Had He used-up all His power to heal any more; that He needed some kind of support power from the wet clay and the water? I don't think there was more power in the wet clay and the water; though the clay symbolizes the sin and the water symbolizes the Word. I believe what

Jesus wanted was some amount of obedience to His Word by this particular blind man; before he got his healing.

It is therefore, obedience is what God would desire more in this subject of water baptism. If that could be the case then; we are bound to comply with every decree of God; even if it looks funny and seems to have no significance from a worldly point of view. It is therefore, being obedient to the command of God is also important as well as the subject matter itself. It is indeed another condition that man has to obey in order to be saved. Anyway, the Bible references that affirm the baptisms by immersion are found in the following texts. (Matthew 3:5-17, John 3:22-23, Acts 8:35-39.

Let's see one more condition here. Sometimes even the Christians have problem with their flesh. The flesh as we know has nothing much in common with the Spirit of God. Therefore, the flesh and the Spirit will never agree with each other's desires. The condition in situation as such is that; no matter how hard it would be, we are charged by Apostle Paul not to show any respect for the desires of the flesh that are in contrary with the Spirit.

This is what Galatians 5:17-21 says; *"For the flesh lusts against the Spirit, and the Spirit against the flesh; and these are contrary to one another, so that you do not do the things that you wish"* (vs.17). *"But if you are led by the Spirit, you are not under the law"* (vs.18). *"Now the works of the flesh are evident, which are: adultery, fornication, uncleanness, lewdness, idolatry, sorcery, hatred, contentions, jealousies, outbursts of wrath, selfish ambitions, dissensions, heresies, envy, murders, drunkenness, revelries, and the like; of which I tell you beforehand, just as I also told you in time past, that those who practice such things will not inherit the kingdom of God"* (vs.19-21).

You see, the condition here is that; no matter who we are; if we practice any one of the above desires of the flesh, we will still not inherit the Kingdom of God. The Bible is very clear that even the so-called Christians must be very careful about their conducts. This is Paul writing to the Christians of Galatia urging them to be careful and mindful in what they do.

We are still talking about conditions though heaven is free. I therefore, would like to take a step forward with Paul and would also like to urge you that not one bit of the desires of the flesh be entertained. If we keep on entertaining our flesh, we might as well loss the eternal life that has been granted to us.

Some Christians think that they can still make it to heaven, even if they have practiced evil according to the desires of their flesh. You can't see any where in the Bible that you can go to heaven as you think. It is not what you think (in terms of eternal blessings) that will determine your destiny but it is what you do. I am afraid many Christians might not make it to heaven as they think they would. Because if you really look at it more closely, most so-called Christians' conduct really don't demonstrate and match with what they profess to be. Almost all the New Testament Books warn us Christians to be watchful of our actions.

I don't know why but Jesus was so familiar with the word hypocrite. Why He had to call those so-called religious people hypocrites? I think they were good only on the outside, but on the inside, were full of dead men's bones and all uncleanness (Matthew 23:27). These are real warnings I believe; that we as Christians should not play up with the grace of God and take it for granted.

We've got to be Christians; followers of Jesus Christ's footsteps or else quit and do something else. There must be honesty and genuineness in our profession of Christianity, rather than becoming good religious people without the real substance that will determine our destiny.

Finally, the conditions are that; only if we live according to the Bible; nothing will stop us from entering the Kingdom of God. The key for our salvation is with us and we are responsible for our own souls. Jesus says; He has given us the keys of the Kingdom of heaven (Matthew 16:19). What keys? Keys that will open doors for the blessings of God and of course above all, salvation for our own souls.

It's all within us; we've got to choose life for our selves, for nobody will do it for us. We are the sum total of what we do in our lives every day. Again God the Father said; *"I call heaven and earth as witnesses today against you, that I have set before you life and death, blessing and cursing; therefore choose life, that both you and your descendants may live"* (Deuteronomy 30:19).

It's our own responsibility to choose life simply by observing the Word of God. God has granted eternal life to us but the choice is ours, whether to accept it by obeying His Word or to do otherwise. You see, we are potentially capable of obeying what God is commanding us to follow. It is possible to say no to sin and turn back to God and do right. However, if one is found to be guilty of not obeying God, he will have no excuse whatsoever on that Great Judgment Day. Dear friends, we are made purposely for heaven, so let's make it our aim to be up there with Him, simply by believing and observing His Word rather than condemning ourselves by our ignorance in His Word.

Finally, like we said, we are elected to go to heaven but salvation is a making of our own choice. Truly, it's the job of the saviour to save us, but we must make ourselves available for the saviour to save us. And that's only by observing the above prescribed and other conditions in the Bible that significantly contribute towards our salvation. Hope to meet you up-there only if we do it right!

Chapter 9

Church is a Growing Organism

a: **The Right Food**

It is true of a living thing that its growth depends so much on the kind of food that it takes. In other words, let's say its growth and destiny is the end-result of what sort of food it takes. The Church is no exception, for it is a growing organism. We've already seen in Matthew 16:18 where it says; *"And I also say to you that you are Peter, and on this rock I will build My Church, and the gates of Hades shall not prevail against it."*

That means, it will grow and win new grounds that no power of the enemy will stand against its growth. Well, how will it grow, and to what extent? I will try and explain in the following paragraphs.

First of all, because it is a growing organism, it must be fed well with the right kind of food, in order for it to grow. Well, what is the right food for the Church anyway? There are many things that seem to be right food for the Church but the only right food is no other than the Word of God. Besides the Word of God, there shouldn't be any other so-called Spiritual food items labeled as No.2 or No.3 for the Church. Any other thing or activity that is regarded as Spiritual food for the Church should be tested first of all by the Word of God. For example; Music can be one of it. Music can be referred to as a good thing for the growth of the Church but it must be tested and measured by the Word of God. How the music should be played, who should play the music, how the words of the songs are arranged, and what kind of words should be applied and so on.

These bits and pieces must be tested and measured by the Word of God and if any of it has not yet passed the "Word Laboratory Test" so to say, and if it is not practiced according to the Word, it is not healthy for the growth of the Church. The same can be applied in all the other church activities such as pray meetings, cell groups, youth meetings, conventions and even Bible schools etc.

The Word must be the centre of everything that we do in His name. Even in our main services, the Word must be treated and respected highly above all other things and activities performed in the Church. And they should be done in reverence for the Word and in the light of the Word. In other words, our songs, our prayers, our preaching, our doctrines and so on, must be based only in the Word of God. They are good materials but should only be applied in the light of the Word. For the growth of the Church depends very much on the Word of God than all these other activities. Therefore, the only right food for the Church is no other than the Word of God. That means the Word of God is the main diet for the Church.

Man-made laws, rules and doctrines may contribute something good towards the growth of the Church, but like I said, it should only be done in the light of the Word. However, if the Word is not given priority, the Church will definitely decline in terms of quantity and quality. Some Church leaders prefer quantity more than quality, but I would rather prefer quality more than quantity.

Quality proves or shows how the Word being treated highly in the Church and quantity proves how the man-made laws and doctrines being treated and respected more than the Word. Or in other words, quality is the end-result of how the Church had been fed with the Word of God; and on the other hand, quantity is the end- result of how the Church had been fed with the worldly and social activities more than the Word of God.

You know if the Word is not preached in a church as it should, that particular place and its gathering will become like any other social gathering. People will walk in and out in great numbers for services but that doesn't mean that the Church is growing. It is of course growing in quantity but not really in quality. I believe it is the quality that will stand for Christ and even to make it into heaven than the quantity.

However, we can not deny the fact that some churches can grow both in quality and quantity. Should I tell you one thing that I guess it might ignite you to do that which you've never done before? It is God's desire and His perfect will that He wants to see each local church be filled to its full capacity with quality Christians only. But listen; it requires somebody like you to make it happen.

The time is running out and you are also growing faster and getting closer to your graveyard every day. For heaven sake, should you do something about the growth of your church? My friend, God really needs you more than ever, like never before. It is therefore, this is what it really means in Matthew 16:18 as He says; *"And on this rock I will build My church, and the gates of Hades shall not prevail against it."*

The gates of Hades shall not prevail against it literally means, the Church will grow, and grow and grow both in quality and in quantity that no power of hell will stand against it. Powers of darkness such as alcoholic, drugs, sex, pride, dirty politics and the like of it will no longer have any power to prevail against the power of God. You see, it's God's desire and His perfect will that the Church as a universal or a local congregation should grow. Again how can the Church grow? It will grow, only when it is fed properly with the Word of God.

Jesus knows how important the Word is and therefore, He says; *"Go into all the world and preach the gospel to every creature"* (Mark 16:15). He didn't say; go into all the world and establish mission stations, or little kingdoms of your own, or Bible schools or whatever it is. It is also true that these things are very important and we really need them to run our work more effectively and efficiently. Yet the most important of all is the Word of God.

He deliberately said; go into all the world and preach the gospel. He knows that it is the gospel, or the Word alone can establish the Church. Because the Church is not a physical entity that can it be built by any physical materials. But it is a Spiritual institution that it can only be built by the Word. I believe it's our priority number one to listen very carefully to the Chief Architect/Chief Builder as to how we can build and feed the Church.

No wonder, Jesus said in Matthew 16:18 that; *"And I also say to you that you are Peter, and on this rock I will build My church, and the gates of Hades shall not prevail against it."*

And on this rock, I will build my Church. Which rock do you think Jesus was talking about? The rock foundation Jesus was talking about is, like I said earlier; the Rock of all ages, which is Jesus Himself. There are numerous of references prove that Jesus is the Rock of all ages; and here are just few for our purpose (Genesis 49:24, Deuteronomy 32:4,18, 2Samuel 22:2, Psalms 18:2, 19:14, 31:3, 92:15, Isaiah 17:10, 26:4, 1Corinthians 10:4).

And you know that Jesus who is the Rock is also the Word (John 1:1-16). *"In the beginning was the Word, and the Word was with God, and the Word was God"* (vs.1). In that case, it is paramount important that the Church should be built on the Rock the Word, by the Word, and be fed in the Word.

In the closing remarks in His great commission Jesus said; *"Teaching them to observe all things that I have commanded you; and lo, I am with you always, even to the end of the age"* (Matthew 28:20). What is it that Jesus actually talked about when He said; "teaching them to observe all things that I have commanded you?" It is very obvious that Jesus was telling the Disciples to teach and feed the Church with the Word and to observe the Word. It's all Word, nothing else.

Furthermore, Jesus told Peter that he should feed His sheep with the Word. This is what Jesus said; *"Simon, son of Jonah, do you love Me more than these?" He said to him, "Yes, Lord; You know that I love you." He said to him, "Feed My Lambs"* (John 21:15). *He said to him again a second time, "Simon, son of Jonah, do you love Me?" He said to Him, "Yes, Lord; You know that I love You." He said to him, "Tend my sheep" (vs.16). Again, Jesus said to him the third time, "Simon, son of Jonah, do you love Me?" Peter was grieved because He said to him the third time, "do you love Me?" And he said to Him, "Lord you know all things; You know that I love You." Jesus said to him, "Feed My sheep" (vs.17).*

Jesus knows how important the Word of God is for the growth of the Church. Therefore, He repeated Himself three times, urging Peter to feed the Church. Jesus did not specify what sort of food should Peter use to feed the sheep but it is very obvious that Peter would use no other than the Word of God to feed the sheep.

Jesus even went into the extreme of saying that He who is also the Word is the bread of life. Man is made to eat in order to live, both in physical and spiritual lives. The truth of the matter is that; if one does not eat, he will obviously not live any longer. It is not an option but it is a must that one must eat in order to live.

If one does not eat, or does eat but only deadly food for a certain period of time, he should not expect to live any longer, because he will definitely not. How can he expect to live, knowing the fact that he is not eating anything at all, or does eat but only deadly food? If one thinks that he can live without eating anything or eating only deadly food, then he might be out of his mind. For no man with a good sense of mind can ever do that. That is why food is only the most important essential basic that one can not afford to live without.

Man can live without other essential basics like shelter or clothing, that can also be substituted by other means but food can not be substituted by any other means. Therefore, it is a must that man either eats and live or quits eating and ceases to live. In the same token, Jesus knew how important the spiritual food for the Church and He said; *"Do not labour for the food which perishes, but for the food which endures to everlasting life, which the Son of Man will give you, because God the Father has set His seal on Him"* (John 6:27).

Jesus tells us not to labour for the food, which perishes, but for the food that endures to everlasting life. What is this food which endures to everlasting life? It is the bread of God, which is also the bread of life that comes down from heaven and gives life to the world (vs. 33, 35, 41, and 48). It is wise to eat at least a piece of this bread of life so that it can endure to everlasting life. It is also very, very crucial that we must eat of this bread, for it is the only bread that gives eternal life (vs.51).

It was not easy for the religious Jews to swallow the fact that; *"Jesus is the bread which came down from heaven"* (vs.41). They hardly believe and quarreled among themselves saying, *"How can this man give us His flesh to eat"* (vs.52)?

I am very sorry that the Jews were always thinking about the physical life situation, when Jesus said something about the spiritual life. Their mind-sets were always pre-occupied with the physical things of this world. Jesus was not talking about literally cutting His physical body into pieces to feed the sheep. All He was talking about is the Word. He referred to Himself as the bread of life for He was, and He is, and He will be the bread of life, which is the Word, for all generations. For we know that He is the Word (John 1:1-4).

Jesus further says; *"Most assuredly, I say to you, unless you eat the flesh of the Son of Man and drink His blood, you have no life in you"* (6:vs.53). *"Whoever eats My flesh and drinks My blood has eternal life, and I will raise him up at the last day"* (vs.54). *"For My flesh is food indeed and My blood is drink indeed"* (vs.55).

It has been a tradition in our churches that whenever we come together in our churches for communion services, we usually read these verses, referring them to the bread and wine that we prepare for the communion table. I don't think Jesus was talking about the bread and wine that we participate in our churches every Sunday or Sabbath morning for the communion service. Truly there is no eternal life in such physical bread and wine that we prepare in our churches for communion services. The communion service is just a token of respect and remembrance of what Jesus had done for us on the cross of Calvary (1Corinthians 11:24-25).

And therefore, the bread symbolizes the Word and the wine symbolizes the Blood. It is the flesh (the Word) of Jesus gives eternal life, for His flesh is food indeed for the growth and durability of the Church (vs.54-55). Therefore, the Word of God is indeed the only right food for the Church and its growth. So let's say the healthy growth and the quality of the Church will be very much determined by the level and amount of the Word being preached in the Church.

b: Can Anybody Feed

In the previous segment, we have seen that the Word of God is the only right food for the growth of the Church. The Word therefore, must be prepared and presented properly to the Church. The Word of God is very important in its status and it is also very important for the growth and health of the Church. The Word of God is the ultimate authority for every situation, both for physical and spiritual lives on earth. Everything, both visible and invisible, things that are here on earth and that are in heaven, big or small, were all created by the Word and through the Word.

We've seen what John said in his Gospel 1:1-3 that; *"In the beginning was the Word, and the Word was with God, and the Word was God"* (vs.1). *"He was in the beginning with God"* (vs.2*). "All things were made through Him, and without Him nothing was made that was made"* (vs.3).

With the provision of sufficient evident as such, I see that the Word of God is in fact the source of everything. You talk about life, wealth, knowledge, power or whatever it is, the source of all is the Word of God. God spoke the Word, and all these things came into existence from nothing but the Word (Genesis 1:1-28). That's how powerful and mighty the Word of God is. If the Word is that powerful, mighty and holy as such, I don't think it is right for anybody to just grab anything from the Bible and preach it anyhow. Man, He is the Great I Am, the Awesome God who lives forever, the Creator of the universe, All Powerful and Mighty; and He is indeed a Consuming Fire (Deuteronomy 4:24, Hebrews 12:29).

Therefore, those of us who are dealing with the Word must be very careful and cautious in what we are doing. If we don't do it right, we are in trouble. That is why; from the very beginning, God had been mindful of His Word. King David knew how important the Word of God was to him and he commented the Word in many forms. Here is one found in Psalm 12:6; *"The words of the Lord are pure words, Like silver tried in a furnace of earth, Purified seven times."*

I guess in the furnace of the Holy Ghost Fire, the Word had been purified seven times. A common Christian belief or creed; that I guess most of you may agree with me that figure seven (7), is a number of God that speaks for completeness and wholeness in the things of God. With such belief in the Christian community, there shouldn't be any doubt that the Word of God which is purified seven times, is in its completeness and fullness; in terms of life, power, blessing, healing etc. That's why we are forbidden not to add or take away a dot of it, for it is perfectly complete and it needs nothing, neither to add nor to subtract.

Because the Word is purified seven times for all purposes, those of us who are translating this Word, must only do what a translator should do, or in other words, we must only do the job of a translator. God's Word is forever True and Amen that we are obliged to translate the Word as it is. We must know the fact that we are not preaching our own ideas and messages; but we are only translating what has been said. I've been translating messages for many times in my area, and as a translator, I don't preach what the preacher doesn't say. I only say what the preacher says, for I am not the preacher but the translator. We are trustfully called by God only to translate no other than His Word as it is in its fullness. As translators of the Word, our job is to translate no less or no more of what had been said by God.

That is why, whoever preaches the Word, should know that what he is doing is what God called him to do. It is not right; just to preach the Word, for the sake of preaching it. Preaching the Word of God has nothing to do with our education, our finance or wealth, our position, our title, our status in society and so on. Your education, finance or whatever it may be can only help; but it has got to be God's call upon your life, whether to be a full time or a part time minister to preach the Word. I would therefore, encourage you to prayfully find out what you are made to be and faithfully serve Him through whatever the call it may be to the best of your ability.

We should know the fact that all of us are not called by God only to preach the Word but to serve Him. Serving Him doesn't only mean that you have to preach the Word from the pulpit but there are many other ways in which you can serve God. Let's see what Paul tells us in 1Corinthians 12:29-31. *"Are all apostles? Are all prophets? Are all teachers? Are all workers of miracles"* (vs.29)? *"Do all have gifts of healings? Do all speak with tongues? Do all interpret"* (vs.30)?

No, the answer is not all can preach as an apostle, or a prophet, or a teacher, or a pastor, or an evangelist. But Paul also reminds us that some can be helpers, or administrators (vs.28). You can help with finance and others, you can help in your prayers, you can help in administration work and so on. There's so much to be done in the service of God; that every one of us should prayfully find out what God has intended for each one of us.

Preaching the Word is not the only way of serving God. But it has been granted to some as He wills. Apostle Paul further says in Ephesians 4:11 that it is *"He Himself gave some to be apostles, some prophets, some evangelists, and some pastors and teachers."*

If you are a preacher of the Word, I want to challenge you that your ministry should operate under the banner of one of these five-fold ministries. Why under the banner of these five-fold ministries? I'll tell you why. If you are really enthusiastic in preaching, I want to appeal to you that you also read verses 12-13 and all through verses 14-16 of Ephesians chapter 4.

I will explain more on the purposes of your calling and ministries in chapter 10. But for this purpose, let me say that he, who is not called by God into one of these five-fold ministries; whether full-time or part-time, will definitely not help to build the Church, in line with or in accordance with verses 12-16. He will instead produce negative results. The simple reason is that; because God did not appoint him or had given him the ministry as such; he does not have the mandate from God to do so.

He can be a good character for the ministry but if God hasn't called him, He also doesn't know him. Jesus says in Matthew 7:21-23 that at the Day of

Judgment, He will say to some of us that; He never knew us. *"Not everyone who says to Me, "Lord, Lord," shall enter the kingdom of heaven, but he who does the will of My Father in heaven"* (vs.21).

What sort of will is He talking about? In everything, if God is not in it, even the ministries for that matter, then it is not God's will. If it's not God's will, then God's hand of approval and special ministry anointing and the mandate from on High is not there. The man will act as if he is an anointed one but in actual fact he is not. He is a foolish and he can only fool the likes of himself but eventually this sort of foul ministry can destroy the Church of God.

That is the ultimate purpose for such people and ministries thereof, for they are not from God but from the enemy of God. *"Many will say to Me in that day, "Lord, Lord, have we not prophesied in Your name, cast out demons in Your name, and done many wonders in Your name"* (vs.22)? *"And then I will declare to them, "I never knew you; depart from Me, you who practice lawlessness"* (vs.23).

There will be people standing naked in the eyes of God complaining about what they had done in His name. Unfortunately, the self-appointed ministers (they are found not in all but in some countries) and of course the unfaithful servants will be there among the crowd complaining about their services rendered in the work of God. But Jesus will declare to them, I never knew you.

It's a good thing to preach the Word, but you must be called and ordained by God to do what you are doing. It doesn't matter whether it is a full-time or a part-time service. If not, the good works done in His name will be done in vain according to Psalm 127:1.

False prophets the Bible talks about don't have to be people with long horns and sharp teeth and long ears and so forth, but they can puff-up from within our own churches. They can be some of our good Christian friends or even from our own family members (2Peter 2:1). What are false prophets, anyway? False prophets are prophets who don't preach the full gospel but heresy, only to deceive the people of God. They are used by the enemy of God, purposely to steal, to kill and to destroy the Church of God.

Jesus once highlighted this by saying that; *"The thief does not come except to steal, and to kill, and to destroy. I have come that they may have life, and that they may have it more abundantly"* (John 10:10). The thief comes in a form of a prophet to carry out his evil plans. We have these thieves or false prophets all over the world today. But how can we identify them? Jesus tells us how to identify them in Matthew 7:15-20.

This is what He says; *"Beware of false prophets, who come to you in sheep's clothing, but inwardly they are ravenous wolves"* (vs.15). *"You will know them by their fruits. Do men gather grapes from thorn bushes or figs from thistles"* (vs.16)? *"Even so, every good tree bears good fruit, but a bad tree bears bad fruit"* (vs.17). *"A good tree can not bear bad fruit, nor can a bad tree bear good fruit"* (vs.18). *"Every tree that does not bear good fruit is cut down and thrown into the fire"* (vs.19). *"Therefore by their fruits you will know them"* (vs.20).

To identify a false prophet is not a big deal. All we have to do is to look at the fruits of every so-called preacher of the Word or minister of God. The end-result of a ministry is very important than the ministry itself. Whatever the fruit you see is what the ministry is all about.

If you see that a ministry that does not build the Body of Christ; but instead causes divisions in the Body and steals sheep from one church to another, there is no doubt about this sort of ministry. The person involves in such a ministry is truly a false prophet. Why am I saying that? You go back to Ephesians chapter 4, and read verses 12-16 again. A ministry that is from God and ordained by God cannot preach messages and produce fruits that are contrary to the spoken and written Word of God.

Let's see some of these verses again. It is Jesus who gives the ministries for certain purposes, and here are some of them; *"For the equipping of the saints for the work of ministry, for the edifying of the body of Christ"* (vs.12). *"Till we all come to the unity of the faith and of the knowledge of the Son of God, to a perfect man, to the measure of the stature of the fullness of Christ"* (vs.13).

Any one of these five-fold ministries should equip the saints for the work of ministry, edify the Body of Christ, and unify the faith and knowledge of the Son of God that the Body of Christ should become perfect to the measure of the stature of the fullness of Christ. That's what we supposed to be doing as ministers of the Word. I hardly see anywhere in the Bible that God has ordained a special ministry to cause divisions and split the Body of Christ. However, if there happens to be any, I don't think it is from God.

Let's go back to Matthew 7:15-20 and see what Jesus says. Jesus warns us that we must be aware of false prophets, who come to us in sheep's clothing, but inwardly they are ravenous wolves (vs.15).

I've literally seen couple of prophets come with sheep's clothing. Their clothing speaks of what they do on the outside, and this is what I've noticed. They are really smart and professional in their hypocrisy. They talk well, preach well, and do almost everything well in a gentle way. You'll hardly identify them as false prophets at the initial stage. They seem to be loving and kind to everybody. It is a con spirit which deceives the people and that's how the false prophets operate. By doing that, it is easy to win the hearts of especially the weak sheep and others.

In the process, the impartation takes place. When the impartation is over, the game is also over. Now they slowly begin to say something new. They call it, 'a new and fresh revelation' that has been concealed for ages. As the deceived and fooled flocks hear such a deceitful revelation, they run for it. Because they are deceived and the spirit of deception is already at work in their lives as a result of the impartation, they believe in all fakes that sound new and itchy in their ears.

Paul was inspired by God (2Timothy 3:16) to write the warning in advance and this is what he said; *"For the time will come when they will not endure sound doctrine, but according to their own desires, because they have itching ears, they will heap up for themselves teachers"* (2Timothy 4:3); *"And they will turn their ears away from the truth,* and *be turned aside to fables*" (vs.4).

If you see a prophet or a ministry fall under this category and its fruits as such, he could be one of these false prophets that the Bible is warning us about.

Verses 16-20 of Matthew chapter 7 says; "*You will know them by their fruits. Do men gather grapes from thorn bushes or figs from thistles?*" "*Even so, every good tree bears good fruit, but a bad tree bears bad fruit*" (vs.17). "*A good tree can not bear bad fruit, nor can a bad tree bear good fruit*" (vs.18). "*Therefore by their fruits, you will know them*" (vs.20).

I think this is enough to know the good from the bad. We have ears to hear and eyes to see what the Bible is telling us. Preaching the Word is not a problem. Anybody can grab anything from the Bible and preach it. But a minister can be proven only in the fruits of his ministry. A minister ordained by God could not bear bad fruit and in like manner, a minister that is not from God will never bear any good fruit. That is why, it is not healthy for the Church to allow anybody to get up and preach anything as he wishes. In that regard, I as for one would really want to judge the vessel more then the message. For if the vessel is good and clean, then the message will surely be good anyway.

Jesus once said in Matthew 9:17 that new wine cannot be stored in an old wineskin. Why new for new and old for old? Because the chance of the new getting dirty in an old wineskin, is more likely than the old getting new in a new wineskin.

Having said that, it is also true that sometimes God may use anybody to accomplish His purposes, but that only happens in very rare occasions in certain situations. Such people should not be reckoned as called and ordained ministers of the gospel. I call them one day or one hour ministers with a donkey mouth as it was with the case of Balaam in Numbers 22:28-30 in the Old Testament. I therefore, strongly want to emphasize that preaching the Word of God should be highly respected and honoured above all, for it is indeed an honourable task according to 1Timothty 3:1.

When we preach, we are actually imparting something into the lives of our audience. Whatever it is that we are preaching, will be planted in the hearts and minds of those listeners. Unless they reject the message and the spirit behind the preaching, it will definitely be planted in their hearts and minds.

Every word that a listener is attending to, (whether it is a Word of God or any other word) does not stop at the ear-drums of the listener. It penetrates deep into the bottom of the heart and changes the course of man's reasoning in life. As the Word of God or any other word begins to lubricate the system of reasoning in man's life, the course of action takes place either for good or bad.

This is what the Bible says; *"For the word of God is living and powerful, and sharper than any two-edged sword, piercing even to the division of soul and spirit, and of joints and marrow, and is a discerner of the thoughts and intents of the heart"* (Hebrews 4:12).

In fact the Word of God is the sword of the Spirit (Ephesians 6:17). The danger here is that; it is not only the Word of God that it penetrates and does all these. But the same principle is applied when any other form of word or message that enters into the ear-drums of a listener.

The principle of penetrating into the bottom of the heart, piercing even to the division of soul and spirit, and of joints and marrow, and discerning the thoughts and intents of the heart, can be caused by either the Word of God or any other word spoken by man, with whatever intention it may be. It may be a mixture of the Word of God plus worldly messages, or it can be any other worldly words with messages that are verbalized intentionally for the hearer. When such words are presented to the hearer, the words sink into the bottom of the heart, and at due time, it will surely produce its own kind. Therefore, if we are not careful in what we are hearing, our lives can be destroyed by what we take into our hearts.

The Bible warns us to keep our heart from all evil. In proverbs 4:23 it says; *"Keep your heart with all diligence, for out of it spring the issues of life."* If we are not careful but attend to all sorts of flying words, destruction is inevitable. For what we hear, will surely sink into our hearts. Let's see what Proverbs 18:8 says, *"The words of a talebearer are like tasty trifles, And they go down into the inmost body."*

As the Word of God pierces even into the division of soul and spirit, so as the negative words. Let's see Proverbs 12:18. *"There is one who speaks like the piercing of a sword, But the tongue of the wise promotes health."* Here we see that man's words can also pierce like the sword of the Word of God.

Therefore, before it's too late, we must keep our hearts from all poisonous words as we are directed by Proverbs 4:23. How can we keep our hearts from all evil and poisonous words? Our answer is found in Proverbs 18:21, *"Death and life are in the power of the tongue, And those who love it will eat its fruit."* Isn't this very clear to us? It is a spoken word that gives either life or death only to those who love it. But listen to this. All spoken words are just like flies flying around and over our heads. It's only when we open doors for them, they will enter.

Like Proverbs 26:2 says; *"Like a flitting sparrow, like a flying swallow, So a curse without cause shall not alight."* Jesus says; *"And I will give you keys of the kingdom of heaven, and whatever, you bind on earth will be bound in heaven, and whatever you loose on earth will be loosed in heaven"* (Matthew 16:19). Like I said, it's only when we open doors, we are bound to destruction. We have the keys to open our doors and accept it or close our doors and let go the words that are not of God.

Let's go back to Proverbs 18:21 and read the second part of the verse. *"And those who love it will eat its fruit."* Though death and life are in the power of the tongue of the speaker, only those who love it will eat its fruit. Whether it is for good or bad, whatever you accept, you'll eat of its fruits.

Don't forget that we are still under our sub-topic 'can anybody feed?' What I am trying to expose for your clear understanding in this lengthy explanation or discussion is that; we must be consciously careful in what we are listening to. Unlike in the past in the human history, we have now all kinds of people puffing up everywhere in the name of Lord, preaching His Word. Some are truly ordained by God but others are not. Somebody said the other day that, "some are truly sent by God but others picked the microphone and went."

With all these Bible authorities that we've read so far, there shouldn't be any doubt that there are people who are not appointed or ordained and sent by God, to preach His Word. Therefore, we should be cautious in whoever is preaching whatever message to us. Because in accordance with Proverbs 18:21, whatever you love it, you'll definitely eat of its fruits.

The Bible is talking about false prophets (Matthew 7:15-20, 1John 4:1-3) and Antichrist (1John 4:3), that we must be aware of them. They preach the Word but not pure Word of God in love. May be for some of them they do in their ignorance. The spirit of Antichrist had blinded their eyes that they don't know what they are doing (2Corinthians 4:4). These kind of people think what they are doing is always right and will never give in to get advice or listen to others. The spirit of self-righteousness, pride and boastful takes control and over-rules their lives. Others deliberately preach heresy so to go against the truth. We should pray that the Spirit of God may enlighten our spiritual eyes and our minds that we will understand every bit of it. Or we should wholeheartedly ask God for the gift of discernment.

However, if we are not alert in our spirit, the enemy will deceive us as he deceived Eve and later Adam in the Garden of Eden (Genesis 3:1-6).

Satan came to Eve and preached something that seemed right to her. At the first place, it seemed right and good for the woman, but after a matter of seconds, the real colour of Satan's colourful message turned into soar and bitterness (3: 7-19).

Satan's message had a bit of truth that was twisted and it was a great lie. The greatest mistake of Eve was that she paid attention to the half-truth and didn't bother to judge the whole message. The great lie was painted colourfully with nice words. Satan was smart in his presentation (not in wisdom but in foolishness) that he started off with a simple question. This is what he said; *"Has God indeed said, You shall not eat of every tree of the garden"* (vs.1)? You see, he could have said something else, but he said; *"Has God indeed said?"* He started off with what God had said.

To start off with what God had said, is the easiest way to pull somebody's attention to deceive him. It was a tricky question only to pull Eve's attention.

The question was asked not to seek information for he (Satan) knew the answer already. Satan was only seeking an avenue where he could present his greatest lie. Only if the woman knew what was hidden behind the question, she wouldn't have said what she said. The very answer the woman gave was exactly what the devil was looking for. The woman got up and said what God said, but she also added something that was not said by God.

This is what she said. *And the woman said to the serpent, "We may eat the fruit of the trees of the garden"* (vs.2); *"But of the fruit of the tree which is in the midst of the garden, God has said, You shall not eat it, nor shall you touch it, lest you die"* (vs.3).

As Eve said this, Satan was laughing in his heart, for he knew that he had now won the avenue that he was looking for.

The second mistake Eve made was that she got up and answered the question that supposed to be answered by Adam. But to make it worse, she said something that God did not say. It was her own addition to what God said; that really spoiled the whole thing. This is what she said; *"Nor shall you touch it"* (vs.3). God did say; *"You shall not eat it"* (2:17), but He didn't say, *"Nor shall you touch it."* Touching and eating are two different things. Both of them are verbs for they are doing words that will obviously produce their own kind.

I'll explain a little bit on this later, but first of all let's see what the devil had said. *"Then the serpent said to the woman, You will not surely die"* (3:4). *"For God knows that in the day you eat of it your eyes will be opened, and you will be like God, knowing good and evil"* (vs.5).

In this great lie said by the devil, there was half-truth, and the lie thereof was mixed in the truth. *"You will not surely die;"* in this statement, both half-truth and the great lie were all together in it. Let's distinguish the half-truth and the lie.

The half-truth was that, truly they could not die physically at the time of committing the sin though it was sure to occur eventually. But the first great lie was that they would surely die spiritually, as they eat of the tree; that Satan twisted around. There was one more mistake made by both the man and the woman. And their mistake was that they did not know that God was first of all talking about their spiritual death as well as their physical death. God said; *"For in the day that you eat of it you shall surely die"* (2:17).

Here God was talking about the spiritual death that would immediately take place and of course the physical death that would follow eventually. But the two poor man and woman didn't understand God properly and they thought He was only talking about their physical death.

That miss-understanding of God's Word led them to add something that God did not say. Their action proves what God says in Hosea 4:6; where it says; *"My people are destroyed for lack of knowledge."* What knowledge did He talk about? I believe, it generally talks about the knowledge in the Word of God that should be applied in any situation that arises. For that reason we must at least understand the context of the Word properly. For it is the only way to gain knowledge in the things of God. If not, we are opening doors for heresy to creep into our level of faith and understanding of the Word.

It was their own addition to the Word of God that contributed much in their eating of the fruit. I said, I'll explain little bit more on it so here it is. As I said, God did not say; *"Nor shall you touch it."* But because of their own addition to the Word of God, they'd gained a knowledge that was not true, for it did not have any base on God's Word. The very thing that made them not to go close to the tree or to touch it was; *"Nor shall you touch it."* 'Nor shall you touch it' was a knowledge gained from their own making that really spoiled the soup.

No wonder, God's Word says that we should not add or take away any dot from the Word of God

(Deuteronomy 4:2; 12:32, Proverbs 30:6, Revelation 22:18-19). If we do, we'll surely be in trouble, as a result of preaching heresies. And that was exactly what had happened to Eve and Adam.

I think they didn't touch even a dry fallen leave for that matter, before they felt into sin. But it was only when responding to the devil; the woman must have taken her few steps for the first time closer to the tree. And Eve's first test was I believe the "touch" test. It is very obvious that she could not swallow the fruit without touching it. She must have for the first time touched the stem of the tree, the branches, the leaves, as well as the fruit itself, before she gave her first bite to the fruit.

This is what I am trying to say. When she touched the tree and its fruit for the first time, surely nothing happened as they thought it would. Everything was still the same. There was no sign of sudden death and destruction. Eve had passed her first "touch test" and thought, 'wow; that's it, this fellow (Satan) could be right.' Without delaying anymore and giving a second thought, she ate the fruit.

Unfortunately she had no idea about the later consequences that would follow in disobedience. It was a fortune moment for that one-second's happiness.

Surely any sort of death; whether physical or spiritual did not occur even after Eve had eaten the fruit. She was still alive; everything was okay, instant death did not occur as she thought it would. She had passed her second "eating test."

Why not death, after touching? The answer is; God did not say; *"You will surely die as you touch it."* But He did say; *"You will surely die as you eat of it."* That's why death did not occur at the first instance of touching the tree.

Then you would think why not death occur at the second instance of eating the fruit by Eve? Because the command was not given to Eve but to Adam.

Another thing we can also learn from here is that God will not do or act upon anything that He did not say. He does not act on what man says, but He only acts upon His own Words. Let's read again verse 6 of Genesis chapter 3 to confirm that nothing really happened after she touched the tree and ate the fruit. This is what it says; *"So when the woman saw that the tree was good for food, that it was pleasant to the eyes, and a tree desirable to make one wise, she took of its fruit and ate. She also gave to her husband with her and he ate."*

Why am I saying that death did not occur when Eve touched and ate the fruit? My answer is; Adam did not pick the fruit and ate the fruit together with Eve at the same time. If you read it properly with understanding, you will notice that, the woman touched the tree and its fruit first and she also ate the fruit first. She came first in everything.

While she was busy touching and eating the fruit, your friend Adam was watching. The last part of verse 6 says; *"she took of its fruit and ate."* That was Eve on action. She picked the fruit and ate first. After she had eaten, she also gave to the man. Like I said, I don't think she just grabbed it and swallowed it down as fast as she could and gave the other to her husband which he did likewise in less than a minute.

Come on, we are human beings, lets play some common sense here for a while. It must have taken not that long but frankly enough, some few seconds, if not, some few minutes for Eve to go into the short process of walking closer to the tree for the first time, slowly begin to touch the tree only to notice no harm, picking up the fruit and imagining about the life that Satan was talking about, looking at the fruit and swallow some slaver, and eating the fruit at last. This is Eve on action like I said, and not Adam (vs.6 of Genesis 3, 2Corinthians 11:3; 1Timothy 2:14).

These bits and pieces of incidents that had obviously taken place one after the other as Eve was on action, was indeed very, very important moment for Adam. Adam was just standing there watching Eve with big opened eyes in silent wonder.

Some people believe that Eve ate the fruit in the absence of Adam. I don't think so because the Bile says that; *"She also gave to her husband with her, and he* ate" (Genesis 3:6). If Adam was not there when Eve ate the fruit, the Bible would have definitely specified the time when he (Adam) really joined in; could be an hour later or so. However, the Bible does not say anything along that line but in fact it says that; *'She also gave to her husband who was with her.'* I believe it all happened in the presence of Adam the husband, who was with her that he deserved equal punishment together with his wife. Adam was also in the scene of the crime that he could not able to justify his defence of innocence. One way or the other, it is obvious that Adam's presence in the garden amounts to him being the accomplice in what Eve was doing and of course, his own act of eating the fruit. Adam also did not play the role of a man as the head over his wife. He therefore, deserved equal punishment with Eve.

I think he saw what Eve was doing, and so he believed Eve and did likewise. I don't think he would have believed in that bunch of nonsense; that she ate the fruit while he was away but still alive. No; Adam had to prove it by seeing. He saw that nothing really happened to Eve, and that alone had tempted him to do likewise.

If death or nakedness had occurred to Eve prior to Adam's eating, Adam could have thought twice. But he saw that nothing had really happened to Eve, Adam must have thought; 'I think this woman is right.' Without giving a second thought, he just followed the woman's ill advice and he also ate the fruit (vs.12 of Genesis 3). As soon as the man completed his eating, unfortunately, spiritual death occurred instantly (vs.7), but of course physical death occurred some years later as it is recorded in Genesis 5:5.

Anyway, why death did not occur after Eve's disobedience but Adam's? Simply, because the woman did not disobey God but man, and man disobeyed God. For the command; "*You shall not eat*" (2:15-17) was given to man by God (3:17), without the presence of the woman. The woman was not there when God commanded the man. She was created after when God already had given the command to man. You read verses 15 through 25 of Genesis chapter 2 and 3:17 to confirm this. Adam must have informed the woman, his beloved wife afterwards. So let's say, the man was commanded by God and the woman was commanded or informed by the man. Therefore, when breaking the command, it was Eve disobeying the man, while man disobeying God. That could have been the reason why, death and destruction had to wait until the responsible person (none other than Adam) disobeyed God.

Why do you think, the woman disobeyed man and man disobeyed God? Because the woman believed in what she heard from the serpent and did not believe her husband, while the man believed in what he saw his wife was doing and did not believe in what God said.

This tells me one thing that the women folks can be easily influenced by what they hear and the men folks can also be influenced by what they see. Women folks can be easily influenced by what they hear because they are emotional beings. That's why they just jump up and down in what they hear and are quick to act. They don't sit down to reasoning things and think twice but they are very quick to act no matter what.

Of course this is not true altogether for all female gender, but the fact is that generally, women can be influenced by outside force so much so; to influence the men. On the other hand, men folks are creatures that are too rational that they take time to reasoning things, even if things are obvious. They don't give in to believe quick as they hear things but it is what they see that causes them to believe. Eve believed in what she heard from the Devil but Adam believed in what he saw from the woman.

Thomas is a good example in the Bible for the men folks. In John 20:26-29 records the narrative of

Thomas who didn't believe until he literally saw the torn body of Jesus. *Jesus said to him, "Thomas, because you have seen Me, you have believed. Blessed are those who have not seen and yet have believed"* (vs.29).

Another thing I also want to show you here is the second lie that the serpent lied to Eve. It is also found in Genesis 3:4-5. This is what the serpent said; *Then the serpent said to the woman, "You will not surely die"* (vs.4). *"For God knows that in the day you eat of it your eyes will be opened and you will be like God, knowing good and evil"* (vs.5). *"You will not surely die,"* was the first lie. The second greatest lie was that; *"For God knows that in the day you eat of it your eyes will be opened, and you will be like God, knowing good and evil."*

In this great lie, there is also half-truth as well as the lie. The half-truth is that; *"Your eyes will be opened, knowing good and evil."* However, the greatest lie is that; *"And you will be like God."*

You see the Devil's lie was a mixture of truth. Much of it was true, but the bit of lie in the midst of the truth, was a worse one. And it was sufficiently effective to wash away the truth. The Devil said, 'you will be like God, or you will become like God, as you eat of the tree.' That was a great lie and I'll show you why.

Lets go back to Genesis 1:26-27; *Then God said, "Let Us make man in Our image, according to our likeness; let them have dominion over the fish of the sea, over the birds of the air, and over the cattle, over all the earth and over every creeping thing that creeps on the earth"* (vs.26), *So God created man in*

His own image; in the image of God He created him; male and female He created them (vs.27).

God created male man and female man, just like Himself to have dominion over all His creation. In fact they were not created to become another God, or to be equal with God but like God; for they were created in the likeness of God. Wasn't that enough for them? What else, did they long for? There was nothing far better than the position they were placed as to be like God. Unfortunately, Satan came with the flattery words and twisted the truth. He (Satan) said; *"In the day you eat of this tree your eyes will be opened, and you will be like God."*

It's very sad to see that Satan only took advantage of their ignorance in the knowledge of themselves and of what God did for them. Our old friends Adam and Eve did not know that they were already like God; for they were created in the image and likeness of God. If they had the knowledge that they were already like God, they could have refused to heed to what the Devil said. The sad thing was that, they didn't know who they were in God and the position they were placed. They also didn't know that God created them perfectly well, just like Himself. There was nothing left incomplete by God in their creation, that a little fellow like Satan may come and complete His work afterwards. No wonder God says; *"My people are destroyed for the lack of knowledge"* (Hosea 4:6).

It is God's character that when He creates one thing, He creates it in its complete perfection and its fullness. The Bible tells me in Genesis 2:1 that God had finished and completed all His creations and nothing was left unfinished, that Satan may come afterwards and finish it for God. Who was Satan to help God in His creation, and offer advices to His children? What a tragedy for Eve and Adam to listen to a poor man who had absolutely nothing to offer? In like manner, it is a tragedy for one who does not know his position in Christ Jesus and ends-up listening to all kinds of voices but only garbage.

When I read the narratives of these two old friends of ours, I use to wonder whether they had really listened to what God said, and knew that there was none besides Him who could be His proxy. To me, it looks like they really did not know their Father, the Marker, and they did not listen to Him carefully. And as a result, they said something that God did not say, and disobeyed Him by end-up eating the fruit.

But the worse of all is that, they did not know that they were already like God; in all aspect of life, except that they did not have that knowledge to distinguish good from bad or bad from good. I suspect one of the reasons why Eve obeyed Satan was that, she wanted to be like God, which she already was. I would therefore want to say that, to be ignorant in the things of God, is the gateway to destruction.

I don't think she was hungry and the fruit was far better than the others. If it was, in according to Genesis 3:6, then it was only in the woman's eyes that *"The tree was good for food, that it was pleasant to the eyes, and a tree desirable to make one wise."* It was only in the eyes of Eve that the tree looked like the way it looked like.

Should I tell you why? Let's read verse 6 again. *"So when the woman saw that the tree was good for food, that it was pleasant to the eyes, and a tree desirable to make one wise, she took of its fruit and ate.*" The three things that attracted the woman to eat the fruit are as follows: Firstly; "*When the woman saw that the tree was good for food*," she ate the fruit. Secondly, "*That it was pleasant to the eyes*," she ate the fruit. Thirdly, "*And a tree desirable to make one wise*," She ate the fruit.

I don't know whether Eve knew that it was Satan in the form of a serpent speaking to her. Let's say if she did not know that it was Satan speaking to her, how could she dare to believe a serpent that seemed to know it better than God? Or if she knew that it was Satan, then how could she also dare to believe that Satan knew it better than God? She only found out after few minutes that she was deceived by the serpent (3:13).

When I see this, I draw my conclusion by saying that; all she was lacking was the knowledge of the spoken Word of God to them. Hearing the Word is one thing but it is another thing to have knowledge in the Word. Though faith comes by hearing the Word (Romans 10:17), hearing alone is not good enough (James 1:22). We must be doers of the Word, for hearing and doing of the Word will produce knowledge of the Word. Eve opened the floodgates of destruction and death to mankind because she was lacking knowledge in the Word of God. No wonder the Bible says; "*My people are destroyed for the lack of knowledge*" (Hosea 4:6).

The three attractions that caused the woman to eat the fruit were not genuine. The tree was neither good for food, nor was it pleasant for the eyes or was it desirable to make one wise. Like I've stated above, if it was; then it was only to the eyes of the woman that the tree looked like the way it looked like. The truth of the matter regarding this tree is that, it was not a good tree for food. In fact it was a poisonous tree only to kill and to destroy.

The basis for my theology is found in Genesis chapter 2:16-17. Let's see what it says in these verses. *"And the Lord God commanded the man, saying, of every tree of the garden you may freely eat"* (vs.16), *"But of the tree of the knowledge of good and evil you shall not eat, for in the day that you eat of it you shall surely die"*(vs.17).

What can you really see in these two verses? I see nothing else but God was talking only about food. The Bible is telling me in these two verses what to eat and what not to eat. Verse 16 tells me that anything that was found in the garden, that would be regarded as food was allowed to be eaten freely, especially of every tree in the garden. The trees that would be good for food were there, the trees that would be pleasant for the eyes were there, the trees that would be desirable to make one wise were also there, even the tree of life.

The Garden of Eden was rich in food. Let's also read verses 8-9 of chapter 2. *"The Lord God planted a garden eastward in Eden, and there He put the man whom He had formed"* (vs.8). *"And out of the ground the Lord God made every tree grow that is pleasant to the sight and good for food. The tree of life was also in the midst of the garden, and the tree of the knowledge of good and evil"* (vs.9).

The Eden was a garden. To me, a garden is a place where all kinds of food are planted. And it is also true that it was only Adam and Eve were there in the midst of a big garden that was rich in food.

There was no good reason at all, for any one of them to put their eyes on the tree that was forbidden. Because the forbidden tree was not needed for any one of the reasons that Eve gave for her surrendering to the Devil. Do you still remember the three reasons for Eve to surrender?

You go back to chapter 3:6 again. "*So when the woman saw that the tree was good for food.*" That was not true because there were other trees, good for food in the garden, not the forbidden one (2:9 first part). "*That it was pleasant to the eyes.*" Reason number two was also not true because there were other trees, pleasant to the eyes in the garden (vs.9 first part). "*And a tree desirable to make one wise.*" Reason number three was also not true because the only tree that could make one wise was the tree of life (vs.9 second part).

Particularly, for reason number three, I think the tree of life was the best of all the best that could able to make one wise. In contrary, like I said earlier, the tree of the knowledge of good and evil was not a good tree for food. It was not a good tree to make one wise. It was not a tree of wisdom as it was with the tree of life. Instead, it was a tree of the knowledge only of good and evil. And as I said, it was a poisonous tree that would only kill and destroy. For God said; "*But of the tree of the knowledge of good and evil you shall not eat, for in the day that you eat of it you shall surely die*" (vs.17).

You see, God clearly said, it was not a good tree for food; He said if you eat of it, you will surely die.

That means it is a poisonous tree that can only kill. To God, it was not a desirable tree to make one wise, and it was also not a good tree for food and pleasant to the eyes. I don't know where Eve got that eyesight from.

In our situation, if we don't listen carefully and properly, to what God is telling us to do, we also can be deceived by the same Devil and end up doing wrong things and preaching heresies.

History can repeat itself, if we act smarter than God. I believe what God says is final and we as simple creation of God should not by any means try to twist His Word. Twisting the Word of God and creating heresies everywhere is the most powerful weapon of the enemy to destroy the Church of God. It has been the weapon ever since the fall of first Adam and it is more active than ever. It was through one man that the all world is under condemnation because he and his wife did that which God told them not to do.

However, then again it is also through one man's righteousness and obedience that the all world can be justified and made righteous (Romans 5:15-19). *"For as in Adam all die, even so in Christ all shall be made alive"* (1Corinthians 15:22). It further says in verse 45 that; *"And so it is written, the first man Adam became a living being. The last Adam became a life-giving spirit."*

Let's elaborate on what these verses are telling us. For in Adam all of us are bound to die, even so in Christ all of us shall be made alive. Why do you think all of us die as a result of Adam's sin? Because we are born into this world, through the chain of his (Adam's) blood. It is through the blood of Adam that sin entered the world, and death through sin, and thus death spread to all men, because all have sinned (Romans 5:12). *"For all have sinned and fall short of the glory of God"* (3:23).

Nevertheless, the last Adam became a life-giving Spirit (1Corinthians 15:45) that through the last Adam's righteous act the free gift came to all men, resulting in justification of life (Romans 5:18). But how can this happen to a sinner's life? The answer is found in Romans 6:8, and it says; *"Now if we died with Christ, we believe that we shall also live with Him."*

We were dead as a result of Adam's sin, but in order for us to be alive in Christ; our old life must die together with Christ's death (vs.1-13). It was a death in the Garden of Eden that separated us from God and so a death should again join us back to God. The sinful blood of Adam that we have inherited, should be renewed by the life-giving blood of Jesus Christ. For without being washed or renewed by the blood of Jesus, we are still bound to sin and subsequent death. There's no other easy way to escape than to be set free by the blood. For the last Adam had passed the test and has proven record to give life to mankind, of those who are dead in sin. Do you want to know where He had done this? Let's go to Matthew 4:1-11.

After the water baptism in the Jordan, *Jesus was then led into the wilderness to be tempted by the devil (vs.1). And when He had fasted forty days and forty nights, afterward He was hungry (vs.2). Now when the tempter came to Him, he said, "If you are the Son of God, command that these stones become bread" (vs.3). But He answered and said, "It is written, Man shall not live by bread alone, but by every word that proceeds from the mouth of God"* (vs.4). **Jesus passed the first test.** *The devil then took Him up into the holy city, set Him on the pinnacle of the temple* (vs.5). *And said to Him, "If you are the son of God, throw Yourself down. For it is written"* (vs.6): And he quoted Psalm 91:12. *Jesus said to him, "It is written again, You shall not tempt the Lord your God"* (vs.7). **Jesus passed the second test.** *Again, the devil took Him up on an exceedingly high mountain, and showed Him all the Kingdoms of the world and their glory* (vs.8). *And he said to Him, "All these things I will give You if You will fall down and worship me"* (vs.9). *Then Jesus said to him, "Away with you, Satan! For it is written, You shall worship the Lord your God, and Him only you shall serve"* (vs.10). *Then the devil left Him, and behold, angels came and ministered to Him* (vs.11). **Jesus passed the third test.**

The Devil came to Jesus the way and manner he did to Eve. He said similar things to Jesus as he did to Eve. He was quoting the Bible verse from (Psalm 91:12) as well as touching the areas in which Jesus could give in if He wanted to. He said, *"Command the stone that it be turned into bread."* The Devil used the same strategy on food to tempt the Lord. Jesus was very hungry so if He wanted to, He could have done that. But He didn't want to do it because first of all, it was Satan instructing Him. He knew that Satan was a liar and anything that he says is always a lie.

Secondly, He knew that it is written that man shall not live by bread alone, but by every Word that proceeds from the mouth of God. In the second and third temptations, Jesus was still not convinced by what the Devil said. He knew that even if the Devil changes his language, he is till Satan, the deceiver and liar forever. And therefore, Jesus continually said; it is written. Having said all these, I want to repeat two things again.

Firstly, Jesus knew it was Satan tempting Him so He was very stubborn not to listen to a liar and a loser. Unlike Eve and Adam who were lacking knowledge in what God said to them; Jesus had full knowledge in the Word of God. He was fully equipped with all His attributes even with His Omniscience. He knew who He was, and He also knew the purpose for which He was here on earth. He knew that He was here for a mission and that was to serve God and to save the world; not to listen to a stranger who is also a liar.

Secondly, in every temptation, He responded to the Devil by referring to the written Word of God. He said; "it is written, it is written." For Jesus knew that referring to the written Word, was a good one for the Devil. The Devil is not scared of any other thing except the Word of God. For it is sharper than any two edged sword that it cuts and judges every thought and it is the final authority of God (Hebrews 4:12). The Word of God is creative that it can do any thing.

Only if the woman said, exactly what God had said, and if she was stubborn not to listen to the stranger, then the all human race would have been saved and the story would have been different altogether. But unfortunately, she said something that was not said by God and yielded to Satan.

However, fortunately Jesus said, it is written, and because of what He said; the Devil was defeated. It was not an angelic military power or any other form of power but it was the knowledge in the written Word of God. Eventually Jesus completed His victory on the cross of Calvary to fulfill the Word that He should die. The first Adam failed three tests with his wife as a result of lack of knowledge in the Word. But the second Adam passed His three tests and overcame the Devil by the sword of the Word of God. Therefore, it is a must that whoever deals with the Word of God must do it right with fear and reverence for the Word.

And finally, to conclude this very lengthy chapter, I would like to say that whoever feeds the sheep must feed only with the pure Word of God, rather than a mixture of truth and a bit of lie and one's own make-up stories. To participate in the work of God, especially to preach the Word or to feed the people with the Word, is something very, very crucial that we should not take it lightly.

Whoever deals with the Word of God must know for sure that he is called and ordained to do what he is doing. And he must also know that what he is doing is the right thing to do. Only then the Church will grow into its maturity and it will be in a better position to be ready for her wedding ceremony when the bridegroom (Jesus) comes. However, if we take this honourable and noble task of preaching the Word of God for granted, then we might as well open doors for the enemy to creep in with heresies and destroy the Church of God; as he did to the first man and woman in the Garden of Eden.

Therefore, it is wise not to allow just anybody to feed the Church with the Word, without prior testing and approval from the Church Leaders in the light of the Word of God (1Timothy 3:10).

If you are a preacher of the Word, I want to leave this challenge with you. It is a good thing to preach the Word, but at the same time, please bear in mind that whatever we preach will be our judge. Our rewards and even our eternal life will be very much determined by what we preach. We will leave everything else behind but will take ourselves and our actions with us, to stand before the King of kings and the Lord of lords in His great judgement.

The top preachers of the Word will be made known and crowned on that day to rule and reign with the King of kings and the Lord of lords, in the heavenly places forever and ever (John12:26). Do you want to be one of them? Make sure, you do it good and do it right according to the Word, for nobody else will do it for you!

Chapter 10

God's Calling

a: The Purpose of a Calling

A "Calling" is a call unto a person by God for a
certain task. It is God's character that He does not call
anybody for doing nothing. When God calls someone,
He calls that person for a certain task and for a certain
purpose. All He wants and desires to see upon that
person is the fulfillment of the calling. And a calling
must be a call for the task of a ministry and a gifting.

Therefore, a minister who has been called by God
should first of all know the purpose for which he was
called. Unless he knows the purpose for his calling,
he will never accomplish his purpose. When one does
not accomplish his very purpose in his ministry, it
will lead to confusion, destruction, chaos, division
etc, in the Church of God. Hence, to avoid such
deterioration in the service of God, a called minister
should be very careful in what he does.

Paul says; *"If a man desires the position of a
bishop, he desires a good work"* (1Timothy 3:1) and
therefore *"He must be blameless"* (vs.2) in his life and
his ministry. In order for one to be successful in his
ministry, he must be very careful in what he does. He
should also avoid things that are unnecessary for a
minister of God to involve. His priority in life is to
identify the ministry and the gifting for his calling and
should be busy in his ministry so to fulfill the calling
in his life.

Like I said, God does not call anybody for doing nothing or to get mixed up in His service. In the service of God, there are certain tasks that only certain people who are called for such can perform. It is very true that not everybody can do everything in the service of God. Each one of us is called for a certain task and that's where God wants us to be and successfully complete our ministry before we are called to be with Him in the glorious land.

I don't think it is right for a minister of God to look for ministries in the service of God. Sometimes, it is right for a minister to look for a better location where he can perform his ministry, but not the ministry itself. For the ministry is of the heart, that we should at least know before we are engaged in the service of God.

Prophet Isaiah knew who he was in the service of God. He did not join the prophets club just to find out whether he was also called as a prophet. He knew who he was and what he was supposed to be doing. He knew that he was even called from the womb of his mother. This is what he says in Isaiah 49:1-2. *"Listen, O coastlands, to Me, And take heed, you peoples from afar! The Lord has called Me from the womb; From the matrix of My mother He has made mention of My name"* (vs.1). *"And He has made My mouth like a sharp sword; In the shadow of His hand He has hidden Me, And made Me a polished shaft; In His quiver He has hidden Me"* (vs.2).

Isaiah says; he was called even from the matrix of his mother's womb. No man has ever called him and made mentioned of the title of his ministry. I don't know who really told Isaiah that he was called from his mother's womb to be a prophet. He somehow knew that he was called even from his mother's womb. I think it was an insight that he got from God. His intimate fellowship with God made it very easy for him to listen and understand what God said to him. He knew the voice of his Father, the maker. He knew without a shadow of doubt that he was called from the matrix of his mother. It was all done by God even when Isaiah was only a tissue in the womb of his mother. He was therefore born purposely for what he was doing.

The same thing happened to Prophet Jeremiah. He also said something similar about his life and his ministry. In Jeremiah 1:4-10 it says that he was also called from his mother's womb to be a prophet to the nations. *"Then the word of the Lord came to me, saying* (vs.4). *"Before I formed you in the womb I knew you; Before you were born I sanctified you; I ordained you a prophet to the nations"* (vs.5).

God told Jeremiah that he was called even before his formation in his mother's womb. He knew what Jeremiah would do after his birth and therefore, He sanctified him even before he was formed. Jeremiah had a clear vision. He knew that he was a prophet ordained by God to be a voice to the nations of the world. He was not a confused man, didn't know what to do in the service of God.

Paul repeatedly said something similar to that of Isaiah and Jeremiah said. This is what he said in Romans1:1. *"Paul, a bondservant of Jesus Christ, called to be an apostle, separated to the gospel of God."* In 1Corinthians 1:1, 2Corinthians 1:1, and Ephesians 1:1, he repeatedly said to all of those churches that he was an Apostle of Jesus Christ called by God according to His will and not by man. Paul also knew who he was and for the purpose for which he was called.

I've seen one of the most effective weapons that a minister of God should have for the good of the Church of God and for his own ministry, is to know who he is and to what ministry the Lord has called him to be. Until he knows his ministry and his position in the work of God, he wanders around praying. In the process, sometimes he ends up fighting for ministries and positions with his fellow colleagues in his church.

Sadly, if he doesn't get one, he has to get it by force or else break the fellowship and form his own group with the likes of himself. It is not so much so, in some centralized and very well organized churches. In those churches, a single minister has no freedom of choice but he is bound to comply with the orders given by the church hierarchy. However, it is truly a problem in churches where all ministers and people have equal rights and powers.

I like what Paul did. Straight after his conversion, he went around preaching the Word of God. He didn't bother to visit the elderly Apostles in Jerusalem but went ahead and did what the Lord had called him to do (Acts 9:20). That doesn't mean, that he formed his own little church or ministry apart from the Apostles. No; not at all. All he did was to share the love of God to others and did what he was called to do. But he then went to Jerusalem to see the Apostles and to join with them in the Apostolic Ministry sometimes later (vs. 26-28).

In Jerusalem, he went in and out with the Apostles preaching the Word. Because of his understanding in his calling, and his eagerness in his Apostolic Ministry, and his cooperation and unity with the elderly Apostles, the churches throughout all Judea, Galilee, and Samaria had peace and were edified. For they were walking in the fear of the Lord and in the comfort of the Holy Spirit; that their number was multiplied (vs.31). And it's not only that but he eventually became the leading Apostle in ministry and in his epistles to the churches. The likes of Prophets Isaiah and Jeremiah and Apostle Paul knew who they were and to what ministry they were called to engage with.

No wonder the Church of God was started off with perfect knowledge and understanding of the Word of God. And as such, ministries thereof were perfectly executed according to the perfect will of God. The few bigheads rose in their midst who caused division in the Church were easily identified and were dealt with. Paul was heavily motivated by the actions of those few bigheads to say so much on the issue of causing division in the Church. By no means, should we imitate the evil actions of those bigheads.

Our fore runners showed us an example that we should not by any means cause divisions in the Church of God. No matter how smart we are or anointed we are; we must execute our ministries within the boundaries of the respective ministries in the Church. We must know that our calling of whatever the ministry it may be; should be executed only to benefit the Church; the Body of Christ. God does not call anyone for the purpose of causing division and destroying His Church. God's calling upon a person is generally to build and edify His Church.

Let's see the purpose for the call of the first disciples. Matthew records the narratives of the first disciples in Matthew 4:18-22. *And Jesus, walking by the sea of Galilee, saw two brothers, Simon called Peter, and Andrew his brother casting a net into the sea; for they were fishermen* (vs.18). *Then He said to them, "Follow Me, and I will make you fishers of men"* (vs.19). *They immediately left their nets and followed Him* (vs.20). *Going on from there, He saw two other brothers, James the son of Zebedee, and John his brother, in the boat with Zebedee their father, mending their nets. He called them* (vs.21), *and immediately they left the boat and their father, and followed Him* (vs.22).

What can you see in this story? As different people have different views, you might see something differently than what I see. Well, I see two things and both of them are very important. I see 'the very purpose for the calling' as well as 'the condition for successful accomplishment of the purpose for their calling.'

In this story the condition is extremely important as well as the purpose of the calling. Because in order to accomplish the purpose of the calling (to win souls) successfully, to me the condition here is the key that will open doors to achieve the goal.

The condition is that; they must follow Him in order to catch men. He said; *"Follow me and I will make you fishers of men."* I think following Jesus is priority number one in order to catch men. First thing must come first and in this case, the disciples must first of all follow Jesus and then catch men. Sometimes following Jesus and winning souls can run hand in hand for either of them is very important for the call; but the number of men you catch will speak for the commitment in following Jesus.

To follow Jesus means to follow His instructions and His foot steps in every thing that we do. As ministers of the gospel, we must first of all, follow Jesus in His footsteps. The more we become like Jesus, the more we will catch men. The simple technique to win more souls is to follow Jesus and His instructions. If we can only study the life style of Jesus and His Word and do accordingly, winning more souls will not be a problem at all. Therefore, a minister should first of all make sure that what he does is what Jesus approves to fulfill His calling in his life.

In one of those very cold nights, Apostle Peter and others have exhausted whatever their strength to catch fish; yet they got nothing. All over sudden, Jesus appeared and gave instructions as to where they should throw their nets. As they followed His instructions though it was against their tradition and conscience, they got a very huge number of fish in a matter of few minutes (John 21:1-6).

Many times, ministers of the gospel really do not accomplish their purposes in life because they don't follow Jesus and His Word. As ministers ou the gospel, we should understand that we are only the voice for God; calling unto the world for their salvation. Like the first disciples, those of us who are ministers, are called to follow Him and to become fishers of men. And therefore, we will only gain credit if we have caught any fish from the ocean. The great sea speaks of the sinful world and hence, we should be winning souls that are lost in the sinful world and not from the Church. Lost souls are normally found in the sinful world and are not in the Church.

Therefore, we must set our fishing nets right; even out there in the deep sea, rather than to set our nets in front or gates of other sister churches. Jesus instructed the Apostles to throw their nets at the right side of the boat (vs.6). Jesus knows the right place from where we can catch fish in multitudes. So it's worth listening to the expert (Jesus) and follow His instructions rather than setting our fishing nets at the wrong places like church gates.

Sometimes it's acceptable because there are unsaved souls at the church gates as well as in the churches like the crippled beggar sitting at the church gate who needed Jesus (Acts 3:1-10). Yet our focus must be right; whether it is from the world or church gates; the souls that we are trying to win must be unsaved souls.

Or in other words, let's say; it's not good to throw our fishing nets into somebody else fish-ponds. Because any fish found in a fish-pond should belong to the owner of the fish-pond. Likewise, if a soul is saved from within a church, then that soul should remain in his church; unless otherwise relocated or transferred for a good course.

However, if they are already saved, then we are only wasting our time. For you can't save a saved soul for the second time. How can you save somebody who is already saved by the same Saviour? That's where most ministers go wrong, when they steal sheep from one sheep fold to another, thinking that they are saving their souls. I don't think it is the right thing to do and it shouldn't be the purpose for our calling. The purpose for our calling is to follow His Word and to win unsaved souls, through whatever ministry we are engaged with.

You don't have to be an Evangelist to win souls. As long as you follow Jesus by obeying His Word and live accordingly, surely enough, you will catch some. Your living testimony will surely draw men unto God. Winning of unsaved souls shouldn't be the only reason for our calling, but at least it is good that we present a soul to God, on that Great Day of Judgment. It's my own personal belief that a special reward and recognition will be granted to those who have at least won a soul. In the book of Daniel 12:3 it says; *"Those who are wise shall shine; Like the brightness of the firmament, And those who turn many to righteousness; Like the stars forever and ever."* *"And he who wins souls is wise"* (Proverbs 11:30).

Shining like the stars in heaven forever and ever means a lot more to me. You know in order to give light; the shining element should always be placed above the other households. That's exactly what it will be to those who have led many to righteousness, for they will be shining like stars in heaven.

Anyway, it is very important to know the purpose of a calling. Because it's only when you know the purpose of your calling, you will do it right. However, not knowing the purpose of a calling, will lead to destruction and division in the Church. Why? Because a minister who has no idea about the purpose of his calling, will definitely do something that he is not called to do. Or sometimes he will abuse the power of a gift and ministerial duties or physical materials such as cars or things like that have been offered to him to support his ministry.

Knowing the purpose of a calling will help the minister to set his focus on none other than the goal of his ministry. Apostle Paul showed us a good example of how we can press on to our goals. This is what he says in Philippians 3:12-14. *"Not that I have already attained, or am already perfected; but I press on, that I may lay hold of that for which Christ Jesus has also laid hold of me"* (vs.12). *"Brethren, I do not count myself to have apprehended; but one thing I do, forgetting" those things which are behind and reaching forward to those things which are ahead"* (vs.13), *"I press toward the goal for the prize of the upward call of God in Christ Jesus"* (vs.14).

In these verses, you will see that Paul was pressing on to something that had more value than things behind him. He knew what he was doing and the purpose for his calling. The goal for the prize of the upward call of God in his life was the very thing that caused him to do what he was doing in his ministry. Like I said, unless one knows the purpose for his calling, he will never press on to receive his reward.

In these series of studies, we see that there are two purposes for a calling. First of all, the purpose of a calling is to do that which a person is called to do. Like the first Apostles were called to become fishers of men, or to catch men into the Kingdom of God. And of course, it is not only to catch men but also to teach or feed them and look after the sheep that are already in the Kingdom of God.

The second purpose for a calling is to work hard and press on to receive the reward or prize that is waiting for us in heaven.

I think when we are well aware of these two purposes; we will surely perform our ministries properly to the best of our abilities; irrespective of what. Sometimes as we think of the eternal rewards that we will receive in a matter of few years from now, it really motivates us not to loss focus on the purposes of our callings. But then again, we should not forget the fact that the latter will be the reward for the former. If the first purpose for our calling or the former is not identified properly and done accordingly, the latter will have no ground or reason to be presented to us. Then all our hard works and our sacrifices will be done in vain.

Paul also had concern for his ministry and his reward. He was very careful not to do things other than what he was purposely called to do. He knew that if he was not careful about the purpose for his calling, he would definitely be disqualified for the latter. This is what he says in 1 Corinthians 9:26-27. *"Therefore I run thus: not with uncertainty. Thus I fight: not as one who beats the air"* (vs.26). *"But I discipline my body and bring it into subjection, lest, when I have preached to others, I myself should become disqualified"* (vs.27).

Paul is telling us that Apostles like himself can be disqualified for eternal life and rewards thereof. It can also happen to us if we are not careful and mindful in the purpose of our calling. I believe whatever the purpose for our calling, must be the essential reason for our services rendered for the Kingdom and our life on earth.

b: The Purpose of a Ministry

Any Ministry that is given by God is divinely ordained by Him; and its paramount purpose is for the good of all. No ministry is ordained by God that one can use it for personal gain and exaltation. All ministries are to be used for the common good of all for the healthy growth of the Church and for the glory of God.

The Church is only one as we have seen earlier and therefore, a ministry has got to play its role for the benefit of all the members of that one Body, the Church. God does not give any ministry to anyone that he may preach against the others and overlook them as if they are inferior ministries and have no significance. There is no such thing as superior ministry who can play down on the inferior ministries, in the fivefold ministry found in the book of Ephesians chapter four. If any ministry happens to be of such, that particular ministry should be questioned and screened properly to know whether it is from God or otherwise.

For a ministry that is given by God and led by the Holy Spirit will definitely not go against the other similar ministries from the very same source. How can this God of unity and love go against Himself by playing different roles to cause division through the different ministries? He can only go against the spirits and ministries of Satan, who is His arch-enemy. Therefore, the purpose of a ministry is to be executed and performed for the common good and benefit of all the members of the Body of Christ.

The Apostle Paul by the leading of the Holy Spirit explicitly explained the real purpose of the ministries. He openly explained all about the ministries that we have no reason to get mixed up with sophisticated worldly ideas. The Bible is straight-forward but I don't know the reasons why some of the ministries in the Church of God are operating the way they are operating.

Paul is telling us not in parables or in metaphorical words but in plain words that even an ordinary layman can able to understand it. This is what he says about the five fold ministries found in Ephesians 4:11-16. Let's read them and see what we can learn from these verses. *"And He Himself gave some to be apostles, some prophets, some evangelists, and some pastors and teachers"* (vs.11).

According to this verse, the ministries are given to us by Jesus Christ. They are not given to us by our so-called church organizations or by any of our church leaders or anybody else. If they are given by Jesus, then we should first of all know what He (Jesus) wants us to do with the ministries. I mean, if anything goes wrong or if we do not know what to do with the ministry that has been granted to us, we should always go back to the giver of the ministry. It is not right for us to ignore the giver and seek advice from anybody else who does not know much about the purpose of the ministries.

Why do I have to say all these? Because I see that some ministers of the gospel are more concerned about the man-made rules and doctrines, than the Word of God who is also Jesus, the giver of ministries. When we encounter problems and situations that are beyond our control, we should always refer back to the Word of God. The answers that we seek are all in the Word, for the Word is Jesus (John 1:1-3) and Jesus is the Word. The Word of God will surely tell us what we should do and how to face the situations that we encounter in this long journey.

The purpose of a ministry is clearly stated in verse 12. And this is what it says; "*For the equipping of the saints for the work of ministry, for the edifying of the body of Christ.*" Doesn't it clearly spelt here?

I think the purpose of a ministry is very clear in this one sentence. Hence, any other theology that seems right to provide guidelines as to how and what the ministries should operate for, but in contrast to verse 12; I think it is not from the right source.

The purpose of a ministry is to serve two important distinctive areas in the Church according to New King James Version. The first one is "*For the equipping of the saints for the work of ministry*" and the second one is "*For the edifying of the body of Christ.*"

Equipping of the saints for the work of ministry and edifying of the Body of Christ are supposed to be the paramount reasons for the granting of the ministries. If any one or both of these important reasons of a ministry are absent, then that ministry should be questioned and we should talk it over, before it is too late. I think you are aware that we will only report or to bring an account to God (Matthew 12:36, Romans 14:12 and 1Peter 4:5) according to what scale we were given and what we were told to do. In that case, God will expect us to give an account on whether we've been equipping the saints for the work of ministry and edifying the Body of Christ. However, if the answer is negative, then we'll be in trouble, and it will be too late for us.

I want to challenge us not to waste our time on things that we are not called to do. As ministers, we should be equipping the saints and edifying the Body of Christ. When we equip the saints for the work of ministry, the saints will in return perform their duties that will also help to build the Church and extend the boundaries of the Kingdom of God. And as we edify the Body of Christ, the Church will obviously grow into maturity and bear spiritual fruits.

Again, as ministers according to this verse, our priority number one is to equip and edify the Church, the Body of Christ. Sometimes a minister is like a coach in a game. Like a coach who trains the players how to play the game, a minister's duty is to equip the saints for the work of ministry; that the saints will then go out and bear their own kinds as they spread the gospel.

In whatever ministry we are engaged to, we must not forget the fact that we have a ministry not to criticize, cause divisions and split the Body of Christ, steal sheep from one sheep fold to another, be judgmental to another fellow minister and his gifting, be proud and boastful of our gifting and talents, and etcetera, but only to equip and edify the Body, the Church of God. I think that's very important than our sideline agendas. We must be smart enough to serve God, as He has ordered and directed us to do so. Any other sideline agenda that seems right for a minister to do, should be given double thought before going ahead with it.

To conclude, the fivefold ministries found in Ephesians 4:11 should play their roles by equipping and edifying not only one local church or one church group but if possible, they should minister to the Body of Christ. Like we've seen in this verse, the ministries thereof are actually given to be exercised for the good of the Body of Christ. And the Body of Christ is not made up of only one local church or one church group, but like I said earlier, it is the universal or collective body of believers from all Christian churches around the world. In that sense, we should do away with the mentality of independent ministry. There is in fact no such thing as independent ministry in the Church of God.

Even though a minister's performance is not that big enough to cover the all world, if a fraction of the great world is touched and blessed by whatever the level of ministry it may be, then it is accepted by God for this is what it matters with God. So long as your level of ministry touches, blesses and encourages in helping to build the Church of God in your area, is exactly what God wants you to do. Therefore, the Bible says that be faithful to whatever the little you have that at due time God will entrust to you with big things (Matthew 25:21, 23).

Now let's see that Ephesians Chapter 4 verses 13 through 16; talks about the end result of verses 11-12. When the purposes of the ministries are fulfilled, the end results of the ministries will be achieved. Verse 13 records the key message in these verses. *"Till we all come to the unity of the faith and of the knowledge of the Son of God, to a perfect man, to the measure of the stature of the fullness of Christ"* (vs.13).

Finally, if all the ministries play their roles correctly and effectively as they should, the believers from all the Christian churches around the world will definitely come to the unity of the faith and of the knowledge of the Son of God. That's exactly the very purpose for the ministries and who knows, it might cause God to act quickly by sending Jesus for the rapture (2Peter 3:11-12) followed by His Second Coming after the marriage wedding in heaven for seven (7) years!

Chapter 11

The Position of the Church

It is true that the position of the Church both here on earth and up in heaven, should be identified and made known not only by the Church but also by the general public as well. The identity of the position of the Church (though it is crushed down by worldly pressures) is very important for its recognition. Only until it is made known, the Church will be taken lightly as if it has no value at all.

The Church is not like any other social organization as it seems to be, but it is in fact the only institution to which the all of heaven and earth are clung to. Like I've noted in chapter one, both heaven and earth, the great universe was created for the Church. Therefore, the Church should have pre-eminence over all things and as such, its position should be highly placed and respected. The identification and recognition of its position by the all world, is I guess the most powerful medication that will heal the sick generation of this time. (We should not deny the fact that we are living in a sick generation).

a: The Church in the Physical World

Among all the other organizations, institutions, bodies, the governments and even the different ethnic people groups around the world, the Church should be regarded as something very, very special for it is indeed sacred and holy. Unlike any other institutions, it is the only Spiritual institution in the all world that has Spiritual connection to the Great Throne of God. And it is the only Spiritual property of God in the physical world.

It is therefore, when God wants to do something in this world, it is His fashion that He never by-passes the Church. It's only through the Church that God does whatever He wants to do in this world. For the Church and its office is a separate entity of its own for the Spiritual matters and hence, the only Spiritual embassy of God established in this world some two thousand years ago.

Therefore, whoever is engaged with this embassy is known as an ambassador for Christ. No wonder, the Apostle Paul stated this in his second Epistle to the Corinthians 5:20, where it says; *"Now then, we are ambassadors for Christ, as though God were pleading through us: We implore you on Christ's behalf, be reconciled to God."*

I want to repeat myself again for your sake that; the Church is God's embassy in this world that He is willing to do whatever He wants to do in this world only through the Church. I am more concerned and emphasizing more on this because whoever wants to see God in action, will only see Him in and through the Church, for there's no other short-cut besides the Church. It is therefore; God is in the business of causing the people to change their lives through the Church; in order to know the real substance of humanity and its surroundings.

Its God's desire and His priority number one that man; whom He also created in His own image and

His likeness should know Him. Truly the man is lacking in the knowledge of God; the knowledge that is superior to any other knowledge that the world may offer. But it will only eventuate through the fulfilling of all the ministries allocated to the Church. It is therefore, no other physical organization, institution, body or any government can offer the best that will bring solution to all the problems of this world as the Church would do.

That's why, even if the world likes it or not, there's gonna be a time when God will cause the all world to come before the Church and have reverence for the Church. When that time comes, the Church will be recognized far above all other institutions like never before in the history of Church. By then, the position of the Church will be exposed, that the all world will have no choice but to feel the taste of defeat from their evil actions that have been practiced for many, many years.

The world will ultimately come to the Church and confess before the Head of the Church; that He is the Lord of lords and the King of kings who is also the Lord of all. The world will kneel down before the Head of the House of God and have reverence for Him. They will literally confess that, that's what they've been waiting for ages according to Romans 8:17-25. *"For the earnest expectation of the creation eagerly waits for the revealing of the sons of God"* (vs.19). *"For we know that the whole creation groans and labors with birth pangs together until now"* (vs.22).

The Apostle Paul clearly says this in Philippians 2:9-11. *"Therefore, God also has highly exalted Him and given Him the name which is above every name"* (vs.9). *"That at the name of Jesus every knee should bow, of those in heaven, and of those on earth, and of those under the earth"* (vs.10). *"And that every tongue should confess that Jesus Christ is Lord, to the glory of God the Father"* (vs.11).

Here we see that the name of Jesus is above every other name. No matter how powerful and famous the other names are; the name of Jesus Christ, the Son of the Almighty God is the only powerful and highest name that is named on the face of this earth. Therefore, at the name of Jesus every knee should bow, of those in heaven and of those on earth, and of those under the earth. And that every tongue should confess that Jesus Christ is Lord.

Through these portions of scriptures, God is telling us something that we should understand. I believe the names that the Bible talks about; are not only personal names as we may think, but organizational names, government names, titles, positions and even some names of materials that seem to rise above the name of Jesus. God is telling us that all other names besides the name of Jesus should come under His name. The name of Jesus Christ is the only name that should rise above every other name.

There is one interesting thing the Church of God will experience in the history of Church; is to see the name of Jesus rises above any other name. That means the Church of God will be highly respected and placed in the prominence of all. Paul also stressed more on that in Ephesians 1:20-23. *"Which He worked in Christ when He raised Him from the dead and seated Him at His right hand in the heavenly places"* (vs.20). *"Far above all principality and power and might and dominion, and every name that is named, not only in this age but also in that which is to come"* (vs.21). *"And He put all things under His feet, and gave Him to be head over all things to the Church"* (vs.22). *"Which is His body, the fullness of Him who fills all in all"* (vs.23).

I see that God raised Him from the dead and had seated Him at His right hand in the heavenly places, far above all principality and power and might and dominion, and every name that is named. That's what God the Father did to Jesus but lets see what He did to the Church. In verse 22 it says; *"And He put all things under His feet, and gave Him to be head over all things to the church."*

You see, God has given the highest name and the position to Jesus; and the consequent blessings and benefits thereof, He has also given to the Church. *"And He put all things under His feet."* Which feet? The feet of Jesus Christ.

God gave everything to Jesus that Jesus would share it all together with the Church, the Body of Christ; which is also referred to as His feet. The feet here speak of the Body of Christ for Jesus is the Head of the Body. That simply means all things are under the Body, the Church of God in which you and I are part of it. Again, God gave the most Highest Name and the position to Jesus, that this highest and the most distinguish position of Jesus may bless the Church. For the Church is the Body of Jesus that direct benefit to the Church from this honorable position and title of Jesus is inevitable.

One might say; how could that be? Again, the answer is found in verses 22 and 23. The Church is part and parcel of what God is doing for Jesus. Therefore, when Jesus is glorified by the Father, the Church which is also Jesus' Body will automatically be affected by the glory of God. Verse 23 tells me that the Church, which is His Body, contains the fullness of Him (Jesus) who fills all in all. In other words, Jesus is honored and glorified by the Father to the Church. That simply means the glory of Jesus will be easily reflected and its radiation will be seen in the Body of Jesus, the Church.

When that literally happens, the Church will be in a better position to be identified and respected as it should, for it is in fact the Body of Jesus. For the Church is made to be transparent at all time; that all men and authorities on the face of this earth will be attracted by the glory of God like never before in the history of Church. You will see more of it in the book of Isaiah 60:1-22 that I will explain in a later paragraph.

The governments around the world will run to the Church to seek solutions and answers for their unsolved problems. Truly every knee will bow before the Lord and every tongue will confess that Jesus is Lord. The Word of God in Philippians 2: 9-11 and Ephesians 1:20-23 will surely and literally come to pass. Prophesies recorded in the Old Testament books like Isaiah 2:1-3 and Haggai 2:21-22, will definitely be fulfilled at that time.

Let's see what Prophet Isaiah says; "*Now it shall come to pass in the latter days, that the mountain of the Lord's house, shall be established on the top of the mountains. And shall be exalted above the hills; And all nations shall flow to it"* (2:2). *"Many people shall come and say, "Come, and let us go up to the mountain of the Lord, To the house of the God of Jacob; He will teach us His ways, And we shall walk in His paths." For out of Zion shall go forth the law, And the word of the Lord from Jerusalem"* (vs.3).

Now let me elucidate every important point in this portion of scriptures. Here in verse 2 it says; *"Now it shall come to pass in the latter days."*

"Latter days" speaks of the time and the season in which these prophecies will literally come to pass. I think we all know that we are now beginning to tap into these days. And it is also true that we are not too far from these wonderful days. I guess most of us believe that these days are around the corner. May be anytime in this 21st Century towards the next millennium, or it might come little bit later than that, but what is certain is that soon or latter it will definitely come to pass, for the Word of God says that it will come.

It doesn't matter if it happens in our generation or the generations to come, the truth of the matter is that; these latter days the Bible prophecies point to, are certain and no prophet of doom can preach something otherwise in order to extinguish this belief.

Let's continue in verse 2. *"That the mountain of the Lord's house, shall be established on the top of the mountains."* This is what it will actually come to pass in the latter days. "The mountain" here speaks of the position and "the Lord's house" speaks of the Church of God. And "the top of the mountains," not only one but many mountains speaks of the nations, governments, organizations, all kinds of systems and beliefs, situations and circumstances, both poverty and luxury life styles, pain and sufferings, sicknesses and diseases, fame and famous, all sorts of names; titles and positions, the world of materialism and etc, etc.

Can you see what this prophecy is talking about? I see that in the latter days, the Church of God will be positioned in the highest place of all. For so many years, the things which I have referred to as mountains above, have one way or the other become big mountains in people's lives around the world; and the so-called church thing has been neglected and taken for granted. But praise God; there's gonna be a time when all of them will come under the feet of Jesus which is indeed the Church of God.

It further says; "*And shall be exalted above the hills; and all nations shall flow to it.*" The Church shall not only be exalted above the big mountains but also the small hills as well. "The hills" here speak of even the very small issues that affect human lives. For it is true that both big and small, anything that which is not of God can be a mountain or a hill to desecrate the Church and to dislocate and disrupt the growth of the Church.

But thank God, the big mountains or small hills will no longer be there to progress in their evil plans. And when that happens, all the nations shall flow to it. Like never before in the history of the Church life, not only some but "all the nations" around the world will flow to it to seek peace, solutions and answers to their unsolved problems and issues. Surely that's what the Word of God says, and it will definitely be fulfilled.

Now let's see more of it in verse 3. Not only few or some but "*Many people shall come and say; Come, and let us go up to the mountain of the Lord, To the house of the God of Jacob.*" "Many people" speaks of many different race or ethnic people groups around the world. They will say; come, let us go to the house of the God of Jacob. Why would they go up to the mountain where the Church of God is? The answer is; "*He will teach us His ways, And we shall walk in His paths.*" "He," speaks of Jesus, the Head of the Church, who will teach them His ways, and they shall walk in His paths. "*For out of Zion shall go forth the law, And the word of the Lord from Jerusalem.*"

Again, "Zion" speaks of the Church, and that out of the Church shall go forth the law. At that time all people, mostly the Political Leaders will seek Godly advice to run the affairs of their nations. And further more it says; "*And the word of the Lord from Jerusalem.*" "Jerusalem," the city of God, which is located in the center of the all world, speaks also of the Church, which is also the central control centre (CCC) of the world.

For it says; the Word of the Lord shall go forth from Jerusalem. Words from any other place or city have no value and Spiritual significance as the Words from Jerusalem, the Church. For the Words of life and true peace for the all world will only be delivered from the Church.

Why Jerusalem? It is not only talking about this physical Capital City of the Nation of Israel, but it is also talking about the Spiritual City, the New

Jerusalem of God. The New Jerusalem, the City of God, is the place where actual Throne of God is (Revelation 21:10, 22:3). That's where all the Christians are heading to; to spend their eternity.

However, before that happens in the Spiritual world, the heart of a Christian man is somewhat known to be the place where this Great God is enthroned. Truly God is up there in Heaven, the New Jerusalem, but Spiritually, He is in the heart of a born again Christian man here on planet earth. The heart of a born again Christian man is the sacred and holy place of God where He dwells.

Isaiah 57: 15 states that; *" For thus says the High and Lofty One; Who inhabits eternity, whose name is Holy; I dwell in the high and holy place, With him who has a contrite and a humble spirit, To revive the spirit of the humble, And to revive the heart of the contrite ones."* A short paraphrase of this verse can be something like this. *'The Most High God lives in the high and holy place; but He also dwells in a born again and humble heart to revive the broken and contrite heart.'*

You know that the heart of a man is the central part of the whole being of a person. It is in that heart where God is enthroned. And from it, He executes all His plans, particularly anything that is to do with this world. The heart of a man is where the Kingdom of God is located; spiritually speaking (Luke 17:21). In that sense, we can also say that Jerusalem speaks of the heart of man; which is in fact the spirit-man, where God dwells and sends forth His Word through the man as he preaches.

So let's conclude this portion of scriptures by saying that; in the latter days, God will literally be enthroned in the hearts of all born again Christians around the world. And that body of Christians is the Church of God that the all world will run to; to find solutions and answers for this problem world. That will be the most highest and distinguished position the Church will ever have in its history.

Anyway, Prophet Micah records the very same Words as Prophet Isaiah did, in chapter 4:1-2, that we really do not need to look at it again. However, let's see what Prophet Haggai says in chapter 2:21-22. *"Speak to Zerubbabel, governor of Judah, saying: I will shake heaven and earth (vs.21). I will overthrow the throne of kingdoms; I will destroy the strength of the Gentile Kingdoms. I will overthrow the chariots, And those who ride in them; the horses and their riders shall come down, Every one by the sword of his brother"* (vs.22).

This portion of scriptures is talking about overthrowing of Gentile Kingdoms and the thrones thereof. However, it does not mean that the governments of the world will literally cease completely from functioning and running the affairs of the nations as independent states. But it talks about overthrowing of the demonic and humanistic spirits that are at force behind the governments.

Ever since the ideology of people getting independence from God and looking after themselves through the political offices had come into existence, almost all the government leaders seem to know the answers relating to the problems and issues that are affecting this world. In the process, over the years, leaders deliberately or not knowingly ignore and neglect the guidance and wisdom from God; the Maker. In fact the idea of people looking after themselves (even the Israelites for that matter) through the political offices was not from God, but it was an initiative instigated by the people themselves (1Samuel 8:1-9).

It was not altogether wrong to do so but the biggest mistake was that the people became independent from God and thus, leaders didn't allow the Almighty God, the Creator and the Source of all wisdom to intervene in their situations.

Because the concept of man becoming leaders rather than God was from the people themselves, there were other personal agendas attached to the idea of serving other fellow human beings. In fact God revealed the evil motives as the first incident took place. This story is recorded in 1Samuel 8:1-22. Here is what it says from verses 4-20.

Then all the elders of Israel gathered together and came to Samuel at Ramah (vs.4), and said to him, "Look, you are old, and your sons do not walk in your ways. Now make us a King to judge us like all the nations" (vs.5). But the thing displeased Samuel when they said, "Give us a king to judge us." So Samuel prayed to the Lord (vs.6).

And the Lord said to Samuel, "Heed the voice of the people in all that they say to you; for they have not rejected you, but they have rejected Me, that I should not reign over them" (vs.7). "According to all the works which they have done since the day that I brought them up out of Egypt, even to this day-with which they have forsaken Me and served other gods-

so they are doing to you also" (vs.8). *"Now therefore, heed their voice. However, you shall solemnly forewarn them, and show them the behaviour of the king who will reign over them"* (vs.9). *So Samuel told all the words of the LORD to the people who asked him for a king* (vs.10). *And he said, "This will be the behavior of the king who will reign over you: He will take your sons and appoint them for his own chariots and to be his horsemen, and some will run before his chariots"* (vs.11). *"He will appoint captains over his thousands and captains over his fifties, will set some to plow his ground and reap his harvest, and some to make his weapons of war and equipment for his chariots"* (vs.12). *"He will take your daughters to be perfumers, cooks, and bakers"* (vs.13). *"And he will take the best of your fields, your vineyards, and your olive groves, and give them to his servants"* (vs.14). *"He will take a tenth of your grain and your vintage, and give it to his officers and servants* (vs.15). *"And he will take your male servants, your female servants, your finest young men, and your donkeys and put them to his work"* (vs.16). *"He will take a tenth of your sheep. And you will be his servants"* (vs.17). *"And you will cry out in that day because of your king whom you have chosen for yourselves, and the Lord will not hear you in that day"* (vs.18). *"Nevertheless the people refused to obey the voice of Samuel; and they said, "No, but we will have a king over us,"* (vs.19). *"That we also may be like all the nations, and that our king may judge us and go out before us and fight our battles"* (vs.20).

From verses 11-17, the Bible tells us about the evil plans and motives behind the man they have asked to be their king. The Lord revealed the hidden motives behind the man even before he was officially appointed as king for Israel. When you read verses 11-17, you will surprise to notice that the man was full of nothing else but only selfishness and greediness.

Prophet Samuel prophesied exactly what the coming king would do to the people of Israel. Since then, almost all the governments that came to power on the face of this earth were controlled and led by this same spirit. I guess the works of this same evil spirit is evident in the governments around the world today. I really do not know much about many other governments of the world but with due respect, the National, Provincial and Local Level Governments of which I know very well, are classical examples of the kind of governments that I am talking about here. The ancient governments of both BC and AD dispensations are no exception. I think I at least know that these governments have proven beyond doubt that their practice of corruption is really the evident of the spirit of selfishness and greediness that Prophet Samuel prophesied about.

We now see that the initial concept of forming separate government besides the government of God was all motivated by evil. Because it was motivated by evil, God will not tolerate it forever. There must be a time when God will put to an end of everything that came into existence without His perfect will but under His permissive will.

With that note, the governments of today are no exception. Their days are numbered as to when their fate will be; as the days of King Belshazzar were numbered in the Bible days in accordance with Daniel 5:26. No wonder, what the Prophet Haggai says is in line with what God had planned to do. This is what Prophet Haggai says: *"I will shake heaven and earth"* (2:21). *"I will overthrow the thrones of kingdoms; I will destroy the strength of the Gentile kingdoms. I will overthrow the chariots, And those who ride in them; the horses and their riders shall come down, Every one by the sword of his brother"* (vs.22).

God is telling us that one fine day, He will shake the heavens and the earth. I believe when God shakes the heavens and the earth, the authorities and their powers thereof, will be the first ones to be affected. You might argue and say; how and why the authorities first, before the others?

Well, the answer is right there under your nose. Verse 22 will tell you what will really happen to the authorities of both the heavens and the earth as God shakes them. It says; He will overthrow the thrones of kingdoms. And He will also destroy the strength of the Gentile kingdoms. He says; He will also overthrow the chariots, and those who ride in them, that the horses and their riders will definitely come down.

The last part of verse 22 is a very interesting one for me. Here it says; *"Every one by the sword of his brother."* This is the Word of God and so whatever the Word says, will definitely come to pass. "Every one by the sword of his brother" means; every government leader will be affected by the sword of the Word of God through the Church.

At that time Ephesians 1:20-23 and Philippians 2:9-11 as I said little bit earlier, will literally come to pass. When God is in action of overthrowing the throne and destroying the strength of the Gentile kingdoms, no chariot or horse rider will remain in his position anymore.

No matter how powerful and strong they are, or how smart and intelligent they are, big or small, old or new, all of them, both in the heavenly places and on this earth will surely come down before the King of kings and the Lord of lords. (Authorities of heavenly places mean the powers of darkness that Ephesians 1:21 talks about). They will bow down and kneel before His face and confess that Jesus Christ is truly the King of kings and the Lord of lords.

The prophecy about every government shall be upon His shoulders will by that time surely come to pass (Isaiah 9:6-7).

That really doesn't mean that they all will literally repent and become born again Christians (hopefully some may do) to worship God. All I am saying is that directly or indirectly they will some how confess even from the evil status of their hearts; that truly there is a God who is in control of everything. Like never before in the history of mankind, there will be a worldwide fear of God, that will sweep across the all world, even in the deep darkness, according to Isaiah 60:1-22 and Joel 2:1-32.

The deep darkness that both the Prophets Isaiah and Joel talk about; speaks of overwhelming sinful nature that will also sweep across and cover the all world simultaneously. Apostle Paul touched little bit on this in 2Timothty 3:1-17. In fact the power of darkness will compete with the power of God only to be defeated at the end of the day. Certainly the powers of darkness will hardly stand against the power of God (Matthew 16:18), as it literally comes with full force to wipe out the old evil passions and practices.

This is in fact a figurative theory that its actions will be very much evident in the spiritual realm. However, in the natural, the common belief of literal universal peace and righteousness that is sure to happen but gradually, will take place after the rapture in the millennial reign.

The Redeemer of 'Zion' Isaiah 60 talks about is I personally believe (the Zion), speaks of the 'Church' that the Redeemer will redeem in this time of chaos in the all world, as well as the one thousand millennium years of Jesus' rule in the future. Let me tell you what will actually happen at that time. The one thousand years of Jesus' rule on earth will definitely take place after the rapture.

However, what I am talking about here will surely come to pass one way or the other before the rapture. I don't care who says what; there's one thing that is certain is that; this world and everything else, even all the creations for that matter, including you and I will bow down before the King of kings and the Lord of lords, and confess that He is truly the God of all; as it says in Ephesians 1:20-23 and Philippians 2:9-11.

Jesus Christ the King of kings will take His position and reveal His throne in the hearts of believers that His glory will shine from the Church, the Body of Christ like never before. Jesus will be lifted up and glorified from within the Church. And that alone will eventually bring the Church to a higher place of recognition.

There are provisions in the Bible that talk about Jesus' rule of one thousand millennium years (Revelation 20:4-6, 2:26-27, 3:21, 5:9-10, Daniel 7:13-14). And there are also provisions that talk about Jesus' rule in the New Jerusalem that is also yet to come (Revelation 21:1-27, 22:1-21).

What I am actually talking about here should not confuse you with those two (2) great times of Jesus' rule; one on earth and the other one up in New Jerusalem. The Kingship of Jesus that I am talking about is the present one that I guess most people don't know; in the sense that He is right now Ruling and Reigning as He would do in those two great events.

What do you think Jesus is doing right now? Do you think He is just sitting somewhere in heaven dreaming about His future reign? Of course, He said; that He went to prepare a place for us (John 14:2). Do you think He is still busy preparing the place even now? He is Almighty God; who is all-powerful (Omnipotent); who could able to create the great universe in a split second; but it took Him only six (6) days. If it was only for preparing of a place, that should have been already done in some hundred years back since His ascension. But I think, He is also Ruling and Reigning both the physical and the spiritual worlds from the Throne of His Father's Right Hand through the Church. The following Bible references speak of this time of His Reign through the Church (Mark 16:19, Luke 22:69, Acts 7:55-56, Ephesians 2:6, Romans 15:12, Ephesians 1:20-23, Philippians 2:9-11, Revelation 12:5, 19:15, 1John 4:4, Luke 10:18-19, Matthew 16:19, 1Peter 2:9-10, John 14:12-14).

It is also not the theory of Post-millennialism that puts the Millennium before the Coming of Jesus. This is what a Post-millennarian believes, according to Drs. Guy Duffield and Nathaniel Cleave. "According to this theory, based on an interpretation of the parables of the "leaven" and the "mustard seed," the Church will gradually, through the preaching of the Gospel and the promotion of social justice, overcome war and evil in the world; after which, Christ will come. Post-millennarians believe that universal peace and righteousness will be accomplished by the Church gradually, rather than by the Coming of Christ in power. Two world wars in this century, together with increasing crime, violence, and the threat of a nuclear holocaust have largely disproved this optimistic theory."[26]

However, I agree with the theory of Pre-millennialism. "A pre-millennarian believes that when Christ comes again, He will then, and only then, establish His Reign of peace and righteousness over the earth. He believes in a literal rule of Christ on the promised throne of David, when He, together with the Redeemed of the Church age, will reign over the regathered and saved remnant of Israel and the righteous Gentile nations. The pre-millennarian does not confuse Israel with the Church, nor the Church age with the millennial age; for him the schedule of future prophetic events is: (a) the Rapture, (b) the Tribulation, (c) the Final Coming of Christ as King, (d) the Millennial Reign of Christ on Earth, (e) the Eternal State of a New Heaven and a New Earth."[27]

But what I am trying to explain here is the current Spiritual Reign of Jesus from within our hearts. Don't you know that Jesus is the King of kings and the Lord of lords who is currently Ruling and Reigning from

---

[26] Ibid, (2006). p. 543.

[27] Ibid, (2006). p. 544.

the hearts of all believers? Paul says that every born again Christian is ruling and reigning together with Jesus in the heavenly places; spiritually speaking. And this is what it says; *"And raised us up together, and made us sit together in the heavenly places in Christ Jesus"* (Ephesians 2:6). Seated together with Jesus in the heavenly places means ruling and reigning together with Him. I hope some of you really do not know what I am talking about. For the sake of those ignorant people, let me elaborate little bit more on that.

I think most of us know the fact that the Kingdom of God has already come into this world, according to Matthew 4:17, where it says; *"Repent, for the kingdom of heaven is at hand."* The Kingdom of God has already come according to this verse but where does it locate? Let's read Luke 17: 20-21. *Now when He was asked by the Pharisees when the kingdom of God would come, He answered them and said, "The kingdom of God does not come with observation"* (vs.20)*; "Nor will they say, see here! or see there! For indeed, the kingdom of God is within you"* (vs.21).

You see the Kingdom of God has already come and is within us, the born again Christians. We, the Christians are the Kingdom people and that Kingdom is not like any other kingdom with corrupt kings or leaders of this world. Our Kingdom is the Kingdom of God with King Jesus who has His residence in us.

The Kingdom of God is in us and it's from within our hearts that King Jesus is ruling and reigning; spiritually speaking. Listen folks, this is not just another theory, doctrine, thesis or theism or even a new revelation for that matter. It is indeed a solid fundamental truth that the King with His Kingdom is in us, that this world and everything thereof, should have reverence for King Jesus and His Reign in His Kingdom through the Church.

The other time Jesus said; *"Let your Kingdom come, Your will be done on earth, as it is in heaven"* (Matthew 6:10). Jesus prayed that the Kingdom should come and that God's perfect will be established on this earth. My friend, I don't know about you but I am convinced so much so to say what I am saying.

Truly Jesus Christ is the King and we are the Kingdom people. That's why we are spiritually ruling and reigning together with Him even from the heavenly places, according to Ephesians 2:6, 1Jhon 4:4, Luke 10:18-19, John 14:12-14, Matthew 16:19, 1Peter 2:9-10. Even though we the Christians and the King are spiritually reigning from the spiritual world, the effect should be felt by the physical world. That's exactly what Paul is talking about in Ephesians 1:20-23 and Philippians 2:9-11.

Currently, Jesus is seated on the right hand of the Father in heaven (Mark 16:19, Luke 22:69, Acts 7:55-56, Hebrews 1:3, and 12:2); yet spiritually, He is ruling and reigning in us and through us the Church. It is therefore, every knee should bow and every tongue shall confess that He is Lord of all and should have reverence for Him. I am not trying to spiritualize all references relative to Christ's physical Reign on earth as an Amillennarian does.[28] Yet the current Kingship of Jesus that I am talking about is very

---

[28] Ibid, (2006). p. 543.

much real in its concept; that its teaching should not play any contrary message to any one of these similar theories.

If you carefully read the portions of scriptures in the following verses of Haggai 2:6-9, 20-21, Ephesians 1:20-23 and Philippians 2:9-11, they talk about how the present Church and its glory should affect the nations of the world.

Let's read Haggai 2:6-9 again. *"For thus says the Lord of hosts: Once more (it is a little while) I will shake heaven and earth, the sea and dry land"* (vs.6)*; "And I will shake all nations, and they shall come to the Desire of All Nations, and I will fill this temple with glory, says the Lord of hosts"* (vs.7). *"The silver is Mine, and the gold is Mine, says the Lord of hosts"* (vs.8). *"The glory of this latter temple shall be greater than the former, says the Lord of hosts. And in this place I will give peace, says the Lord of hosts"* (vs.9).

In this prophecy, God is saying something about shaking the nations and causing them to have desire for others. That means the agape love of God will reach every nation on the face of this earth. Consequently, the knowledge of God will cover the earth as the waters cover the sea as Habakkuk 2:14 says. The knowledge of God will increase as a result of the intensive fear of God at that time. No wonder it says in Proverbs 9:10 that, the fear of God is the beginning of all wisdom, knowledge and understanding.

When God shakes the nations, closed doors will be opened for the Good News about the Kingdom of God to penetrate. Subsequently, the glory of this latter temple (the Church) will be greater than the former (the tabernacle). As the glory of God from within the Church is so thick and glorious, its radiation will be felt across the world.

When that happens, the nations of the world will not only bow down before the Lord and confess that He is Lord but they will also bring their wealth to the Church of God. Verse 8 of Haggai chapter 2 also states that. *"The silver is Mine, and the gold is Mine, says the Lord of hosts."* The Prophet Isaiah prophesied more on that in chapter 60:1-22. Verses 5-11, 13, and 16-17 talk about the Gentile nations with their kings coming to the Church of God with their wealth. Let's see verses 5, and 11. This is what it says in verse 5. *"Because the abundance of the sea shall be turned to you, the wealth of the Gentiles shall come."*(vs.5). *"That men may bring to you the wealth of the Gentiles, And their kings in procession"* (vs.11).

Verses 1-4, 14-15, and 18-22 talk about the Church's radiation from the glory of God that will cause the Gentile nations to come to the Church. Well, let's see few of these verses. *"Arise, shine; For your light has come! And the glory of the Lord is risen upon you"* (vs.1). *"For behold, the darkness shall cover the earth, And deep darkness the people; But the Lord will arise over you, And His glory will be seen upon you"* (vs.2). *"The Gentiles shall come to your light, And kings to the brightness of your rising"* (vs.3). *"Lift up your eyes all around, and see; they all gather together, they come to you; Your sons shall come from afar, And your daughters shall be nursed at your side"* (vs.4). *"Then you shall see and become radiant, And your heart shall swell with joy"* (vs.5). *"Also the sons of those who afflicted you Shall come bowing to you, And all those who despised you shall fall prostrate at the soles of your feet; And they shall call you the City of the Lord, Zion of the Holy One of Israel"* (vs.14). *"The sun shall no longer be your light by day, Nor for brightness shall the moon give light to you; But the Lord will be to you an everlasting light, and your God your glory"* (vs.19). *"Your sun shall no longer go down, Nor shall your moon withdraw itself; For the Lord will be your everlasting light, And the days of your mourning shall be ended"* (vs.20).

The above portion of scriptures may literally be applied in the natural but for the one thousand millennium years. Yet it can also be applied in this current Spiritual Reign of Jesus Christ through His Church.

As the Apostle Paul was trying to explain how deep the intimate relationship between a husband and a wife, he was taking the Church and Jesus as an example for the matter. In the process, he said something in line with what the Prophet Isaiah had said. This is what he said in Ephesians 5:27. *"That He might present her to Himself a glorious church, not having spot or wrinkle or any such thing, but that she should be holy and without blemish."* A glorious church is all that Jesus wants of His Church.

When prophesies lined up like this, there is no point in having doubts whatsoever about the position of the Church. The King will take His residence in the Church and the rays of His glory will shine from within the Church. The kings and other leaders of the nations will by then come to the Church with their wealth. It is very obvious that the Church will be lifted to the highest mountain for the glory of God. And that will be the position of the Church of God in this world.

Even Matthew 16:18 will become real at that time, that the gates of Hades shall not prevail against it. The Church will grow into its full shape and power. *"For it pleased the Father that in Him all the fullness should dwell"* (Colossians 1:19). And that's what the creation of God has been waiting to see for many, many years like it says in Romans 8:19. *"For the earnest expectation of the creation eagerly waits for the revealing of the sons of God."* For it is true that the sons of God will only be revealed in the glory of God through the Church. Oh! What a joy to be a member of the Body of Christ, the Church. Praise His Majestic Name!

The Body of Christ the Church is the only Body on the face of this earth, which has members in all the nations of the world. The Church is known to be a nation of its own according to 1Peter 2:9. *"But you are a chosen generation, a royal priesthood, a holy nation, His own special people, that you may proclaim the praises of Him who called you out of darkness into His marvelous light;"*

If it is a nation of its own then, according to human psychology and its reasoning, there is no logic in it and is unbelievable. For a nation with its citizens can not be established as a nation on other man's land. Or else a nation can not be scattered with the citizenship of its citizens all over the place as a nation. But because it is a Spiritual Body, it can surely be established spiritually in all the nations for one reason. And the reason for it is found in 1Peter 2:9 that we've just read. The reason is that; *"That you may proclaim the praises of Him who called you out of darkness into His marvelous light."*

Proclaiming the praises of Him that the people of darkness may go into the marvelous light of God is what the Church of God is commissioned to do. For the Church of God, which is also a nation that supposed to be the glorious nation, should take the lead and set a Godly model on the face of this earth. Of course, the Western World is taking the lead in terms of politics, education, economic and physical developments but spiritually, it is none other than the Church of God which is the holy nation that should take the lead. The Bible indeed declares that the people of God are the head and not the tail; and that they shall be above only and not beneath (Deuteronomy 28:13). That means the people of God are to take the lead in the things of God.

To acquire physical knowledge in order to bring forth physical developments and so on, the only best way is to sit down and learn from the learned or expert person in that particular subject or field. Likewise, those who want to acquire Spiritual knowledge to bring forth spiritual developments to their churches and other areas in their lives; the only best way is to humble themselves and learn from the institution called the Church of God, the holy nation. Truly it is the only institution in this world which has the Word of God, from which the people can learn the Spiritual things of God.

Jesus Christ is the only answer for the world to solve the unsolved problems and issues that are affecting the world today. And the answer from Jesus can only be found through His Body, the Church of God. Therefore, the Church in the physical world is not just another social institution as some may think it is, but in fact it is the only institution that has the answers for this problem world, whether you know it or not.

The global peace that some leading governments of this world are trying to bring on the face of this earth is only a dream and wish for the leaders. I pray that their eyes be opened to see that it really requires a supernatural power beyond human knowledge and understanding. Really it does not require the political leaders only but it also requires the knowledge from on High, which can be transpired from the only Spiritual institution, the Church. Truly the world suffers as a result of the lack of Godly knowledge as it says in Hosea 4:6. Here it says; *"My people are destroyed for lack of knowledge."* Friends, the simple answer for this problem world is nothing more or less of a piece of knowledge from on High that can only be acquired from His Church.

b: The Church in the Spiritual World – The New Jerusalem.

Heaven is where God is and hence, everything thereof, is subject to Him. The heavenly creations, including the angels are under instructions as to what they must do and at what time and how it should be done. Ever since their existence, they were instructed to get themselves ready for a very, very special occasion that all of them eager to see it takes place. That special occasion is no other than the "wedding feast" or "marriage supper" according to Revelation 19:7-9. It is also known as the believer's Bema Judgement of Awards.[29]

Actually the wedding feast (the eternal joy and happiness or intimate relationship between God and His people) will begin straight after the rapture before the Second Coming of the Lord. It will even continue during the period of one thousand millennium years on earth, and it will go on for eternity after the great judgment. That will actually be the position of the Church of God in the Spiritual world, from whence the saints will then rule and reign as kings together with Christ Jesus.

I don't believe the wedding feast will last for only seven years but it will continue forever. For everything and every occasion that is attached with heaven is always eternal. Sometimes there are some spiritual things that human mind can not able to comprehend. But lets ignore our minds and see things from the spiritual perspective as God sees; for we are spiritual people that walk not by sight but by faith (2Corinthians 5:7, Hebrews 11:1).

In actual fact, the wedding feast will be a literal intimate relationship between God and His people. It really doesn't have to be a spiritual banquet that the saints will literally eat and drink with God. In Revelation 3:20, Jesus says something about eating and drinking with us as we open our doors and allow Him to come in. Some of us have already opened our

---

[29] Ibid, (2006). p. 530.

doors and allowed Him to come; but we are yet to experience this type of meal with Him.

I think literal eating and drinking is not part of the Kingdom of God; like Apostle Paul said in Romans 14:17; though it actually talks about physical food. The wedding feast in Revelation 19:7-9, could be a figurative message that it only talks about the church's literal intimate relationship with God, with righteousness, peace and joy in the Holy Ghost. It will not be a banquet that when the table is empty, the feast will then cease after seven years. I also know that it is something really unbelievable and unimaginable; that I have not enough human words to express or describe this great everlasting event of enjoying the wedding feast.

Normally, in a physical marriage, it is a common understanding that no wedding between two couples should last for only a temporary period. It is a lifetime sealing that no circumstance or law should ever rescind it. And we know, a marriage is all about intimate relationship and fellowship between the couples as they are united not as two different bodies but into one body (Ephesians 5:24-32). I believe it is the same thing with the marriage between God and His people, because the Church is in fact one body with God.

The great occasion has not yet come and therefore both heaven and earth are still waiting for it. When that great day comes, the heaven of heavens and the great universe will give way to it. Actually, the real life in the wedding feast will be tasted in three different occasions with two interval periods.

The first one and the initial part of it will be the seven year period in heaven straight after the rapture (Revelation 19:1-10, (vs7-9). The seven year period is calculated from three and half (3 ½) years in Revelation 12:6 and another three and half (3 ½) found in 13:5.

The second part of it is the one thousand-millennium period on earth (20:1-6). That will occur after the initial seven-year marriage celebration in heaven, which will be followed by the Second Coming of Jesus. The wedding feast, a figurative message relating to the literal intimate relationship between God and the Church; will now continue as God and the Church begins to rule and reign for a thousand years on earth.

In the millennial reign, some saints from the Church that has been raptured and had participated in the wedding feast will then be kings to rule and reign with Jesus (vs.4-6). The resurrected and glorified saints will be granted thrones from which they will judge (read again vs.4-6). The Church at that time will have a special position; that it will have easy access; to both the physical and the spiritual worlds.

See what Drs. G. P. Duffield and N. M. V. Cleave say in regard to this theory. "The Church will bear a different relationship to the millennial kingdom than either the restored nation of Israel or the Gentile nations. These latter will be earthly peoples; and even though they will live under the ideal conditions of an earth freed from the curse, they will have mortal bodies and they will pursue normal earthly occupations. There will be universal peace, justice and holiness because of the Sovereign Rule of Christ, but there will not be absolute perfection in the earthly inhabitants (cf. Is. 11:4; 65:20; Zec. 14:17-19). On the other hand, the Church and all saints who have had part in the First Resurrection will rule and reign with Christ (Rv. 2:26, 27; 3:21; 5:9, 10; 20:6).They will not be confined to the earth, for they have glorified bodies and they will have access to Heaven and earth (Revelation 19:6-14, Matthew 22:30-31, Luke 20:35-36)."[30]

The third and the final timeless period of enjoying the wedding feast is of course will be in the New Jerusalem, after the one thousand millennial reign and the final judgment. That will be the final one and truly the Church will then be cut off and separated totally from all the physical and mortal attachments.

Oh! What a great day that will be in the history of mankind. A day full of unspeakable joy and happiness; that will open the gates of eternity. Never again to see, and to taste, and to feel, the gleams of the old heavens and the earth. The old heavens and the earth will literally pass away and the new will begin to take over. Please I beg you to read again Revelation 21:1-27, and 22: 1-6 for your convenience and more confirmation.

The great universe and everything else thereof will cease from its entire work. The sky and the firmament with the stars in the Milky Way or Galaxy (after the completion of their purposes) will cease completely from their operations. The sun and the moon will no longer produce light and heat anymore. The sea will no longer be there to give life to the living things in it. The mountains and the valleys with the river-banks will never be in their positions any more. The plants and all the living creatures won't be there for their humble contributions in the eco-system

---

[30] Ibid, (2006). p. 545.

in this world. Consequently, there won't be any air to give life to anybody. The highways, the byways and the towns and cities will easily disappear without any reluctance.

What will really happen then? The first heaven and the first earth will pass away as the new heaven and the new earth slowly begins to take over. Apostle John saw it in advance for our good in his great revelation. *"Now I saw a new heaven and a new earth, for the first heaven and the first earth had passed away"* (Revelation 21:1-2).

Jesus while on earth declared that one fine day, the old heaven and the old earth will pass away (Matthew 24:35). It is certain that we are living in a world that is passing away. It's not only that but we, the people are also passing through this world. The world that you and I see and live in it was not created to last forever. We haven't come into this world to live forever either. This world and its fullness thereof is only a temporary world for a certain mission.

When that mission is accomplished, the world will have no reason to hang on to the space any more. We, the people were not created to live in this world just for the sake of living an ordinary life and extinguish completely after death. No, not at all; for it's not true. If you are smart enough, you will not believe in all these fakes from the pit of hell. Hence, I once again appeal for the unsaved people to make adjustments in life and turn back to God; for what I've mentioned above is certain, and it will truly and surely come to pass.

Unlike any other animal, we human beings have eternal spirits that will live forever and ever in the eternal world. Nevertheless, this physical world is somehow very important for its mission. It is a place of decision that will determine our destination in one of these two eternal places, either heaven or hell in the eternal world.

When the world of decision is over, human spirits are bound to end up in one of these two eternal places according to their respective decisions. That's why it is very, very important that before we reach the end of our breath or the end of this world, the decision for our destination should be considered priority number one.

Before I elaborate more in the position of the Church in New Jerusalem, let me highlight that the destination of the spirits of unbelievers is no other than hell, the second everlasting place in the eternal world. However, some say that there is no eternal hell as it is with heaven. They say that the spirits of unbelievers will be burnt into dust once and for all, and will never torment the eternal sufferings. I really don't know where they get this sort of foul revelation from.

There are indeed numerous of Bible references prove that there is a burning hell prepared for the wicked ones. Here are just few for our purpose (Matthew 8:12, 23:33, Mark 9:43-48, Luke13:28, 16:23-28, Revelation 20:13-15, 21:8). This is straight forward, and there is no need of any compromising theology.

I am very sorry that they are only deceived and blinded by the god of this world, as 2Corinthians 4:4 says. Sin is sin and no medicine can ever change its colour unless it is cleansed or washed by the blood of

Jesus. Those who are not washed by the blood of Jesus are bound to destruction in burning hell. As the old heaven and earth pass away and the spirits of those who don't believe in Christ are under condemnation, what would then really happen to the Church?

Anyway, the Church and its position in New Jerusalem is obvious. Some members of the Church (those who have scored high) will then begin to have dominion over everything in heaven together with Jesus Christ as subordinate kings.

Is it true that there is, and will be a Church in heaven? Yes; there is and there will be a Church in heaven as it is on earth according to Hebrews 12:23. Here it says; *"To the general assembly and church of the firstborn who are registered in heaven, to God the Judge of all, to the spirits of just men made perfect."*

William Evans says; "There is a Church in heaven just as there is one upon the earth; indeed, it is but a part of the one Church; called the Church militant while upon the earth, and the Church triumphant in heaven."[31] Anyway, the part of the Church in heaven, commonly known as the 'assembly of the saints;' is waiting for that Great Day of the Bridegroom with His bride.

The Church of God is the bride for Jesus that heaven will have high respect for her. Even the angels will surely serve the Church. Angels are aware of this for a long, long time and no wonder, they wish that they become like us, the saints. *"To them it was revealed that, not to themselves, but to us they were ministering the things which now have been reported to you through those who have preached the gospel to*

---

[31] Ibid, (1987). p. 142.

you by the Holy Spirit sent from heaven – things which angels desire to look into" (1 Peter 1:12).

Can you see how important the work of preaching the gospel is? Preaching the gospel and serving God in any means in this world is something that the angles have desire for it. Why? Simply because the Church that has been washed by the blood of Jesus and saved by the grace of God will rule and reign together with Jesus as kings forever, while the angels will only serve both Jesus and the saints. For the Bible says that the angels are only ministering spirits. *"Are they not all ministering spirits sent forth to minister for those who will inherit salvation"* (Hebrews 1:14)? It also says in verse 7 of Hebrews chapter 1: that; *And of the angels He says: "Who makes His angels spirits–And His ministers a flame of fire."*

According to this verse, we the ministers of the gospel are also flame of fire, though it actually talks about the angels (the Cherubim) who are only spirits. This is also telling me something that in heaven, we the ministers and of course all the saints, in togetherness known as the Church of God will be a flame of fire. We will be a flame of fire because we are a glorious Church.

One good thing about the Church to be glorious in this world is that; the Church will continue to be glorious and be a flame of fire in New Jerusalem, the City of God forever and ever. Apostle Paul was led by the Holy Spirit to remind us of this precious time in heaven. This is what he says in Romans 8:17-18. *"And if children, then heirs – heirs of God and joint heirs with Christ, if indeed we suffer with Him, that we may also be glorified together"* (vs.17). *"For I consider that the sufferings of this present time are not worthy to be compared with the glory which shall be revealed in us"* (vs.18).

The subject matter that these two verses talk about is the glory of God that will continue to shine on us even in heaven. Verse 17 says; *'Because we are children of God, we are heirs and heirs with Christ.'* Heirs with Christ for what particular purpose? The answer is; *"That we may also be glorified together with Christ."*

I see that, to be glorified with Christ is all the reason why or the ultimate purpose or intention of God to make me His son and to make me become an heir with Christ. He goes on to say in verse 18 that; *"The sufferings of this present time are not worthy to be compared with the glory which shall be revealed in us."*

To Paul, the sufferings, the pain, the turmoil and anything of that manner is just nothing comparing with the glory of God. In other words, the glory of God is the reason for the sufferings of this world. Anything that the Word of God prescribes as valuable is indeed valuable; that it is worth dying for it.

We really don't know the value and the weight of the glory of God. I therefore find it very hard and have not enough words to express what I feel and imagine about the glory of God. I would only use my simple words with simple terms to express the glory of God in the following manner. The 'unspeakable' in a human dialect and the 'immeasurable' glory of God is too heavy to be weighed by any scale that we know.

Therefore, I can only say that the glory of God is like a long cloth (robe) that clothes God. Why do I have to say that the glory of God is like a cloth or robe? According to my own imagination and personal conviction, I only see nothing but He is indeed covered by His powerful and awesome glory from the top of His head to the soles of His feet. He is all-glorious that I can not see any bare part of His body. The glory of God is like a flame from a burning fire (Exodus 24:17; Hebrews 12:29). He is too glorious and full of power. The rays of His glory give light to illuminate and electrify New Jerusalem, the city of God.

Truly John saw this and it is recorded in Revelation 21:10-11, and 23-25. *"And he carried me away into the Spirit to a great and high mountain, and showed me the great city, the holy Jerusalem, descending out of heaven from God"* (vs.10*), "having the glory of God. Her light was like a most precious stone, like a jasper stone, clear as crystal"* (vs.11). *"The city had no need of the sun or of the moon to shine in it, for the glory of God illuminated it. The Lamb is its light"* (vs.23*). "And the nations of those who are saved shall walk in its light, and the kings of the earth bring their glory and honor into it"* (vs.24*). "Its gates shall not be shut at all by day (there shall be no night there)* (vs.25).

It is this same glory that will be shared with the Church; for we are heirs together with Christ Jesus like Paul says in Romans 8:17-18. To share God's glory with Jesus is something that I can not take it lightly. Just imagine; we'll become little kings, glorified together with Jesus to rule and reign with

Him forever. We should be proud of that and be happy and joyful all the time, no matter what; like Paul says in Philippians 4:4 and 1 Thessalonians 5:16.

For to be glorified with Christ and to rule and reign with Him forever, is the only ultimate reason why God had to do all that He has done (Ephesians 1:3-12). And it is only with man that God will do all these things and not with any angels. Angels will not be glorified with Christ and reign with Him; for no angel has ever been washed by the blood of Jesus and saved by the grace of God.

It is therefore; no angel will be seated together with Him to rule and reign, as the Church will definitely do so. That's how powerful and glorious the position of the Church of God will be in New Jerusalem, forever and ever. Doesn't that sound nice to your ears? Please, make it your aim to be there even if it costs your life. Amen!

Chapter 12

Church Ought to Love

The Church ought to love, for without it Church can be equalized and labeled with other organizations in this world. There are many components that make the Church different from all other man-made organizations. But the foremost of all is love. The love that we are going to look at here is no other than the agape love, which is the divine love of God. As a matter of fact, the Church has to exercise this love for God and for man. It must be first of all for God because only then, the love for man will have meaning and substance.

a: **Love for God**

Before anything else, the Church has to love God first, for it is the fundamental component to which all the other activities in the Church are clung to. As a Church, before going out into the world to preach the gospel and baptize the people, teach them in the Word and to get them involve in many other Christian activities, we should not forget the fact that all of these must be done only in love. It is indeed the fundamental component that without the love for God, all these other components or activities in the Church will truly mean nothing to God. Besides anything else, God wants to see somebody really loves Him with all his heart, with all his soul and with all his mind or strength. For all these other things defend so much on this only and one great commandment.

Let's see what Jesus says about this great commandment. It says in Matthew 22:36-38 that; *"Teacher, which is the great commandment in the law"* (vs.36)? Jesus said to him, *"You shall love the Lord your God with all your heart, with all your soul, and with all your mind"* (vs.37). *"This is the first and great commandment"* (vs.38).

The first and great commandment here is not an Old Testament Law. The first commandment in the Old Testament Law is slightly different from this one. It talks about not to have any other god before God the Creator. It indeed says; *"You shall have no other gods before Me"* (Exodus 20:3). In the Old Testament, God did not want anybody to have any other god before Him. However, in the New Testament, God does not want anyone to love anybody in His place or to love anything else in this world before Him. It is also true that we should love others but loving God must precede the others and none as such should rise above His name.

No wonder, He is demanding for an undivided love from the three important components of a person. All He wants is complete love from the 'all heart,' which is the spirit-man, with 'all soul or mind,' which is the soul-man and with 'all strength,' which is the physical-man. The whole person should love God, for only then, God will be satisfied with our worship that we offer to Him. Or in other words, it is the holistic love or worship that God requires from us.

Why love comes first than the others? Because when we have love for God, all the other activities will have meaning and substance. Then God will be honoured and we will be blessed. However, if there is no love for God the Creator, our act of worship in whatever manner or form it may be, will be an act of abomination only. No matter how we sacrifice in His service, God will have no regard for our services. No higher level of preaching will ever please God. No highest amount of tithes and offerings will ever change Him. No challenging or convincing songs will ever cause God to dance in our music. No sophisticated models or ideas applied in modernized Church buildings or Church institutions will ever invite God to draw more closer to us. No so-called anointed this ministry or that ministry will cause Jesus to come little bit earlier than He should; and the list goes on, unless we have love for God before we make an attempt to act on whatever ministry or gift or talent that we are entrusted with.

Most people actually don't have love for God in whatever they do in the service of God. They do whatever they do only for their personal benefits. When they really don't love God, first of all, they would not bother to give God the glory and honour that He deserves.

Secondly, they also would not bother to bless others. Blessing others and have concern for others in the Body of Christ may be the least thing in their all programme. When they do that, they will be guilty of breaking the second most important commandment. The second most important commandment is; *"You shall love your neighbor as yourself"* (Matthew

22:39). Why the second commandment is important as much as the first one? Because, *"On these two commandments hang all the Law and the Prophets"* (vs.40). Anyway, we'll see more on the second commandment in the next segment.

There are many reasons why loving God must be foremost activity number one, but first; God says; with the absence of love for Him, all the other activities are no better than abominations in His eyes (Isaiah 1:11-17). For when we really love Him, we will have no space to commit sin against Him. What sin? *"Every wrong doing is sin"* or *"All unrighteousness is sin"* (1John 5:17).

That means, when we do anything that is not in line with the Word of God, we are committing sin. No matter how small it is, all unrighteousness is sin. A wrong is a wrong and will never turn out to be right. In the same token, a small sin is like a tip of the iceberg that will remain sin forever and produce its own kind, unless it is washed and cleansed by the blood of Jesus. No matter how best we try to cover it up or paint it with colourful words, it will never turn out to be good. Therefore, when sin controls one's life, there's no room for love for God in his life.

Love for God is priority number one for a minister's life as well as the Christians as a whole. For it is love that will cause us to do it right. Jesus knew how important it is to love God before serving Him and thus, He asked Peter three times whether he loved Him or not. *So when they had eaten breakfast, Jesus said to Simon Peter, "Simon, son of Jonah, do you love Me more than these?" He said to Him, "Yes, Lord, You know that I love You." He said to him,*

"Feed My Lambs" (John 21:15). *He said to him again a second time, "Simon, son of Jonah, do you love Me?" He said to him, "Yes, Lord You know that I love you." He said to him, "Tend My Sheep"* (vs.16). *He said to him the third time, "Simon, son of Jonah, Do you love me?" Peter was grieved because He said to him the third time, "Do you love me?" And he said to Him, "Lord, You know all things; You know that I love You." Jesus said to him, "Feed My sheep"* (vs.17).

Why do you think Jesus had to ask; 'Do you love me' for three times? We can come up with many different answers. But for our purpose in this segment, let's see what Jesus pointed out to be very important. There are two things Jesus was talking about here. First; loving God and second; feeding the sheep. I see that it is the love for God that should cause us to feed the sheep. Or in other words, love for God should be the reason for us to feed the sheep. It should not be the other way around. For instance; we should not feed the sheep in order to love God. Loving God must be the first thing that we should have in our hearts. It is the unconditional love that should be the base, and it must be this love for God that should cause us to do all these other things in the service of God. For if we don't love God, we would not do it right. Jesus knew how important it is to love God before feeding the sheep.

Secondly, Jesus wanted to show us that if we love Him, we should also love others by feeding them with the Word of God. In that sense, we should say that; loving others is the fruit of loving God. That means, we can love others with the agape love, only when we love God with all our heart, with all our soul and with all our mind or strength. Anyway, like I said earlier, we'll see more about love for others in the next segment.

Love for God is the only fundamental component that will help us to serve God in the way we should. When we love God, it will be easy for us to follow all the other commandments and other teachings of the Bible. Jesus knows all these far better than anyone of us. No wonder He said; *"Loving God is the first and great commandment"* (Matthew 22:38). *"For all the Law and the teachings of the Prophets hang on this commandment"* (vs.40). If Jesus says that this commandment is the first and the greatest of all; then, who are we to substitute it for another? I see that when we love God, it lubricates our system that every part of our life, functions well for the glory of God and for the benefit of our own lives. To me love for God is like oil that lubricates any moving machines to operate without any complication.

When there is no oil, where it is needed, we will only force the machines to cause frictions, if we try hard to use them. Consequently, the machines will surely break down and cease to operate. Like- wise, when the love for God is absent in the life of a believer, the end result will surely be destruction and death. Simply because the very essence of life is missing.

I mean, when love for God is absent, how can you serve God without loving Him? Serving God without love for Him will surely produce unfaithfulness and carelessness in His service. When you are unfaithful and careless, you will surely do anything on an ad hoc basis. You might not show any care and reverence for the God Almighty whom you are serving. You might preach anything anytime or do anything without giving a second thought.

People, who don't have love for God as priority number one, will be easily identified in their actions. For the lovers of God will obviously imitate God in everything they do. They are like a good tree that can not bear bad fruit. On the other hand, those who don't love God, are like a bad tree that can not bear good fruit. If you don't love God, don't you ever expect anything good to come out of you. Therefore, loving God is not an option but it is a must.

Love is of the heart, so when we love God, we are actually sharing our heart with God. Sharing our heart with God is all that God wants of us. When you really do a careful and Systematic Bible Study, you will notice that all other things that we do, will count down to the heart of a man, in loving God, serving God, praising God or whatever it is in the service of God. God wants everything to come out from the heart. For the heart is the centre of man. And it is the most important part or organ of the human body.

Anyway, the heart the Bible talks about is not the physical heart but in fact it talks about the spirit-man that we have on the inside of us. Therefore, our act of worship must come from the inner-man rather than from the surface of our being.

No wonder, the Bible says; *"Keep your heart with all diligence, For out of it spring the issues of life"* (Proverbs 4:23). You see, when we do whatever it is from the heart, we are actually producing life. What sort of life? The Godly kind of life or Christ-like life that is full of love and compassion. But don't forget this; it must all germinate and initial beginning should only be conceived in the matrix of love for God in the heart of a person. The elements that are essence, particularly in forming a life should not be taken lightly. Therefore, in our case, love for God in a heart of a man should be kept with all diligence as it says in Proverbs 4:23; *"For out of it spring the issues of life."*

Therefore, there must be love for God first of all in a heart of a person before he engages himself in other things in life. You know, in everything, first thing must come first for the smooth operation of whatever the object it is without any complication. Likewise, in our case, it must be the love for God first and it should not be substituted with whatever that seems to be right and acceptable in our sight. We must be careful, not to be fooled and tricked by our own little minds.

b: Love for Man

For us to love our fellow man is the second most important commandment in the Law of God. Let's read it again in Matthew 22:39-40. *"And the second is like it: You shall love your neighbor as yourself"* (vs.39). *"On these two commandments hang all the Law and the Prophets"* (vs.40). Like I've touched in the first segment about the love for God, the second commandment or the second to it is also important as much as the first one. Because its not only the first one on which all the Law and the teachings of the Prophets hang on to, but it is together with the second commandment as well. That tells me that these two commandments run in parallel but hand in hand to one another, just for one purpose. That means you can't practice one and ignore the other. Truly they are two separate commandments but operate together in oneness to achieve the common goal or purpose.

First of all, when you love God, the second commandment, which is to love other person, should automatically fall in line. When the first commandment has its roots deep down in our hearts, the second commandment will have no problem. It will be very easy for us to love others. However, if the first commandment is absent, you will find it very difficult to love other fellow human beings. You will some how love people with some amount of love but that love is not agape love. You will only exercise the human love and with such, there is no forgiveness and it is not eternal. The agape love that we are talking about is completely different from human love. The human love is the affection of friendly and relatively love. It is known as "philia" or "phileo" and "storge" love" in Greek.

The other human love is the expression of sexual love known as "eros love" also in Greek. The agape love has nothing to do with the above two human love or whatever love it may be. It is truly the love of God that He shared with us as His children. When we have that same love of God, we will love other people as much as God does.

I think we are aware that God's love has no condition. It is not merited and is an unconditional love that has been poured out for the sinners of this world. Let's see what Paul says about this love. *"Now hope does not disappoint, because the love of God has been poured out in our hearts by the Holy Spirit who was given to us"* (Romans 5:5). *"For when we were still without strength, in due time Christ died for the ungodly" (vs.6). "But God demonstrates His own love toward us in that while we were still sinners, Christ died for us"* (vs.8).

Isn't this very clear that God loved us with no condition, whatsoever? This is called "agape" love, the only love in the all world that knows nothing about condition. All other kinds of love have conditions like; if you do this for me, I'll do that for you. Many people in this world have a tendency to do things for other people for a return only. But with God, His agape love has no boundary and is indeed a free gift altogether.

We've already talked about the love of God in texts like Romans 8:29-39 and also John 3:16 in Chapter 8 of this book. When you read all these portions of scriptures, truly you will notice that there is no boundary in the love of God. *"For God so loved the world that He gave His only begotten Son"* (John 3:16), is a package that has everything about the love of God is all in there.

The following verses in Romans chapter 8 are classical examples of how deep, wide and broad the love of God is. *"What than shall we say to these things? If God is for us, who can be against us"* (vs.31)? *"Who shall bring a charge against God's elect? It is God who justifies"* (vs.33). *"Who shall separate us from the love of Christ? Shall tribulation, or distress, or persecution, or famine, or nakedness, or peril or sword"* (vs.35)? *"For I am persuaded that neither death nor life, nor angles nor principalities nor powers, nor things present nor things to come"* (vs.38), *"Nor height nor depth, nor any other created thing, shall be able to separate us from the love of God which is in Christ Jesus our Lord"* (vs.39).

When you have this agape love of God in you, you will just feel like to love anybody, no matter who he or she is. This love will literally cost your life for them. It will cause you to lay down your life for others. Jesus shows how effective the new commandment that will cost one's life for others. In John 15:12-13 He says; *"This is my commandment, that you love one another as I have loved you"* (vs.12). *"Greater love has no one than this, than to lay down one's life for his friends"* (vs.13).

Here He was talking about His own life that He laid down for the all world but at the same time, He was trying to show us how powerful this love is. When the agape love is effective in one's life, it is so powerful that it will surely cost his life for others. He will forget all about himself and put others first in everything that he does. The self-man on the inside of him is already dead and he is sold out for others. Or in other words, he only lives for others.

I've heard and read books about some people of such character and even seen a few Christians with such life style and I guess you also might have seen some. The classical examples are the first Apostles who gave up everything and laid down their lives for the sake of others. This is the kind of love that I am talking about here.

I know it's very easy to preach about love but to really apply it in your own life; you must be man enough to lay down your life for others. To lay down one's life for others means, to really make a living sacrifice by giving up the best you can possess in life or to offer your best talent for others. Sometimes it will really cost you to become enemy with your self-man on the inside of you. Only when you have overcome and defeated the self-man, you will be a qualified candidate to lay down your life for others in the name of love.

Otherwise, you can be a good and smart preacher about love but only sounding brass or a clanging cymbal as Paul says in 1Corinthians 13:1. I don't know about you but to me, it is something that I am still working on it, even after so many years in the ministry.

When I do my general exegesis in my personal Bible Study, I see that truly the whole Bible is summed up in only one subject and that is no other than love.

I know that the subject of love is very huge with all its ingredients that I cannot able to cover everything and write them all in this little book. But what I am trying to touch here is only the tip of the iceberg for the purpose of this book. No wonder, Jesus said; the greatest commandment of all is love.

Well, why the subject of love happens to be the greatest of all than the other subject matters in the Bible? The question here has many answers but let's see some of them one at the time. Let's start off with John 13:34-35, where it says; *"A new commandment I give to you that you love one another; as I have loved you, that you also love one another"* (vs.34). *"By this all will know that you are My disciples, if you have love for one another"* (vs.35).

My paraphrase for these two verses read like this. The new commandment Jesus gave to us is that, 'we should have love for one another, in the same measure as Jesus loved us, that the world may know that we are His disciples.' Jesus says; it is a new commandment for the New Testament believers; because such commandment was rarely found in the Old Testament Law. In the Old Testament, if you had slapped somebody on his face, the victim had legal right to slap your face. Eye for an eye and a tooth for a tooth was the law in the Old Testament; and it is found in Exodus 21:24-25; and is quoted again in the New Testament in Matthew 5:38.

However, Jesus had to repeal that law and its substitute is to love your enemy (Matthew 5:39-48). Isn't this tough for some of us? Of course, it is; but that's what God wants us to do. We must have to have love for one another even for our enemies as Jesus loved us. Because that's the only scale on which the world will judge us to know whether we are truly Jesus' disciples.

I have a message titled 'Stephen's Love' that I have not enough space to insert everything about it here, but let me briefly say that; Stephen's Love is what we really need now. What was Stephen's Love then? Stephen's Love was a kind of love that could able to forgive even the very murderers who murdered him right there on the hot spot. Only few can pray even to forgive their enemies like Stephen did (Acts 7:54-60). Stephen was a man just like us, but how could he able to forgive the very murderers who murdered him? The answer is found in verses 55 and 56. His eyes were opened and he could able to see the glory of God with Jesus standing at the right hand of God.

It was what he saw in the heavenly places that made it possible for him to forgive those who murdered him right there on the hot spot. Likewise, we also need to see Jesus and love Him before we can also love and forgive others. Seeing the Man Jesus, who gave up everything with all His attributes even His love for the world, just to save us, will make us very easy to love others. It is what we see in Jesus will truly help us to love even our enemies.

Jesus also says; we must have love for one another, as He loved us. This is also a challenging one, isn't it? Can we able to love others in the measure He loved us? It sounds very easy but in reality, to love others with the same amount and measure as Jesus did, will definitely and surely cost our lives. Truly, it will cost us to see things in the spiritual realm. And it is only when we see Him as He was and He is, it will then make us able to love others.

To be frankly honest with you, I don't think I have love for another person, as Jesus loved me. If I say that I do have, I think I am a hypocrite. For me to have the love for others in the same measure as Jesus had for me, I must be well prepared to lay down my life for others.

That means I have to give up so many things in life that would have benefited me and elevated me to a respectful status in society. That doesn't mean that I have to become a poor man with only rags in the name of the love for others. But what I mean is that you can be a wealthy person with high status in society, only to offer them in the service of God for others. Only then, the world will know that you are truly a disciple of Christ.

Let's go to the Epistle of John and see what he says about love. In 1John 2:9-11, John says; *"He who says he is in the light, and hates his brother, is in darkness until now"* (vs.9*). "He who loves his brother abides in the light, and there is no cause for stumbling in him"* (vs.10). *"But he who hates his brother is in darkness and walks in darkness, and does not know where he is going, because the darkness has blinded his eyes"* (vs.11).

Here is my paraphrase for these verses. 'He who says that he is in the light of God and hates his brother and does not love him, is still in the darkness and doesn't know where he is going, for the darkness has blinded his eyes.'

That means you can not be in the light of God and still hate your brother. It is very obvious that if you are in the light of God, you will still love your brother, no matter what. In your own personal judgment, if you see that you still hate your brother, or whoever he is; then, I think you really don't need anybody to tell you that you are still in the darkness. Your own action tells you that you are still in the darkness and therefore, the way you are going is not right.

For it is common sense that no man does anything good or better in darkness. In that sense, the spiritual darkness is even worse than one may imagine. At least to do things right and good in the service of

God, we must be in the light of God. And you know, it is the Word of God that produces the light of God (John 1:1-9). And the right test or scale to weigh our standing in God is to see if we have love for others.

Here is another reason why we should love others. Let's see what the Bible says in chapter 3:14-16 of 1st Epistle of John again. *"We know that we have passed from death to life, because we love the brethren. He who does not love his brother abides in death"* (vs.14). *"Whoever hates his brother is a murderer, and you know that no murderer has eternal life abiding in him"* (vs.15). *"By this we know love, because He laid down His life for us. And we also ought to lay down our lives for the brethren"* (vs.16).

If we love our brethren, then we've passed from death to life. But if we don't have love for others, the Bible describes us as dead people and have no eternal life, for we are murderers. I think this is also a challenging one, isn't it? I therefore challenge you not to take the grace of God for granted, thinking that you are His child while hating others. Brother, it won't work out for us, no matter how smart we are in our intellect.

Furthermore, let's see what John says in chapter 4. *"Beloved, let us love one another, for love is of God; and everyone who loves is born of God and knows God"* (vs.7). *"He who does not love does not know God, for God is love"* (vs.8).

In this portion of scriptures, it tells us that if we are born of God, then, we should love others for God is love. But if we don't love others, we are not born of God and therefore, we do not know God. This is also frightening; for if we are not born of God, then we don't know Him and He also does not know us as His children.

Another thing is, if we are not born of God and don't know Him, then what sort of message do we have to tell others. Actually we have nothing to offer to this world. We are just as good as decorating flowers that are beautifying the Church.

Here is still another one. *"Beloved, if God so loved us, we also ought to love one another"* (vs.11). *"No one has seen God at anytime. If we love one another, God abides in us, and His love has been perfected in us"* (vs.12).

These scriptures are telling us something different again. Here John says that; 'if God so loved us, we also ought to love one another.' To me, this is a command and an obligation that I have to love others. It is not a choice that I may choose to love. No, it is an obligation that I am obliged to love. Verse 12 tells us that no one has ever seen God at any time. But if we love one another, it shows that God abides in us. How can we prove that we are born of God and that He abides in us? According to these verses from the Word, it is only through love for one another.

Verse 16 also has something that really touches me. It says; *"And we have known and believed the love that God has for us. God is love, and he who abides in love abides in God, and God in him."*

Isn't the second part of this verse also challenging? You see, God is love, and if we abide in love, we abide in God and God abides in us. It is very easy to say that I am a Christian and therefore I have God in me. But if love is absent, then it is a clear indication that we need to do some homework to make sure that God in us. Therefore, love is not just any other religious ritual, but it is in fact a scale on which we weigh our standing in God. And therefore, whatever this love scale tells us is what really we are.

We have some more good things in verses 20 and 21. *"If some one says, "I love God," and hates his brother, he is a liar; for he who does not love his brother whom he has seen, how can he love God whom he has not seen"* (vs.20)? *"And this commandment we have from Him: that he who loves God must love his brother also"* (vs.21).

There is something little bit different here. Here it says; 'I say that I love God and yet hate my brother, I'm a great liar. For how can I profess that I love God and at the same time hate my brother'?

Loving God your Father on one hand and on the other hand hating your brother is like; you are telling somebody that you have something on your hand to give, but when the receiver reaches out his hand to get what you have on your hand, actually you have nothing on your hand to offer. As soon as the receiver finds out that you have nothing to give, he will automatically give you a good name called liar. Do you want your friend to call you a liar?

This is exactly what it happens when someone says that he loves God and hates his brother, he is automatically fit to be called a liar. For when we love God, it is natural that we will also love others. But if we don't love others, that means we don't love God; simple as that. It's a two way thing that the former will be determined by the latter. Love for God and love for man operate hand in hand that one cannot survive in isolation of another.

Let's see one more verse in John's Epistle in Chapter 5:2. *"By this we know that we love the children of God, when we love God and keep His commandments."*

Here John is telling us the things that would cause us to love others. Sometimes it is not that easy for us to just get up and love anybody for the sake of loving him. That's why John is showing us the way that will make it easy for us to love others. In order for us to love others, we must first of all love God the Father and keep His commandments.

Only then, it will be very easy for us to love others. John also recorded this in his Gospel Chapter 14:15. *"If you love Me, keep My commandments."* First thing must come first; so in our case, loving God and keeping His commandments must come first, for without it, it will be very hard or even impossible to love others; even our enemies.

Now let's see what Apostle Paul says about love. In 1Corinthians 13:1-8 and 13, it says; *"Though I speak with the tongues of men and of angels, but have not love, I have become sounding brass or a clanging cymbal"* (vs.1). *"And though I have the gift of prophecy, and understand all mysteries and all knowledge, and though I have all faith, so that I could remove mountains, but have not love, I am nothing"* (vs.2). *"And though I bestow all my goods to feed the poor, and though I give my body to be burned, but have not love, it profits me nothing"* (vs.3).

In the first three verses of this portion of scriptures, Paul is really disqualifying us from whatever the ministries or gifts that we have, if we don't have love. We can speak many languages fluently and even of angels, but if we don't have love, we are just as good as the crying instruments in the Church.

We can able to produce whatever it is to bless the people, but our products will be just like good music produced by instruments that have no life. There won't be any reward or even life for that matter, for we are categorized as sounding brass and a clanging cymbal. Even the gifts of prophecy, and depth understanding of all mysteries and all knowledge, the strongest faith, even to remove mountains, bestow all our goods to feed the poor and to give our bodies to be burnt, and many more, yet if we don't have love, we are nothing and our hard works and our sacrifices will also profit us nothing.

This is really telling me something that I should not take it casually, but rather be serious in it. I mean this is the Word of God and everything that the Word says is True and Amen; and it will surely come to pass. Therefore, I believe that it must be our priority number one to spend much time, effort, energy, money or whatever it may cost to work on love, before engaging ourselves in gifts, ministries, titles, and positions etc in the Church. For it will be a total waste of having all these others, when there is no love in us. Love for others should be the essence and fundamental component of the Church, for all things hung unto it (Matthew 22:40).

Anyway, the following verses taken from 1Corinthians chapter 13 are self-explanatory that I really don't need to explain or define. Therefore, we should examine ourselves to see whether we've passed the test in some of these areas in our lives.

However, if our conscience is not clear and feels guilty of our own makings, it is better to change our minds and do it right before it's too late. *"Love suffers long and is kind; love does not envy; love does not parade itself, is not puffed up"* (vs.4); When we have love for others, we will not complain when things go wrong. Even if we suffer for what we are doing, we will endure it.

Love is also kind; so no matter how harsh the people around you, you will be kind to everybody in every situation. Love does not envy for other people's success and try to parade with them. Puffing up with all kinds of evil motives to be equal or match with others is not of God. *"Does not behave rudely, does not seek its own, is not provoked, thinks no evil"* (vs.5).

Love is a good medicine to make you cool down even if you are provoked to think or to act evil to protect your own interest. *"Does not rejoice in iniquity, but rejoices in the truth"* (vs.6); It is an opposite thing altogether for most people to rejoice in iniquity than to rejoice in the truth. Those who are filled with the love of God will make it their habit to rejoice in the truth always. Rejoicing over iniquity is a sign of a rebellious person who knows nothing about God, for God is holy and is love. *"Bears all things, believes all things, hopes all things, endures all things"* (vs.7).

When the power of love is so strong, you can able to bear all things, no matter how tense the situation is. For love endures forever that it will cause you to have faith and hope that will surely take you through for many miles. *"Love never fails but whether there are prophecies, they will fail; whether there are tongues, they will cease; whether there is knowledge, it will vanish away"* (vs.8).

Love never fails, for it is eternal. It never fails for love knows the way to go about in every situation. Love has many ways to escape from destruction and death. Love is more powerful that no other power can stand against it. Love never quits for it completes its purposes. Love is everything that concerns our lives.

It was a thing called love that caused God to send Jesus Christ into this world (John 3:16). And again it was only love that led Jesus to the cross, even to die for the ones who actually crucified Him. He loved them as well and forgave them on the same day (Luke 23:34). That's how powerful the agape love of God is.

Truly, it is love that will be the climax of all the joyful activities, which will involve the saints and angels together in heaven. Again love is eternal while all the ministries and gifts will cease after the accomplishment of their purposes. For love is of God and God is love. *"And now abide faith, hope, love, these three; but the greatest of these is love"* (1Corinthians 13:13).

Apostle Paul concludes chapter 13 by saying that though the Church is gifted with all kinds of gifts, there are three important elements that last forever which are faith, hope and love. Among them, love is the most important of all. I therefore, also want to conclude this chapter by saying that; anything that the Bible says that it is most important and number one; should not be substituted for another. It must remain number one forever, even love for that matter. I believe as a Church, our job is to extend the boundary of the Kingdom of God in no other than in love, for it is love that matters the most.

Finally, it was the love of God that happened to be the motivating factor behind God to send Jesus into this world (John 3:16). And it was the love of God that also happened to be the foundation of the Church of God. Again, I am convinced so much so to say that really, God is love (1John 4:8), from His head down to the soles of His feet, from the inside of Him to the outside, God is all love. The great universe the creation of God, speaks not only of the power of God but of God's love. So it must be the love that should build the Church and the Church should also grow into her maturity in love.

The title for this book, *'Church the Reason for All'* covers most activities of God from day one to the final day of judgement. And the only medicine that keeps them all fresh and alive is no other than love. For it is love that abides forever and ever: Amen!

Conclusion

I have nearly exhausted myself in the subject of the Church of God however, that does not guarantee me to say that I have covered everything about the Church. What you have read so far in this book is only a hint of what one can come up with. There are many recommended books on the same subject that you can also read to increase your knowledge about the subject matter.

The Church is an institution that is sole property of God. Before everything else came into existence, the Church was conceived in the heart of God. He saw a people washed and cleansed by the blood to serve and worship Him not only in this world but also in the eternity. In His great wisdom, He did all that He has done just for the Church. This is really a mysterious theory that can not be easily swallowed, yet as simple creations of God, we have no other options but to accept it as it is.

The incarnation of Jesus, (God becoming man) is the only easiest way to know this mysterious God. God wouldn't have bothered to send His Son, if things would have worked out into its perfection without Him (Jesus Christ). The spoken Word (the logos) was already in the land yet the Word had to get a form of a man in order for us to imitate Him. The simple creation of God to sit back and questioning or reasoning the works of this great Almighty God, is like a foolish man trying to draw the whole sea into a small cup. We should know the fact that no human brain can able to contain the infinite knowledge of God, for His is indeed the Omniscient God. All we have to do is to just accept it and have faith in what He says and imitate Him.

To understand this mysterious Church and its ingredients, why not follow Christ and simply obey His Word? I mean, if the Word says that Jesus Himself is the builder of the Church, or the head of the Church, or if the Church is His Body, and His Body is only one, then we have no other option but to accept it and have faith in it and act accordingly.

Even the salvation is the fruit of one's own makings; though eternal life is a free gift from God. We've got to comply with the written (logos) Word of God and work it out accordingly as it requires for such.

The position of the Church is very important for its recognition. Without the recognition of the status of a high position or title, it would not have any respect as it deserves. Likewise, it is very important to recognize the position of the Church. The Church is an institution that has the very highest position of all; both here on earth and the world to come.

The only fundamental essence in the Church of God is God's agape love. The paramount material used to build the Church is of course His Word. And His Word of life is the expression of His great love for mankind. And the Church is the fruit of the Word.

Because the Church is the fruit of the Word and the Word is God Himself, who is also glorious, the Church is a glorious Church. And its glory should be reflected to the world through the expression of His agape love!

Reference

All Bible references applied in this book are taken only from the **New King James Version.** I was tempted to use other Bible Translations as well, but I also felt strong in my heart to use only one Bible Translation, and that I chose the New King James Version. As each Bible reader has his or her own preference of using different translations, I prefer New King James Version for my own good and understanding.

For your better understanding of this book, I suggest that you should also have a copy of the New King James Version (only if you can) or a copy of your own choice in front of you as you read this book. For this book like I said, is a study book that needs to be read with a Bible in front of the reader!

Bibliography

*Don Clowers, <u>Spiritual Growth</u>, Book Production by Image Source, Inc. Tulsa, OK 74237, USA. 1995.

*Guy P. Duffield and Nathaniel M. Van Cleave, <u>Foundations of Pentecostal Theology,</u> OMF Literature Inc. Manila, Philippines. 2006.

*Graham Fitzpatrick, <u>How To Recognize</u> <u>God's Voice</u>, Spiritual Growth Books, Queenslands. 1985.

*Oxford Advanced Learner's Dictionary of Current English, Chief Editor: A P Cowie, Oxford University Press, LONDON, 1993.

*The Holy Bible, The New King James_Version, Thomas Nelson Publishers, Inc. Nashville, USA, 1992.

*The NIV Study Bible, General Editor, Kenneth Barker, Zondervan Publishing House, Grand Rapids, MI 49530, USA, 1995. (Only for cross-checking).

*Williams Evans, <u>Great Doctrines of the Bible</u>, OMF Literature Inc. 777 Boni Avenue, Mandaluyong, Metro MANILA: 1974.

About the Author

Pastor Clement B.Talipan is an ordained Pastor of the Assemblies of God Church of Papua New Guinea. He was converted under a **(Joseph Yans Lepatu's Evangelistic Ministry**, one of the top Ministries in those days) in February 1975 in Mount Hagen Town in the Western Highlands Province of Papua New Guinea. Straight after his conversion, he went back to Enga Province where he comes from to evangelize the Province. He was then working with the Finnish and Swedish Pentecostal Missionaries who had their base in Mount Hagen, in the Western Highlands Province to coordinate their mission work in the Highlands Region. Since then, he has been faithful in serving God in both good and bad times for the last thirty-three (33) years.

Back in the 1970s, there was a massive revival that swept the Nation of Papua New Guinea and thus, Pastor Talipan happened to be one of those revivalists to revive the Enga Province. As a young and energetic minister in those days, Pastor Talipan had the energy to spread the Gospel all around the Province. He was the only young Pentecostal preacher in the Province who then worked side by side with the PNG Apostolic Church which was already established some two decades ahead of him beside the three mainstream Churches namely, the Catholic Church, the Lutheran Church and the Seven Day Adventist Church.

Under his young Evangelistic Ministry many new churches were built in almost all the six (6) Districts. Some of these churches still exist this time under the banner of the AOG Church, Four Square Church, Christian Revival Crusade (CRC) Church, Christian Life Centre (CLC) Church and so on.

He is a graduate from the AOG Jubilee Bible College (now Jubilee University). He is married with five (5) children. Pastor Talipan says that he is still a student in the Word of God and hence, he's really keen in studies for that matter!

To contact the author on any queries or comments or even critiques regarding this book, please write:

Pastor Clement B.Talipan
P.O.Box 76
WABAG
Enga Province
Papua New Guinea.
or
 Email address:
clementtalipan@gmail.com
or
Call: (675)71163088 / (675) 3415494